F.V.

THE ETIQUETTE OF RACE RELATIONS
IN THE SOUTH

THE ETIQUETTE
OF RACE RELATIONS IN
THE SOUTH

A STUDY IN SOCIAL CONTROL

By

BERTRAM WILBUR DOYLE

Professor of Sociology, Fisk University

KENNIKAT PRESS, INC./PORT WASHINGTON, N. Y.

KENNIKAT PRESS SERIES IN NEGRO CULTURE AND HISTORY

THE ETIQUETTE OF RACE RELATIONS IN THE SOUTH

Copyright 1937 by The University of Chicago
Reissued in 1968 by Kennikat Press
Library of Congress Catalog Card No: 68-25198
Manufactured in the United States of America

TO
MOKEE-HI AND PETER

PREFACE

THE American people seem to exhibit a perennial interest in problems pertaining to the contact and association of the many races which constitute the general population. Not the least uninteresting of the problems is that of race relations, and not the least unregarded is the Negro racial group. It is, indeed, frequently assumed that "the Negro problem" is *the* problem and that Negro-white relations are *the* relations which should stimulate, although they may not require, the greatest attention.

Publications in the field of race relations, especially within the last two decades, testify to a flourishing and continual interest in the subject and have provided a motive, if they have not furnished an excuse, to publish this volume.

In an appraisal of books, which dealt less frequently with analysis than with solution of problems of race relations, Dr. Donald Young was moved to remark that "solutions to the problems of race relations have been offered freely, but not by scholars." He implied, even if he did not state in the generalization, that such volumes, generally benevolent in tone or political in purpose, have for the most part presented plans or programs for reform of the existing conditions in race relations.

Dr. Robert E. Park, distinguishing between moral, civil, and natural law, says that "if natural law aims at prediction it tells us what we can do. Moral laws, on the other hand, tell us, not what we can, but what we ought to do. The civil . . . . law, finally, tells us not what we can, nor what we ought, but what we must do. . . . . We do not know what we ought to do until we know what we can do; and we certainly should consider what men can do before we pass laws prescribing what they must do."

These statements, taken together, may be said to be the point of view of this work. It is true that attempts to predict the future in race relations have crept into the volume; but, we trust, we have not been overconcerned with solutions. We have rather sought to indicate that solutions must await explanation of those sequences of behavior which can be reduced to what might, in sociological terms, be called "natural laws." This study, then, while analyzing the phenomena of race relations between white and Negro people in terms of the external forms in which the relations are symbolized, attempts to suggest that the control—which solutions of the race problem seek—might better be established after the forces which have developed the existing controls have been analyzed. In other words, as we know what can be done in the field of solving problems, we can also indicate what should be done and require what must be done.

The study, to a great extent, has been a co-operative enterprise. Herbert Spencer advanced the hypothesis that ceremonial government was the most elementary and most persistent form of social control. Other philosophers and sociologists, exerting their influence through the medium of the printed page, have contributed their share to the main thought of the book. The General Education Board provided a fellowship, whose terms allowed us to gather many materials presented here. Students in our classes in Fisk University favored us with documents and case materials from their own experiences. Publishers have been generous with permission to use their materials. Although acknowledgment is given in each instance where the materials are cited, this additional mention is cheerfully made.

Dr. Ellsworth Faris not only imparted intellectual stimulation but also, at a critical stage in the preparation of the manuscript, painstakingly read it, page by page. Dr. Charles S. Johnson has offered advice, encouragement, and aid with technical and financial details, in a manner which makes him an especial collaborator. Colleagues and friends, all of whom cannot be recalled here, have given assistance in many ways. To the two persons who, above all, have shown an abiding faith and have given unflagging support, we have referred elsewhere. To all these we acknowledge our obligation, extend our thanks, and express our appreciation.

We wish to acknowledge a particular personal obligation to Dr. Robert E. Park. His contribution, at once obvious and highly important, is gratefully recognized. He has given constant encouragement, constructive and pertinent criticism, scientific counsel, and wholesome advice.

None of the persons mentioned, however, may be charged with the deficiencies of the book; they may only be credited with whatever merit it possesses.

One last word—the footnotes, ordinarily found at the bottom of the page, are included in the Appendix. They are arranged serially and by chapters, however, in order to facilitate quick reference.

BERTRAM W. DOYLE

FISK UNIVERSITY
NASHVILLE, TENNESSEE
June 26, 1937

INTRODUCTION

A GOOD many years ago when I first became interested in the South and its problems I ran across in a little volume by John Spencer Bassett, entitled *Slavery in the State of North Carolina*, a reference to a legal decision by Chief Justice Ruffin of the Supreme Court of North Carolina, which set forth the character of the institution of slavery in such uncompromising terms that I have never since forgotten it, and I can still recall some of its more incisive phrases.

It was a decision, rendered in 1829, dismissing an indictment of a master for an assault upon his slave, the memorable thing about it being the Chief Justice's opinion affirming the master's right to inflict any kind of punishment upon his slave short of death. In support of this decision Justice Ruffin cited the fact that, in the whole history of slavery, there had been no such prosecution of a master for punishing a slave, and added, "against this general opinion in the community the court ought not to hold."

It had been said, the opinion continues, that the relation of master and slave was like that of parent and child. But this was a mistake. It was to the interest of the parent to give his son moral and intellectual instruction in order to fit him to live as a free man. The case of the slave was different. What sense could there be in addressing moral considerations to a slave?

The Chief Justice summed up his conception of the relations of master and slave in these words: "The end [of slavery] is the profit of the master, his security, and the public safety; the subject, one doomed in his own person and his posterity to live without knowledge and without the capacity to make anything his own, and to toil that another may reap the fruits. What moral consideration shall be addressed to such a being to convince him, what it is impossible but that the most stupid must feel and know can never be true—that he is thus to labour upon a principle of natural duty, or for the sake of his own personal happiness. Such services can only be expected from one who has no will of his own, who surrenders his will in implicit obedience to that of another. Such obedience is the consequence only of uncontrolled authority over the body. There is nothing else which can operate to produce the effect. The power of the master must be absolute to render the submission of the slave perfect."

No harsher judgment, I can well believe, was ever passed upon the institution of slavery than that contained in this decision, and if I have ventured to quote it here at some considerable length it is partly because of its intrinsic historical interest but mainly because it seemed to contribute something, by way of contrast at least, to the present study of a very different aspect of slavery, and one which presents that institution in a more amiable light.

The very fact that there existed, in the South before the war, as the title of this volume suggests, a recognized social ritual and a code of etiquette regulating the personal relations of both races is evidence that the regime of slavery was not, everywhere and always, as inhuman as the laws defining the relations of master and slave might lead one to believe. Where there is custom there will always be some sort of justice and equity, and no individual will be wholly a law unto himself.

It is interesting, also, in this connection that having described with remorseless logic the nature of slavery, the Chief Justice should have felt moved to conclude his legal opinion with a personal comment which indicates how little he approved, in his private capacity as a citizen and a man, the institution which, in his public capacity as a lawyer and a judge, he felt compelled to support.

"I freely confess," he says, "my sense of the harshness of this proposition. I feel it as deeply as any one can and as a principle of right every person in his retirement must repudiate it. But

in the actual condition of things it must be so; there is no remedy. This discipline belongs to the state of slavery. It constitutes the curse of slavery both to the bond and free portion of
our population."[1]

There was always, it seems, a conflict in the minds, if not the
counsels, of thoughtful southern people, between the demands
of public policy, interested in the perpetuation of slavery, and
the disposition of individual slaveholders who, for private and
personal reasons, were disposed to emancipate their slaves. This
was particularly true when, as often happened, emancipation
seemed the only way to discharge an obligation which had been
accumulating during a lifetime of intimate personal association and faithful service.

One evidence of this conflict was the uninterrupted increase in
the number of free Negroes, particularly in Virginia, North
Carolina, and the Border States, where the more intimate relations between masters and slaves tended to multiply emancipa-
tions, in spite of the efforts of legislators to discourage them.
The motives of masters in freeing their slaves, in opposition to
accepted public policy, are revealed in their testamentary statements where one encounters again and again the clause "in
consequence of faithful service" such-and-such a one should be
given his freedom. Not infrequently such provision for the
emancipation of a faithful servant was made in final fulfilment
of a promise made long before.

It is clear from these and other evidences that the actual position of the slave in the little world of the plantation, and his
legal status in the world outside, were never in actual harmony;
were finally, in fact, quite irreconcilable. The regime of slavery,
constantly threatened from without, was at the same time
steadily undermined and weakened from within; weakened by

[1] See John Spencer Basset, *Slavery in the State of North Carolina*, Johns Hopkins
Studies in Historical and Political Science, pp. 23–24. Also *Judicial Cases Concerning
American Slavery and the Negro*, Edited by Helen Tunnicliff Catterall. Vol. II. Cases
from the Courts of North Carolina, South Carolina, and Tennesee.

the claims of the slave, on the one hand, and the conscience of the master, on the other.

This contrast and conflict between slavery as a legal concept and as an actual working concern may be regarded perhaps as an instance of the normal reaction of living and conscious human nature against the formal and rational structure of the society which incloses it. We know how friendships sometimes corrupt politics. In a somewhat similar way the intimate association of master and slave may be said steadily to have corrupted the institution of slavery, and in so doing hastened it on its course to its predestined extinction.

Slavery came into existence to meet the demands of the frontier and plantation. The hard conditions that the system imposed upon the slaves were not essentially different from those imposed a little earlier upon indentured servants. In any case they responded to the necessities of the situation and the customs of the time and place. But "human relations," as a noted anthropologist, Malinowski, puts it, "do not rest merely or mainly on constraint coming from without. Men can only work with and for one another by the moral forces which grow out of personal attachments and loyalties."

Men come together ordinarily because they are useful to one another. Under these circumstances they may regard each other for a long time as mere utilities. But human beings do not live for long, like plants, in relations that are merely symbiotic. For men, unlike plants, communicate. In this way they come to know one another's minds and to be responsive to one another's attitudes and sentiments. They find themselves, eventually, living as it were, each in the mind of all his neighbors. It is in this way that a moral order grows up in which, under the happiest circumstances, the individual feels himself constrained only by those obligations which he freely accepts or imposes upon himself.

It is characteristic of such a moral order that it is nonrational. That means that it is not devised to protect any special interest, to serve any policy, and has no ulterior purposes of any sort. On the contrary, it arises in response to the natural claims which one individual makes upon another, as soon as he recognizes that other individual as human like himself.

I am reminded in this connection of an anecdote related of John Randolph, who was a slaveholder and abolitionist at a time when that combination did not seem as much like one of Oliver Hereford's mixed beasts as it did later. John Randolph was himself a great orator, and he had known Patrick Henry. Someone, knowing his reputation, asked him in the course of an interview whom, of all those he had ever heard speak in Congress or elsewhere, he regarded as the greatest orator.

"The greatest orator I ever heard," he replied, "was a woman. She was a slave and a mother and her rostrum was an auction block."

The anecdote illustrates the curious and unexpected ways in which men gain those moral insights which eventually undermine but humanize institutions. To make the record complete, one should know that John Randolph at his death emancipated all his slaves and settled them on free soil in the Northwest Territory, in what is now the state of Ohio.

Thus, long before emancipation had finally put an end to the regime of slavery, that institution was visibly breaking down under the tension of internal conflicts. At the same time, under the urge and pressure of sentiments and attitudes, which the lifelong association of master and slave evoked, one observed the burgeoning, within the framework of the old, of a new and more humane social order.

The emancipation of the slaves did not at once usher in a regime of free competition and democracy, in the sense of the Declaration of Independence, the Bill of Rights, and the laissez faire doctrines of Adam Smith and the Physiocrats.

On the contrary, the social order which emerged with the abolition of slavery was a system of caste—caste based on race and color. The plantation had been organized on the pattern of a familial and feudal, rather than of a civil and political, society. Caste was the form which race relations took under conditions which the plantation imposed.

So firmly was the system of caste fixed in the habits and custom—what Sumner calls the mores—of both races in the South that all the social disorganization incident to the Civil War and Reconstruction were not sufficient wholly or suddenly to destroy it.

Slavery is dead, and no one now defends it. But caste remains, and is still so much a part of the natural and expected order that few people in the South either question its right to exist or discuss its function. The North has never understood either the nature of race relations in the South or the fanaticism with which southern people have defended, wherever and whenever it has been attacked, the caste code in accordance with which these relations were regulated. The failure of reconstruction legislation to effect any fundamental change in the South's caste system is less an illustration of the recalcitrance of the Anglo-Saxon than of Sumner's dictum that it is not possible to reform the mores by law.[2]

People not reared in the southern tradition have sometimes assumed that southern people's insistence on racial segregation is evidence that they cherish some deep, instinctive antipathy for the Negro race. Anyone who accepts that conception of the matter is likely to be somewhat mystified when he learns that the Negro is quite all right in his place. And that place, like the place of everyone else, is the one to which tradition and custom has assigned him.

In 1906 Ray Stannard Baker came South to investigate the background of the Atlanta race riot. Later he recorded his observations in a volume entitled *Following the Color Line*, which is one of the very few books in which an author has succeeded in reporting race relations in the South with anything approaching disinterested objectivity. Baker made, in the course of his

[2] See William Graham Sumner's *Folkways*, pp. 113–14. Boston, 1906.

investigations, what amounted to an important discovery. He found that the "color line" was no mere incident of social life in the South. Rather it was an institution, the influence and ramifications of which entered into and pervaded all the life-relations of both races. The "color line" is, as a matter of fact, nothing more or less than a local variety of what students of society and human nature call caste. It is this institution to which southern people make oblique reference when they speak of "the doctrine of social equality." It is this institution, in what is sociologically, perhaps, its most important aspect—namely, its etiquette—which is the subject of the present volume.

Students of society are indebted to Herbert Spencer for directing attention to the importance of etiquette and social ritual as a form of government or social control, and, indeed, as a subject for sociological investigation. Etiquette—or "ceremonial observance," as he calls it—is not only, he points out, the earliest but the most pervasive form of social control, and for that reason, perhaps, has still "the largest share in regulating men's lives."

As every society that has achieved any sort of permanence has its traditions and customs, so every society has its etiquette. Social ritual is indeed a part of the social tradition, but it has its own special function. Something more in detail needs to be said here, perhaps, in regard to the origin and nature of etiquette. Its social function and the character of the control it actually enforces is amply illustrated in the chapters which follow.

Etiquette is concerned primarily with personal relations. It grows up in the first instance, perhaps, as the spontaneous expression of one person in the presence of another, of a sentiment of deference. Under ordinary circumstances such an attitude of propitiation of one individual implies and is likely to evoke a corresponding expression of benevolent recognition on the part of that other. Expression and response rather than stimulus and response are the natural termini of every instance of social interaction.

Forms of deference and recognition, repeated and imitated, soon crystallize into those conventional and obligatory forms of expression we call "etiquette," or social ritual. But ritual, as Sumner points out, "is not something to be thought or felt. It is something to be done." In fact, "ritual is strongest when it is perfunctory and excites no thought." It is for this reason that a social ritual which was originally the natural and unstudied expression of a social sentiment may serve finally as the masque behind which one controls and conceals his emotions rather than reveals them. Etiquette in that case becomes a kind of social device by which one does the expected thing but preserves his inner freedom.

Etiquette, so far as it can be conceived to be a form of government or control, functions only in so far as it defines and maintains "social distances." Social distance is a phenomenon of a society that is based on primary or face-to-face relationships. In every such society, even in the most casual assembly, every individual will tend to be located at certain social distance in relation to every other. This means that, at a given time and place, every individual may be said to occupy a position, defined in terms of his psychical distance or intimacy, with respect to every other. What this distance may be at any time depends upon a number of things: upon the personality of the individual, for one thing; his office and function in the community, for another. It will depend in part, however, upon the number of persons present and the known relations of each to every other. The principle involved is stated in the aphorism, "Two is company but three is a crowd." In general one may say, therefore, that the larger the number the greater the distances.

A society or community of this sort may be said to have attained stable equilibrium when all the social distances are known and every individual is in his place. Thus etiquette turns out to be, at the same time, a principle of social order and an index of the stability of the society in which it exists. In such a society every individual is "all right," and quite acceptable, in his place and at his proper distance, even when that distance is only symbolically expressed.

Thus it was quite possible, on the plantation, and particularly in the case of the house servants and the master's family, to maintain the most intimate relationships between master and slave provided the social ritual defining and maintaining the caste relationship was maintained in its integrity.

There is a delightfully quaint and touching Negro spiritual of which the refrain is: "I want to be in heaven settin' down."

One misses the symbolic significance of this image of the perfect comfort of heaven if one fails to recognize its reference to a traditional racial etiquette. I suspect that the heaven here referred to is somehow identified in the mind of the singer with the image of the "Big House" on the plantation. When one went there, one did not ordinarily sit down. One stood and waited, on one's feet.

We are largely dependent upon the personal memories of travelers and the reports of writers of a reminiscent and nostalgic literature for our knowledge of the domestic life of the plantation. Margaret Mitchell's novel, *Gone with the Wind*, for example, is a veritable source book on race relations and racial etiquette. From these and other sources one learns that this plantation society, originally a mere *modus vivendi* to insure the co-operation of individuals of two divergent races, had achieved at the end of the era a social stability and a moral solidarity that enabled it to withstand the shock of a Civil War in which its very existence was involved.

In this society, it appears, every individual—from the carriage-driver to the field hand—each according to his office and function, had his place in the occupational hierarchy, and, in his place, each had a certain degree of security and independence. It was a security and an independence, to be sure, that disappeared outside of the limits of the plantation. Within these limits, however, the existing social order was sustained by tradition and a code of etiquette that was binding upon master and servant alike.

Etiquette is the very essence of caste, since the prestige of a superior always involves the respect of an inferior. But this respect is insured only when it manifests itself freely, either in a natural expression of deference or in some more conventional form of ceremonial observance, enforced by public opinion and the general expectation. Any relaxation by any individual of the rigors of the code is likely to involve a loss of prestige not merely to that individual but to the caste as a whole.

This fact explains at once the importance which etiquette assumed on the plantation before the Civil War and the fierce insistence of the southern people upon its observance afterward, when any sign of disrespect of any Negro for any white man was evidence that the whole structure of social life in the South was crumbling, and any toleration of a violation of the traditional code was likely to be resented as a concession to a political and social equality abhorrent to southern tradition.

The caste system as it had existed was maintained not by law but by a body of customs that was more or less self-enforcing. One evidence of the change in race relations, as a result of emancipation, was the efforts of the southern communities to enforce by statute racial distinctions and discriminations which it was difficult or impossible to maintain by custom and tradition.

Most of the racial conflicts and controversies in the southern states during Reconstruction and after seem to have had their origin in the caste system, and in the efforts to maintain it by law and force when it was no longer sustained by the inertia of tradition and the force of public opinion.

It was, I suspect, less the fear of the political domination of the Negro than opposition to any and every form of social equality that was responsible for the Solid South, one of the most notable if incidental consequences of Reconstruction. This solidarity was necessary to insure white supremacy, but it had one unexpected effect. It co-operated with other forces to bring about what has been sometimes described as the emancipation of the poor white man. It gave him an equality with the planter aristocracy he had never had under the old regime. It made him an enthusiastic defender of the ritual of a caste system in which he had once occupied a distinctly inferior position.

It has been the violent, often vituperative, and always tactless efforts of the New South, in which the poor white man has become the dominant figure, to enforce upon Negroes the ritual of a racial etiquette already obsolete that has been responsible for a good deal, including lynchings, of what we refer to as the "race problem" in the South. Negroes acquired in slavery the conviction that a poor white man was an inferior white man, and the course of events since emancipation has not increased the black man's respect for the white man as such.

In a certain sense we may say that the caste system, in so far as it has served anywhere to organize race relations, has been a solution of the race problem. It was when, after the abolition of slavery, the caste system broke down that the disorders and racial animosities that we ordinarily identify with the race problem began.

Generally speaking, there was no such thing as a race problem before the Civil War and there was at that time very little of what we ordinarily call race prejudice, except in the case of the free Negro. The free Negro was the source and origin of whatever race problems there were. Because he was free he was at once an anomaly and a source of constant anxiety to the slaveholding population. He had no place in the system, and although exceptional individuals achieved a relatively high place in their community, and were respected by members of both races, free Negroes, as a class, were feared and often outrageously maligned.

Although caste still persists and serves in a way to regulate race relations, many things—education, the rise within the Negro community of a professional class (teachers, ministers, and physicians) and of an intelligentsia, seeking to organize and direct the Negro's rising race consciousness—have conspired not merely to undermine the traditional caste system but to render it obsolete.

Meanwhile, the slow but steady advance of the Negro, as a result of competition within and without the group, and the gradual rise of a Negro society within the limits of the white man's world have changed the whole structure of race relations in the United States, both in the North and in the South.

The restrictions on intermarriage still persist and continue to make of the Negro an endogamous social group, in much the same sense that the Jews, the Mennonites, and any of the more primitive religious sects are endogamous. On the other hand, in view of the fact that he has developed a society in which all the professions and many, if not most, occupations are represented, the Negro has an opportunity now, which he did not have earlier, to rise within the limits of the Negro world. Under those circumstances the Negro group has gradually ceased to exhibit the characteristics of a caste and has assumed rather the character of a racial or national minority.

The Jewish people have been described as "a permanent minority group," and by the same token the position of the Jew in Europe may be said to constitute a race problem in the same sense as the position of the Negro constitutes a race problem in the United States. But the Jewish people, if they may be described a minority group or nationality, cannot properly be described at the same time as a caste.

The change in the status of the Negro from that of a caste to minority group has not come about without some interesting changes and quaint compromises in the racial ritual, growing out of the contradiction between present conditions and the traditional attitudes of both races as they have become enshrined in the traditional racial etiquette. An anecdote told me years ago by Booker Washington will illustrate better than any exposition the point I am seeking to make.

One of the methods adopted by Washington to spread his gospel of education was to organize from time to time statewide educational campaigns. On such occasions he and his party traveled sometimes for a week in a special car visiting and speaking in every city and center of Negro population. On these occasions he was frequently visited by delegations of white folk from remote villages along the way who, attracted by the legendary reputation he had achieved, wanted to see this extraordinary man. Southern white people have always been interested in Negro prodigies.

On one of these occasions a delegation, headed by a lanky and rustic but enterprising member of the village intelligentsia, waited upon Mr. Washington at the station and introduced himself and his fellow-villagers in good-natured, backwoods fashion:

"Y'u know, Booker, I been hear'n about you, I been hear'n for a long time now, and I sure did want to see you. I been a tellin' my friends about y'u. I been tellin' them you was one of the biggest men in this country today. Yes, sir, one of the biggest men in the whole country."

At this time Theodore Roosevelt was at the height of his reputation, and Mr. Washington, somewhat at a loss for a reply, but thinking it well to discount the exuberance of his visitor replied, "Well, what do you think about President Roosevelt?"

"Oh! Hell, Roosevelt! Well, I used to be all for him until he let you eat dinner with him. That finished him far as I'm concerned."

This retort was not perhaps as naïve as it may at first appear, but it illustrates, at any rate, the curious and incongruous association of ideas and attitudes that arise out of the necessity of maintaining the customary caste distinctions in a world which is gradually outgrowing them.

In the daily newspaper that lies on my desk as I write this

there is a more recent illustration, a little less comic, of a similar incongruity. Congressman Mitchell, the Negro Democratic congressman from Chicago, it appears is suing the Illinois Central and the Pullman Company for fifty thousand dollars damages because in Arkansas, in accordance with local custom and state law, he was compelled to leave the Pullman and go into the "Jim Crow" car.

This is an instance of caste a little less innocent and amiable than the casual mistake of addressing a bishop as "boy." However, if white folk have been disposed, in their intercourse with Negroes, to retain the intimate and familiar forms of address such as "uncle," "auntie," and "boy," which were appropriate to a familial and feudal society but sound rather quaint now, Negroes, on the other hand, are more and more disposed to reject any terms or any racial distinctions that reflect and tend to preserve the memories of an earlier inferior status.

There is, finally, one small but significant change in the ritual of race relations, that it seems to me, needs to be specially noted. The great majority of Negroes now, after a good deal of discussion and difference of opinion, have adopted the term "Negro" as a racial designation in preference to another more logical but less familiar expression like "Afro-American." Having adopted it, however, they spell it with a capital *N*.

ROBERT E. PARK

UNIVERSITY OF CHICAGO

TABLE OF CONTENTS

CHAPTER I

THE ETIQUETTE OF RACE RELATIONS DEFINED

IN THE *Memoirs of Jefferson Davis*, published by his widow, Mrs. Varina Davis, there is reproduced the following letter:

CHRISTINE, NORTH DAKOTA
December 1, 1889

MISS VARINA:

I have watched with deep interest and solicitude the illness of Mr. Davis at Brierfield, his trip down on the steamer *Leathers*, and your meeting and returning with him to the residence of Mr. Payne, in New Orleans; and I had hoped that with good nursing and superior medical skill, together with his great will-power to sustain him, he would recover. But, alas! for human endeavor, an over-ruling Providence has willed it otherwise. I appreciate your great loss, and my heart goes out to you in this hour of your deepest affliction. Would that I could help you bear the burden that is yours today. Since I am powerless to do so, I beg that you accept my sympathy and condolence.

Your very obedient servant,

THORNTON

To MRS. JEFFERSON DAVIS, Beauvoir, Mississippi[1]

The context explains the circumstances in which the letter was written, but one not familiar with the customs and traditions of the South, before and since the Civil War, could not quite understand the form of address—"Miss Varina"—used by a former slave in a letter addressed to the wife of the former president of the Confederate States.

The "Thornton" of the letter was Thornton Montgomery,

whose father had been a slave on the plantation of Jefferson Davis' brother. But Thornton Montgomery himself, at the time he wrote to Mrs. Davis, was twenty-five years removed from slavery and was a prosperous farmer in the Northwest. He used a form of salutation that raised the question—Did slaves address their mistresses with "Miss" and the Christian name? The complimentary close need arouse no speculation, however. It was doubtless a mere formality generally used.

It is well known that the Negroes in the South, before the Civil War, were a polite and ceremonious people. Occasional glimpses into the literature of the period suggest that there was an etiquette used in relations between white persons and slaves. It comprised forms used generally by all persons and those used particularly when white persons and slaves associated. For example, slaves addressed their owners, or whites of high rank, as "Master" and "Mistress."[2] It perhaps happened that, when understanding was established, or upon occasions when the slave would carelessly drop or slur the last syllable of the words, "master" became "massa" and "mistress" became "mistis." Finally, the last syllable was dropped altogether; "massa" became "mars," and "mistis" became "miss."

In the informality of the plantation, or of the household, however, slaves, by addressing their owners as "Mars" and "Miss" and employing the forms with the Christian name, were able to distinguish subtle degrees of intimacy in their relations with persons. This was expected by whites, according to their relation to the Negroes who used the term.

There was, however, a term even more intimate than "miss" with the Christian name, as the following excerpt tends to show:

" 'This is our little Confederate nigger,' explained the lady. 'She is the only one I have been able to keep [since the Emancipation].' 'Did you notice,' she continued, patting the wooly head of the child as it lay with its face buried in her lap, 'that she called me "Missey" just now? All the niggers have been trying to break her of that, but they can't. They tell her to call me "Miss Lizzie," but she says "She may be your Miss Lizzie, but she's my Missey." The other day she made quite a scene in church, by breaking away from the other servants and shouting out, "I will sit with my Missey today." You should have seen everybody's head turning to see who it was in these sorrowful days that was still fortunate enough to be called "Missey." ' "[3]

"Natchez, Mississippi, 1866"

The slave did not at all times use "Mars" or "Marster" in addressing white men. There were other forms quite as respectful, although not so intimate.

"A well-known gentleman of Winchester was crossing the Potomac into Virginia, with his horse, in a ferry-boat. The ferryman said, 'Major, I wish you would move your horse a little forward,' which he immediately did, observing to the man, 'I am not a Major, and you need not call me one.' To this the ferryman replied, 'Well, Kurnel, I ax your pardon, and I'll not call you so any more.' Being arrived at the landing place, he led his horse out of the boat and said, 'My good friend, I am neither a colonel nor a major. . . . . I have no title at all, and I don't like them. How much do I owe you?' The ferryman looked at him and said, 'You are the first white man I ever crossed this ferry that warn't jist nobody at all, and I'll swar, I'll not charge you anything.' "[4]

The Negroes on the Sea Islands of South Carolina used "buckra," both informally and formally, to refer to white persons.[5]

An instance is recorded by Buckingham which indicates that precedence, with reference to superior and inferior, was observed between blacks and whites:

"The order in which the meals were taken in the steamboat was this: at the first bell, the captain and all the white passengers sat down; when all these had finished and left the table, a second bell summoned the pilot, captain's clerk, all the white men of the engineer's department, the white stewardess, and such white servants or subordinates as might be on board; when these had finished, the bell summoned the black steward, and all the mulattoes and colored servants, to take their meal. [However, there were some free Negro women on the boat, and] So equivocal was the position of these ladies that they could not be placed at any of the tables; they were not high enough to be seated with the blacks and mulattoes, so they had to retire to the pantry, where they took their meals standing at the butler's table."[6]

This incident indicates not only that separation of whites and blacks was observed but also that distinction existed among Negroes. It is perhaps true that the two races did not eat together and frequently not in the same place. For example, Miss Martineau remarked of the slaves:

"They have a few customs which are absolutely peculiar. One of these is refusing to eat before whites. When we went on long expeditions, carrying luncheons, or procuring it by the roadside, the slaves always retired with their share behind large trees or stones, or other hiding-places."[7]

The preceding illustrations give evidence that a well-recognized code of observances existed, during the period of slavery, between white persons and slaves. This is to be expected and is but a counterpart of social relations found among the most primitive as well as the most advanced peoples.

The forms discovered in this, and in other codes of manners, do not exhibit, however, too great a consistency among themselves. M. Paul Reboux, for example, has recently published a book in which he shows the need of reform in the code of etiquette because of its inconsistency. He notes that a man is expected to assist a woman with packages, when in public, but not to assist her with heavier burdens in the home.

"Men walk through the corridors of buildings or big shops with their hats on their heads. But if they step into an elevator, etiquette requires that they remove their hats. And yet, as soon as the gentleman emerges from the elevator into a corridor or another floor of the store, he puts his hat on again."[8]

The strain of consistency in the etiquette, or code of observances, is not, however, its most important aspect. What is important is that the forms, accepted as correct, be known by all persons who, under certain conditions, are expected to associate in given situations.[9]

Etiquette enables persons to act freely within the limits which the formal rules of personal relations impose and has, perhaps, no higher sanction than the feeling of superiority one feels when one succeeds, or than the sense of inferiority when one fails. Moreover, the responses of persons differ with what was expected of the person seeking to conform. Persons who are unfamiliar with the formal rules are described as naïve; others who neglect, or are unconcerned with the conventions, are looked upon as boors. If others have striven to acquire "good form" and have not succeeded, it may be regarded as a misfortune but not as a crime or as an indication of moral inferiority. Herein, indeed, lies the elemental authority of etiquette—that when an individual observes the forms of behavior expected of him, and accepted in his relations with others, we may say that he is governed by the etiquette.

Herbert Spencer, in fact, has discussed etiquette under government. The government of which he speaks is ceremonial, but he describes it in such a fashion that it coincides with our notions of etiquette. He says:

"The earliest kind of government, the most general kind of government and the government which is ever spontaneously recommencing, is the government of ceremonial observances. This kind of government besides preceding all other kinds, and besides having in all places and times approached nearer to universality of influence, has ever had, and continues to have, the largest share in regulating men's lives."[10]

One function of etiquette, then, is to exert control over relations between persons and groups. The authority of etiquette is revealed in the fact that the forms generally observed are clustered about with emotions and sentiments; and, since these latter are also customary, they too tend to persist.

The responses of slaves to the presence of white persons seemed at times to be so spontaneous, and occasionally so easy and graceful, that observers would attribute the response to original nature or to instinct. At any rate, the slave moved with an easy familiarity in situations which were at the same time complex and difficult. If he seemed to act spontaneously, it was perhaps due to the fact that the forms which he observed were supported by sentiments which exerted elementary control over his actions and tended to persist along with the forms themselves. For example, Frederick Douglass, a former slave who had escaped, and had subsequently become an antislavery orator, wrote in his autobiography: "Miss Lucretia was kind; but my new mistress, Miss Sophy, surpassed her in kindness of manner."[11] The use of the terms "Miss Lucretia" and "Miss Sophy," in this instance, serves to indicate how the forms of behavior called "etiquette" persist. Douglass had been released from the necessity of using such forms, yet he reverted to them and to the attitudes customary to the relation of beloved mistress and slave.

Under the circumstances, then, when the rules of personal relations have become habitual, are supported by customary sentiments and feelings, and are deemed appropriate to the status of persons in social relationships, they may be said to be "in the mores."[12] They become, then, not only rules but rules which are both right and proper—rules the neglect of which seems to threaten the social organization, and which arouse resentment whenever, or if ever, they seem to change. Moreover, if unapproved things are done, or even contemplated, they shock the underlying sentiments and feelings, bring the person to the defense of the observances, and often create a desire to re-establish the etiquette.

The experience of Mrs. Clayton, a slaveowner, who, on a trip by steamboat from St. Louis to Cairo, had her first contact with the etiquette of race relations in the Border States, serves to illustrate this point:

"We took passage on the steamboat 'Mattie Wayne' from St. Louis. There was only one thing to make me uncomfortable during my stay on this beautiful steamer, and that was seeing the chambermaid, a neat-looking white woman, sit down to the table to take her meals in company with the black men who were waiters on the boat. I had never seen anything like it before. We loved our black servants, but they always had their meals at a separate dining table. The idea of seeing a white woman sit down to the table with those black men was shocking to me."[13]

The feeling recorded by Mrs. Clayton is one which may confidently be expected to recur when observances, established in the mores, are undermined by changed conditions. Under such circumstances bitterness, antipathy, and rationalized prejudices may be expected to manifest themselves, unless some new adjustment, acceptable to the old mores, is worked out. The individual who does not conform to the conduct expected of one of his status is out of place. No one may be expected to have dealings with him from choice; but, if choice is impossible, one's natural reaction is to force the recalcitrant to conform.

On the other hand, if persons have a status different from that which is expected or if, for lack of previous contacts, no status has been assigned, new forms will need to be instituted in order to establish relations upon a plane where communication may proceed. An illustration of this conclusion may be seen in the instance, already cited, of the free Negro women who were put to eat in the pantry. They could not eat with either white persons or slaves, for rules to accommodate them had not been established.

"In Southern Society, before the Civil War," says Sumner, "whites and blacks had formed habits of action and feeling toward each other. They lived in peace and concord, and each grew up in ways that were traditional and customary."[14] The harmony in their relations, if we accept Spencer's thesis, was, no doubt, a concomitant, if not a result, of the code of etiquette in race relations.

How inclusive the code was, and to what extent it followed a general pattern, has, as yet, not been discovered. It has appeared, however, that during the period of slavery a set of observances common to the relation of master and slave, of white persons and black, had been established, conventionalized, and incorporated into the mores. Moreover, it may be shown that a failure on the part of the slave to observe the forms brought forth the charge that he was "out of place" or "impudent." He was acceptable "in his place," however; and within the limits of the code, once accepted, tolerable personal relations were possible.

"Does a slave look dissatisfied? It is said that he has the devil in him. . . . . Does he speak loudly when spoken to by the master? Then he is getting high-minded, and should be taken down a button hole lower. Does he forget to pull off his hat at the approach of a white person? Then he is wanting in reverence. . . . . Does he venture to vindicate his conduct, when censured for it? Then he is guilty of impudence, one of the greatest crimes a slave can commit."[15]

Conceiving, then, that habits of action and feeling, or social usages and customary sentiments, exert control over the relations of individuals and groups, we are led to inquire: What were the social usages, the sentiments and feelings, and the habits of action which, in the period of slavery, existed in the relations of white persons and Negroes, and which resulted in peace and concord? What were the traditional and customary ways in which the two groups grew up? What relations were inharmonious and productive of friction, and under what conditions? What changes have occurred to undermine the code, and what have been the effects of such changes? What happened when persons evinced dispositions to evade or neglect the sentiment of respect which inheres in codes regulating relations of inferior and superior?

The answer to these questions, if they may be discovered, should serve not only to bring to light the forms observed between whites and blacks in the period of slavery but also to test, in a restricted field, the effect of etiquette as an instrument—in fact, as an elementary form—of social control.

Relations between the two races—white and black—have not all occurred under a regime of slavery. Moreover, there is evidence that they have changed. "Often," says Ray Stannard Baker, "I have heard Negroes refer to 'my white folks' and similarly the white man speaks of 'my Negroes.' The old term of slavery, the use of the term 'master,' has wholly disappeared, and in its place has arisen, not without significance, the round terms 'Boss' and 'Cap'n.' "[16]

Perhaps the most significant change in racial relations was brought about by the issuance of the Emancipation Proclamation. At least, changes were inaugurated in response to the proclamation that have become the most far-reaching. Some changes occurred during the war between the states, it is true, yet they were not so widespread as was, or might be, expected.

"The Civil War abolished legal rights and left the two races to learn how to live together under other relations than before. The whites have never been converted from the old mores. Those who still survive look back with regret and affection to the old social usages and customary sentiments and feelings. The two races have not yet made new mores. Vain attempts have been made to control the new order by legislation. The only result is proof that legislation cannot make mores. We also see that mores do not form under social convulsion and discord. It is only just now that the new society seems to be taking shape. There is a new trend in the mores as they begin to form now under the new state of things. . . . . The two races are separating more than ever before. . . . . As we go along with the constructive process, it is very plain that what once was, or what anyone thinks ought to be but slightly affects what, at any moment, is. The mores which once were are a memory.

Those which one thinks ought to be are a dream. The only things with which we can deal are those which are."[17]

Many things have happened since the Civil War which make the old code of race relations seem less tolerable. In many instances the forms have persisted after they no longer conformed to actual race relations. A slave was not called "Mister." Yet Baker relates the following conversation with a southern white man, concerning the use of that title for Negroes in the present day:

" 'Now I admire Booker Washington. I regard him as a great man, and yet I couldn't call him "Mr." Washington. We were all in a quandary until a doctor's degree was given him. That saved our lives! We all call him "Dr." Washington now.' "[18]

It is possible that the status of the Negro in, and since, slavery is related to the problem of race relations and etiquette. The status and rank of an individual determine, to a large degree, the respect in which he is held and the forms considered proper in association with him. Moreover, his response is a function of his conception of his role in the group and is bound up with his status. The status of the Negro in America has constantly changed. Upon his arrival, at Jamestown, he was an indentured servant; he was later reduced to slavery; still later he was emancipated, so that, to all intents and purposes, he became a free man. With each change in his legal status has gone a conception of change in his relations to, and with, white people, though the conception has not always and everywhere been realized. He has had, as Moton remarks, a very troublesome way of outgrowing his status as soon as some interested party had succeeded in fixing it.[19]

The change of legal status indicated in the proclamation which freed the slaves, and the anticipated change in social status, created a problem that has produced not only discussion but also the establishment of organizations, committees and commissions, associations and societies, which look to a solution by agitating the question, by proposing plans or programs of action, or by seeking to remove the discussion from the public hearing. These have not always met with success. Relations between the two races seem somehow to grow in spite, rather than because, of such attempts.

Eventually, then, we are led to believe that the problem and the conditions of its solution lie far beneath the rational desires and purposes of men. Relations which develop between persons in a moral order—that is, in an order where conduct is traditional and customary—are more fixed and lasting, as well as more peaceful, than those established by reason or fiat.

The government exerted by etiquette is not only more elementary than legislation, it also precedes, goes along with, and continues after laws and set rules.

We seek, then, to discover the social usages customary to the relations of the white and black races; how these have operated to control the relations; what effect the success or failure of the control has had upon the ability of the two races to enter into, and co-operate in, an effective corporate life. We shall consider etiquette, or the code of social usages, as the forms required by custom and tradition to be observed in contacts and relations of the two races during the period of their association in America; the ceremonial side of race relations; the behavior that is expected and accepted when white and colored persons meet or associate.

The study will be confined to the southern states largely because (1) the code appears to have developed there and (2) it is still found there, regulating the contact and association of by far the greater number of Negroes in their relations to white people.

The period studied will extend from about 1619 down to the present. The emphasis, however, will be placed upon the period beginning with the nineteenth century.

CHAPTER II

THE ETIQUETTE OF GREETING, SALUTATION AND CONVERSATION

PERSONS visiting in the South, before the war, frequently observed that the slaves whom they met were a courteous set of people.[1] In fact, courtesy seemed to be an innate disposition of Negroes. The forms which Negroes customarily used toward whites had, indeed, become so general that it was easy to assume an instinctive basis for them. Negroes, for example, usually agreed with any statement made by a white person, so that, in many instances, they were accused of evasion, if not of deceit.

" 'Tom,' said his master, pointing to Y., 'this is my brother.'
" 'Ah, massa, him berry like you.'
" 'You did not know that I had a brother, did you, Tom?'
" 'No, massa, him berry good brother.'
" 'And, Tom,' pointing to us, 'these are my cousins.'
" 'All your family, massa?'
" 'Yes, Tom.'
" 'All berry like you, massa. What a family you have, massa.'
I need hardly remark that four persons more unlike could hardly have been brought together."[2]

These forms of behavior were, perhaps, a defense against penetration of the reserves of personality. Moton records an interesting anecdote of two Negro deacons who had been called upon to pray for the success of the Confederacy, during the war between the states. One deacon responded by asking simply that "the Lord's will be done" and left the responsibility on the shoulders of the Lord as to which of the two should win. The second deacon, however, met the issue squarely and prayed fervently for the success of the Confederate cause. Some time afterward he was approached by certain of his constituents and called into question for such an obvious betrayal of their hopes. He was again equal to the occasion and said, "Don't worry, children; the Lord knew what I was talking about."[3]

Politeness on the part of slaves was especially observed publicly. Upon meeting white persons, the men touched or removed their hats—in case they wore hats—and the women bowed or nodded.[4] The women had, however, taken over the curtsey, which, it seems, was a bit more formal than the nod or bow, and in some instances men followed the practice.[5]

If a slave were introduced to a white person, there is reason to believe that he offered to shake hands.[6] This was perhaps not always the rule, for when Mr. Pollard offered to shake hands with "Aunt Debby" she prepared for it "by deprecatingly wiping her hand on her apron."[7] Moreover, the observance, while respected occasionally in more public relations, tended to be confined to the plantations, as, for example, whenever the family had been away on a journey, or a member was returning, or there was a visitor to the plantation. On the Sea Islands of South Carolina the observance was apparently both private and semipublic. Pearson quotes instances from letters showing that, on visits to the slave quarters, and in one case as a visitor went through the street of a tiny sea island, the slaves crowded around to shake hands.[8]

Upon occasions of leave-taking or return from an extended trip, it was customary for "black mammy" to kiss the women and children of the family, but it appears that the young women of the family were her especial charge, toward whom she exercised these prerogatives.[9] The boys were not, however, exempt and were embraced or kissed by the "mammy," even though they protested at times.[10] If perchance there had been a separation between mistress and "mammy," the reunion was occasionally marked by an embrace, perhaps tears, and certainly by mutual felicitations.[11] The "mammy's" position and relation to the mistress and children were perhaps closer than that of any slave. She was a kind of glorified nurse and was the authority in nursery matters. The younger woman who attended the children as guardian and companion, and who was called "nurse," was subordinate to her. Moreover, it is said, the mistress "humoured her claims of authority,"[12] hence the intimacy doubtless begot its own etiquette.

If, then, the greetings advanced beyond the primary stage, so that a conversation was necessary, the slave removed his hat[13] or touched it as if it would be removed, at each sentence,[14] and kept his eye on the ground during the conversation. If, as was the rule in some sections, the slave had no hat, he then proceeded to pull at his forelock while the conversation continued.[15] This latter form was, perhaps, also the accepted behavior indoors.

Once the conversation got under way, the slave replied with "sir," or "ma'am," as the occasion demanded:

"I asked him if Jim had sent for some tobacco, as he said he would. 'Yes, sarr.' 'Did he send the money?' 'Sarr?' Repeated. 'No, sarr.' 'How much does he want?' 'Don't know, sarr.' 'How can I send the tobacco if I don't know how much he wants?' 'He send for him, sarr.' 'Did he send you for it?' 'No, sarr.' 'Whom did he send?' 'Dunno, sarr.' 'How will he get his tobacco?' 'He come hisself, sarr.' 'Where is he?' 'He at home, sarr.' 'He is coming to get it himself, is he?' 'Sarr?' (repeated in nigger phrase). 'Yes, sarr.' 'Did Bruce send you for anything else beside the curry-comb?' 'Yes, sarr.' 'What else?' 'Sarr?' 'Did Bruce tell you to fetch anything beside this?' 'No, sarr.' 'Is this all Bruce told you to get?' 'Yes, sarr.' "[16]

The "sir" or "ma'am" was stressed as the one important word, says one author.[17] If this were true, it would still be true to life, considering that, as Spencer says, "what an obeisance implies by acts—such as reverence and loyalty—a form of address says in words."[18] On the other hand, "sir" was not so intimate as other forms. It was, perhaps, used in conversing with an overseer[19]—who occupied a more formal position than the master—and in relation with persons who were met with in public.

On the plantation, however, slaves addressed the mistress and girls as "Miss"[20] and used the Christian name therewith. If a woman slave felt particularly close to the mistress or daughters, she addressed them as "Missy," without the Christian name.[21] Babies, in some sections, were addressed as "Massa" or "Miss" even in their cradle days.[22] However, as the children grew to maturity, and there grew up also the necessity of distinguishing between "massas" and "misses," their appellations changed to "Young Miss" and "Young Mars," with and without the Christian name.[23] The master's name became "Mars Billy" except when it was necessary to distinguish him from the young master, then "Old Mars Billy" was used.[24] This latter form was not used in address but as a term of reference.

The slave used the term "master" ceremonially. For example, Frederick Douglass relates that he was bought by one Captain Auld, a former ship captain—whence the name—and overseer:

"We seldom called him 'master'; we generally called him 'Captain Auld,' and were hardly disposed to title him at all. . . . . Our want of reverence for him must have perplexed him greatly. He wished to have us call him 'master,' but lacked the firmness necessary to command us to do so. His wife used to insist upon our calling him so, but to no effect."[25]

The term "captain" abbreviated to "cap'n" served perhaps as formal address for white men with whom the slaves were not acquainted, or with whom they had occasion to associate, in one way or another, in public. "Boss" was coming into use toward the end of the war, on the Sea Islands.[26]

From another angle an observance by an inferior toward a superior implies a complimentary observance on the part of the latter since the two are under the control of the same ceremony. When a slave addressed a master or a white man as "Marster" or "Boss," the latter would not only answer with appropriate forms but would also assume the attitude of a master or boss, as the slave had already assumed that of a servant and inferior.

Certain of the old slaves, especially on the plantation, were addressed as "Uncle," usually with the Christian name. Next to "mammy," this title, perhaps, represented the highest respect paid to slaves by white persons. The title was not given in virtue of the age of the slave, as Ingraham seems to think,[27] but in case the slave was considered, more or less, as a part of the family.[28] "With advancing years, if endowed with sufficient personal dignity and other elements of character," the individual became "Uncle Jim."[29] If the term was rather general,[30] it, nevertheless, carried with it some notion of responsibility, as well as respect.

"These old men are always giving the master advice too, in consequence [of their respected position]; and tell him with all oracular dignity whether the moon is just right to plant the different kinds of grain, or how to hoe the tobacco to the best advantage, or when to give the corn the last ploughing, or to harrow the cotton, or to kill the pork-hogs, or to shear the sheep . . . . of how 'they' shall resort to some new and untried experiment to keep 'dem debblish pigs from gettin' in dat ar 'tater patch, and rootin' up dem 'taters'—all of which the master listens to good-humouredly, and in most cases with profit."[31]

Some of these "uncles" took themselves seriously it seems:

"Uncle Jimbo has a good deal of slave pride, and is anxious to appear to visitors as one of great dignity and consequence in household affairs. He is especially proud of his position as general conservator of the order and security of the household, and any interruption of his stilted dignity is painful to him."[32]

"Auntie" sometimes derived her title from long service in the family, or frequently as the wife of a respected "uncle."

The title "Old Man" seems to have been given to "any middle-aged Negro whose name is not known. . . . . The slave is not to be supposed to be beyond his prime of strength."[33] It was perhaps used to express familiarity and respect just a bit

lower than "uncle." One old African, who frequently entertained white people with stories of his native land, was addressed in a familiar manner as "Daddy Cudjo." Bremer noted
a rather general use of the term "daddy" in Charleston, South
Carolina, about 1850.[34]

The slave seldom had a surname. Douglass speaks of one
"Uncle Isaac Cooper," in Maryland, but he adds that "it is seldom that a slave gets a surname from anyone in Maryland."[35]
In fact, in case it were necessary to distinguish between or
among "Tom's" or "Henry's," the accepted form was "Henry belonging to Mrs. Such-an-One," says Ferguson.[36] The usual term
of address to a slave was by the given name—"John" or
"Cicero" or what not.[37] However, Pearson notes, on the Sea
Islands, in 1862, that "all have surnames of one sort or another,
the wife taking her husband's."[38] The islands had, by this time,
come under the domination of the federal government, and perhaps this condition was a response to the new situation in which
the slaves were beginning to imitate the whites.

"Boy" was the term used by whites to address slaves whom
they did not know, or whom they did not recognize, it seems.[39]
Olmsted relates an occasion where a master, near Nachitoches,
Louisiana, addressed the women working in the fields as
"girls."[40] These terms were used not only as direct forms of
address but also with reference to male or female slaves.

The term "nigger" was frequently used as a term of direct
address by white persons who did not know the slave addressed[41]
—and, more frequently, perhaps, by nonslaveholders. Hundley
remarks that "a Southern Gentleman [one of his six classes]
rarely, if ever, says nigger."[42] Buckingham found the term
modified to "nigger-fellow," in Virginia, in 1839.[43] On the
whole, however, by whomever it was used, the literature of the
prewar period abounds with the terms in forms of address, as a
descriptive term, or as a noun and an adjective.[44]

CHAPTER III

MANNERS ON PLANTATION AND FARM

THE more intimate association, and the more numerous contacts between white and colored persons, in the period of slavery, occurred on the plantations and the farms.[1] There were, of course, both slaves and free Negroes in the towns and cities who came into association with white people; but, considering the slave primarily as a laborer and as the chief factor in the production of staples—cotton, tobacco, sugar cane, and rice—it is clear that his life was bound up with the agricultural setting and development of the South.

The industrial units of which the slave formed so important a part varied in organization with the number of acres contained in a given unit, as well as with the size and character of the personnel. The plantation or farm, however large or small it might be, tended to be a kind of kingdom, with a sovereignty all its own. It had its own rules, regulations, and customs; and the laws and institutions of the state touched it seldom, except as plantation customs had been incorporated into those institutions or enacted into its laws.

In general, the organization was bound together, as well as produced, by long family association, by common traditions, by common memories, and certainly by common interests.[2] Contact between the racial groups, intimate or formal, might at one time be cast harmoniously, at another discordantly. But the elementary conditions under which association did proceed tended to be those where forms of behavior, expected and accepted by both races, had been established. These forms tended to define, as well as to support, the distances and reserves that were necessary for effective social action.

Within the "big house"—as the owner's home on the larger

plantations was called—there were certain forms to be observed. The more formal contacts, perhaps, consisted in addressing and in conversing with one another. "No slave," says
Steward, "was ever allowed to sit down in the presence of the
master or mistress." If, perchance, he were sitting when addressed, he would stand; and, if out of doors, would also, if he
had one, remove his hat.[3] On the other hand, it was doubtless a
fact that the slave felt that sitting in the presence of the master
was not proper.

The slaves who acted as waiters stood behind the chairs of
master and mistress at meals, meanwhile attending strictly to
the course of conversation.[4] In some instances, if addressed by
the master, the servant might enter into the conversation, "as
if he were a family friend, better informed on some local and
domestic points" than the master.[5] He did not, however, initi-
ate, or enter into, a conversation unless addressed.[6] This must
have required self-control at times, especially when, as Martineau remarks, the conversation referred to slaves in hearing.[7]

The errand boy was generally required to stand behind the
master's chair, whether or not the latter was at a meal. In this
strategic position he might step up unbidden to light the master's cigar or slip away to bring a ready-saddled horse to the
door.[8]

On the small farm, or perhaps in the case of house servants
on large plantations, the slaves ate in the kitchen. One planter
told Olmsted that the hands ate "right out of the same frying
pan—it was all the same, only they ate in the kitchen and he
ate in the room we were in, with the door open between them."

" 'Massa Hampton 'joyed seein' people have a good time.
He never turned no nigger away hongry—naw, suh,—not even
a po' white! He make 'em come roun' de kitchen, and eat at
de servin' table.' "[9]

On larger plantations there might be a cookhouse for the field
hands, or those hands might be expected to prepare their own
meals in their cabins.

But, if eating in the master's house might at times be acceptable, it appears that slaves might not drink there:

"My mistress said that she would teach me better manners than that . . . . she would have *one* slave that knew his place; if I wanted water, I could go to the spring, and not drink in the house."[10]

On some larger estates, where field hands were not under such direct contact with the master's family, there was established the custom of "visiting" the slave quarters, perhaps on Sundays. On these occasions the slaves met master and mistress with a handshake; then the mistress went into the cabins to see if they were in order, or, perhaps, to inspect some infant who had recently made his arrival.[11] At the cabins of certain favored slaves the family might stop a while to chat. The ceremony was, perhaps, complete when the slave gave the mistress a small present of eggs or vegetables, or offered both master and mistress a glass of milk or a piece of bread.[12]

When the children of the master went to the slave cabins, the slaves would receive them as ambassadors from the "big house" and in much the same manner as they received the adults. They would give the children presents of eggs, "marvels," and cakes.[13] The children would, in turn, bring trinkets from the "big house"[14] and, at times, might be invited to stay and have a bite to eat.[15] Especially was this true in case the person they visited was "black mammy."[16]

There were also occasions when plantation guests visited the "quarters."

"The wife and mother then meets you at the door and with graceful courtesy and kindly greeting invites you in; respectfully yet warmly inquiring about the white folks at the 'greathouse'—Old Marster, and Mistis and Marse John, and Marse Jeems, and Miss Car'line."[17]

Upon one occasion a woman visitor to the Sea Islands stopped at a cabin while the men caught mules to hitch to a wagon, so that they might take her to her home. While waiting the visitor was invited in and given "hominy and chicken" to eat, while the slave women stood around and after the children were sent outside. The meal was passed around among the women after the visitor had finished.[18]

The slaves seldom "visited" the "big house" ceremonially. However, on the Sea Islands, it seemed that the field hands had been in the "habit of coming into the yard on Sundays." They usually brought little gifts, such as fish, a rabbit, eggs, and the like,[19] and perhaps went no closer to the house than the yard.

PLAY AND PASTIME

When the master of the plantation organized fishing or hunting expeditions, he would take his body servants along to assist him. At such times there were certain distinctions to be observed. Ingraham saw a fishing procession in Tennessee, in 1853, which was organized with due regard for precedence and rank. First there went, ahead, a Negro boy who was seated astride a colt; next came the master astride a blooded horse, riding by a coach, in which the guests were seated; after these came an old Negro bait carrier, seated on an old horse; and the pole carrier brought up the rear, seated on a mule.[20]

If a hunt were under way, the master usually rode a horse, and his gunbearer a mule.[21] In the case of a return from a hunt, again described by Ingraham, the master rode in front, his body servant came next, also astride, bearing a wounded dog; after these came the guests, astride; but the game bearers and the game bearers' helpers came last, afoot. Incidentally, the main pack of dogs went by the side of the master, while the puppies and untrained pack went with the game bearers.[22]

Christmas was an occasion in the celebration of which both masters and slaves participated. In the Upper South the celebration might last a week; but, on the large cotton plantations and sugar farms, the time might be cut to three days, or even less, according to the state of the crop. Custom decreed that it should last as long as the "yule log" burned.[23]

At the Christmas season it was the custom to surprise another by calling "Christmas gift" before the other could say it.

"Those of the darkeys who do not intrude upon your slumbers lie in wait behind every door and corner, and the moment your nose appears, they pounce upon you with a whoop, shouting furiously, 'Chrismus Giff, Mas'r, Ah, I cotch you dis time.' "[24]

The one who first called must then receive a present. When the slaves received presents, they responded by bowing "almost to the ground," pulling off their hats, or otherwise pulling at the forelock.

After breakfast a bell would ring, and the slaves would assemble on the back veranda, while the master and mistress gave out presents. To the common slave or field hand they gave knives or packages of tobacco; to the girls and women, dolls or handkerchiefs; and to the favorite slaves, usually money. However, each slave would call out "Merry Christmas" as he passed.[25]

After luncheon, or perhaps later in the afternoon, dinner was served for the Negroes in the back yard. On these occasions the master's family were interested spectators, although they stood while the Negroes sat.[26]

Occasions of a festival nature, such as barbecues, picnics, cornhuskings, and the like were not lacking among the slaves. The first step was to procure permission from the master. If this were given, the slaves then proceeded with their preparations, meanwhile inviting the master and his family to attend and reserving seats at the function for them.[27] At a cornhusking —called "corn-shucking"—Avirett noted that the slaves drew up several chairs in a wagon, "so all de white folks can jest hab deir fun."[28] The slaves, however, stood on the ground.

Before the actual husking began, the slaves filed by the master, who took his stand on the step of a cabin near by.[29] While the husking continued, the slaves might improvise songs, in which they could laud their master and show how kindly disposed he was as compared with other masters:

I

Massa's niggers am slick and fat,
    Oh! Oh! Oh!
Shine jes like a new beaver hat,
    Oh! Oh! Oh!

Refrain

Turn out here and shuck dis corn.
    Oh! Oh! Oh!
Biggest pile o' corn seen since I was born,
    Oh! Oh! Oh!

II

Jones' niggers am lean an' po',
    Oh! Oh! Oh!
Don't know whether dey get enough ter eat or no,
    Oh! Oh! Oh![30]

After the husking refreshments were occasionally served. On an occasion observed by Avirett,

"Uncle Phillip, as master of ceremonies, directed Handy, Cain, and George, and Buck, 'to wait on dem company niggers fus', after dey done giv' the two captains plenty of supper and coffee.' "[31]

It seems, then, that white persons might eat at slave functions, provided that they sat while the slaves stood, or vice versa; and provided they were served first.

When the family had been away upon a journey, the return took on a festival aspect. After greetings had been extended to the white members who had remained, the slaves might then come forward. In one instance given, the house servants came first, then the superannuated slaves. The field hands, however, are not mentioned.[32]

There were also forms to be observed in case of marriage or death among the members of the plantation. Describing a cere-

mony where two young women of a family were participants in
a double wedding, one observer mentioned that house servants
were present along with the family and visitors. After the ceremony the servants approached the two couples and said:

" 'Wish you joy, Mas'r Colonel and Mas'r Major; wish you
joy, Miss Car'line and Miss Le'nora; and may the good Lord
bless you all.' "[33]

The brides, daughters of the master, were greeted intimately, it
will be noticed, while the grooms were addressed very formally.

One young master observed a ceremony when he brought his
bride home. First, he introduced her to his parents, then to
his brothers and sisters, then to the "mammy," and finally to
the house servants.[34]

In case of marriage between slaves, it was first necessary to
obtain the consent of the master.[35] In case the parties to the
ceremony were the property of different masters, both masters
were perhaps consulted.[36]

The permission of the master, or masters, having been pro-
cured, the young women of the master's family assumed charge
of the prospective bride and made her a trousseau, or, in some
cases, provided one from the family heirlooms.[37] Meanwhile,
the young men of the family, or perhaps the master, provided
suitable finery for the groom.[38] In some instances the slave
bride-to-be, her bridesmaids, and attendants were even given
the family jewels with which to bedeck themselves.

"The bride's-maids were dressed very richly. Isabel having
given one of them one of her beautiful dresses, and loaned her
a diamond pin and ruby bracelets. I also decked out my Eda in
a figured white muslin, two necklaces, and a brooch. . . . .
From the neighboring estates were several females, handsomely
dressed, and wearing their mistresses' willingly-loaned jewels,
so that (thanks to the kind indulgence of masters and mistresses) at this wedding of slaves, shone more jewels than are
often seen in elegant assemblies."[39]

When the night of the wedding arrived, the servants repaired to the "big house" where they found the master and mistress and the family waiting. The ceremony was performed in the dining-room or hall—generally in the dining-room[40]—by a white minister,[41] or, perhaps, a colored minister,[42] or in some instances by the master himself.[43] On one occasion the father of the bride gave her away, but in another a white physician assumed the responsibility, although he was not the master of the woman, it seems.[44] When the ceremony was over, presents were given to the bride,[45] and the party repaired to the wedding-supper.

The wedding-supper was held in the kitchen or back yard,[46] but, in exceptional cases, it might be held in the dining-room.[47] In one instance the master "invited" the servants in to supper, "after they had had a dance of their own, on the lower gallery." A slave woman related:

" 'I had a weddin'—a big weddin' for Harlow's kitchen. Your pa gib me a head weddin'—kilt a mutton, a round o' beef—turkeys, cakes, one or t'other trifle. I had on your pa's wife's weddin' gloves an' slippers an' veil. De slippers was too small, but I put my toes in. Miss Mary had a mighty neat foot. Marster brought out a milk-pail full o' toddy, and more in bottles. De gentleman's and marster stood up at de tables. He didn't rush 'round 'mongst the black folks, you know. I had a tearin'-down weddin' to be sho'. Nobody else didn't hab sich a weddin'.' "[48]

Vance and McDonald have testified that the entire occasion was a solemn one, being "entirely devoid of absurdities, and as solemn and imposing as were the same rites when partaken by whites."[49] Page believed, however, that the white persons attended "to get fun out of the entertainment."[50]

Distinctions between house and field hands were likely to be observed in the ceremony. Field hands were perhaps married in the "quarters" or cabins by the master or, occasionally, by a colored preacher.[51] McTyeire records that one master used "an old copy of an English reader" for a prayer-book. Another conducted his ceremony as follows:

" 'Come on in de house you chillun,' Massa say. He set down an' look at us. 'Now,' he say, 'I don't want no fussin' ner fightin'. De way ter live happy is ter be forgivin' an' not start no ruckus. I hopes you have a long life togedder, an' if'n de Lawd send little niggers, dey'll be mos' welcome.' "[52]

After the ceremony the slaves wanted their names put in "the book." This book was the master's record and served, perhaps, as a means to trace descent of slaves.[53]

On occasions where death came to the plantation, there were also certain forms to be expected. If the master were sick unto death, the slaves might be called to the bedside to receive a parting blessing. Thus on a plantation, near Abbeville, South Carolina:

"The master's family and friends were gathered about his bedside when the time came for him to go. Having taken leave of his friends, he ordered his Negro laborers to be summoned from the field to take farewell of him. When they arrived he was speechless and motionless, but sensible of all that was oc-curring, as could be seen from his look of intelligence. One by one the Negroes entered the apartment, and filing by him in succession took each in turn the limp hand of the dying master, and affectionately pressing it for a moment, thanked him for his goodness, commended him to God, and bade him farewell."[54]

Steward relates an occasion upon which the slaves were called in as the mistress died:

"The slaves were all deeply affected by the scene; some doubtless truly lamented the death of their mistress; others rejoiced that she was no more, and all were more or less fright-ened. One of them, I remember, went to the pump and wet his face, so as to appear to weep with the rest."[55]

The presence of the slaves at the sickbed of master or mistress was also expected, perhaps.

"Every night the slaves gather around the house and send up one or two to see how master does. They creep up to the bed and inquire, with very soft voice, 'How is dear massa? O

massa, how we want to hear your voice out in the field again.'
They come down to their *anxious* companions. 'How is the old
man? Will he die?' 'Yes, yes, he is sure to go this time; he will
never whip slave no more.' 'Are you sure?' 'O, yes, he surely
gone for it now.' "[56]

If the master died, the slaves would attend the funeral—if the
master had been exceptionally kind—yet the place of honor was
ordinarily given to house servants.[57]

On the other hand, when a slave died, the master might give
the other slaves a day of rest[58] and meanwhile appoint certain
among them to make a coffin and dig a grave.[59] When time
came for the funeral:

"The procession was formed in the following manner: first,
the old slave minister, then the remains of the dead, following
came the weeping relatives; then came the master and his family; next the slaves belonging to the plantation; and, last,
friends and strangers, black and white; all moved on solemnly
to the final resting place."[60]

When the slave was buried in the plantation graveyard for
slaves, a colored minister might read the service. In one instance a white bishop of the diocese read the funeral service of
an old servant at the request of a Negro minister.[61] The plantation cemetery was an "unfenced quarter of an acre," or perhaps a selected spot, with headstones—some inscribed with
suitable epitaphs. One such epitaph read:

"To record the worthy fidelity of Reynolds Watts . . . .
reared from infancy by an affectionate mistress and trained by
her in the paths of virtue, she was strictly moral in her deport-
ment, faithful and devoted in her duty and heart and soul.
. . . . (The remainder of the epitaph was blotted.)"[62]

Lewis Clarke, himself a slave, suggested that slaves preferred
to be buried "at the greatest possible distance from the master,
lest he whip them dead, as well as he did when alive."[63] This,
however, could hardly account for the slave cemetery on the
plantation.

THE OVERSEER ON THE PLANTATION

Relations between whites and blacks on the farm, small plantation, or large plantation where the owner resided differed from those on the large absentee-owned units and from those on the large resident-owned plantation, where an overseer was needed to manage the slaves. Colonel Starke observed that the introduction of the overseer was the "natural result of wealth, luxury, and indolence."[64]

The overseer obtained a place in the plantation system under varying circumstances, for example, when a plantation grew beyond the limits of a master's capacity to direct; or when an owner had acquired the status of a large planter, for whom it was socially impossible to work with slaves. Again, when an estate was inherited by several minor children or scattered heirs, or when an owner would acquire several plots of land, an overseer would be required to superintend the labor of the separate units.[65] An evaluation of the overseer's presence would then seem to indicate that he was an intermediary—a buffer between master and slave.[66]

The overseer was frequently recruited from among former planters, who, having lost their property, were driven to work as a temporary measure; or he might be the son of a planter, working for a start in life. Occasionally he was an English or German farmer, or member of the native yeomanry, who hoped to make a vocation of superintendence. The result was that some among the overseers were ambitious, some were temporarily established, while still others were purposeless opportunists.[67] All seemed to want to leave the status as soon as possible, either by fiat or fortune.

The almost universal testimony of planters who had occasion to refer to overseers is that they were dishonest, self-indulgent, cruel, and irresponsible. George Washington, as one example, was almost continually complaining of trouble with his overseers.[68] Slaves considered an overseer as "the master's left hand; the burden layer and symbol of the hardest features of bondage."[69] Former slaves who have had occasion to refer to the overseer find little but condemnation to offer. Even in the literature of the plantation, as Gaines remarks, he is usually the uncondoned villain of the plantation cast and, save in the most sympathetic reminiscences, is pictured as brutal, uncouth, and unlettered.[70]

"The business of overseer was not calculated, particularly, to develop the finer feelings of humanity in him, and there was no business interest to restrain his haughty over-bearing and abusive spirit in dealing with Negroes."[71]

Choosing an overseer, in later years, amounted almost to a vocation in itself. Articles contributed to journals, describing the character expected of a good overseer, noted that he would be industrious, careful, prudent, humane, and honest.[72] Owners who were part-time residents of the plantation occasionally found it necessary, however, to include clauses in the overseer's contract, stating that the overseer was required to concern himself with "the care and well-being of the slaves," or declaring that, in dealing out rations to slaves, "measures were to be heaped, and not struck"; or noting that no work was to be done on Christmas, Good Friday, Sundays, and holidays, and only half-tasks on Saturdays, and that extras were to be given for Christmas.[73] One owner required that his overseers "use no abusive language or violence of demeanor" toward the slaves. The slaves on President Polk's plantation complained that their overseer "swore roundly at them; which was not proper."[74] Generally, in contracts drawn up by benevolent slaveholders the overseers were required to treat the slaves "with humanity," and, as one owner stipulated, "submit to make less rice and keep my Negroes at home in some degree of happiness, in preference to large crops acquired by rigor and barbarity to those poor creatures."[75]

Where the plantation was conducted mainly for profit, we must believe that such regulations were neither written nor enforced. But, in any case, the overseer was burdened with the care of slaves, stock, and tools and was expected to make a good crop every year, lest he be not retained the next.

Again, where the owner was a part-time resident or nonresident, the overseer was usually intrusted "with everything on the plantation" and was allowed to manage it about as he pleased.[76] However, in other cases, trusty slaves were given keys to storehouses in order to prevent him from stealing, or doing away with, plantation supplies.[77]

If the slaves thought the overseer too strict or severe, they would occasionally appeal to the master, "who as the dispenser of mercy and forgiveness had some degree of affection for the slaves," or they could "run away," singly or in groups, and remain hidden in swamp or forest until the master arrived to adjust matters.

"The slaves could not negotiate directly at such a time, but while they lay in the woods they might make overtures to the overseer, through slaves on neighboring plantations, as to terms on which they might return to work; or they might await the master's arrival and appeal to him for redress of their grievances. Humble as their demeanor might be, their power of renewing the pressure by renewing the flight could not be ignored. A happy ending for all concerned might be reached by mutual concessions and pledges."[78]

John Evans wrote to his employer that "your Negroes behave badly behind my back and then Run to you and you appear to beleave what they say."[79] He had indicated earlier that one should be careful how one listened to, or repeated, what slaves reported. Said he:

"I Let Chesley go down to Eldesteno [a second plantation belonging to the master] and he ses that the crop was in bad condition and that the mules was very poor and the Negroes also looked bad, and then still I don't Like to talk after Negroes."[80]

The lot of the overseer on the nonresident plantation was,

then, generally hard. There was, on the part of some slaves, a complete lack of interest in their work; and, on the part of others, laziness and occasional actual opposition. Moreover, restrictions imposed by a kind-hearted master, and a lack of confidence too frequently shown,[81] increased the difficulty of the overseer's task.

The terms of the contract between overseer and planter have been styled "the Constitution of the plantation" by Dr. R. E. Park.[82] Many constitutions, perhaps, were found more ideal than practical.[83] The overseer, however, was the enforcing agent and observed requirements when he could but abrogated them when necessary.

"Of the humanizing side of labor he knew nothing, slave labor could not be humanized from his point of view. To lift up the slave was to make him dissatisfied with slavery. To make him accept slavery and to work because he was told to work was the overseer's idea."[84]

This he did by gentleness in some cases but, it seems, by force in most. "The overseer was a development and a destiny."[85]

More light may be thrown on relations of the plantations, in which forms and observances ruled, if we consider the relation of the overseer to other white people and to slaves. He could not live with the planter, and he would not live with the slaves. His house, but little better in size and appearance than the cabins of the slaves, generally lay between them and the "big house."[86]

He might be a member of the same church as the planter, but he generally preferred the evangelical churches—Methodist and Baptist. If, perchance, he did attend the planters' church, he and his family sat apart "quite distinctly." His children did not intermarry with the planters' children, and between them "in social matters was a frozen ocean."[87]

The overseer on absentee-owned plantations was generally a lonely soul. If he were a single man, he would, as a rule, be forbidden visitors.[88] If he desired to marry, he would need to ask the advice, if not the actual permission, of his employer.[89] Yet, even if he were married, he would be expected to receive few visits from his friends, lest he neglect the business of the plantation.[90] His wife was, perhaps, still more lonely. She was the only white woman on the absentee-owned plantation; and generally the only one save the planter's wife and female relatives on the resident-owned plantation. Still, in the latter case, the overseer's wife could associate only very formally with the ladies of the "big house." The following correspondence from an overseer to an owner tends to show how an overseer's sick wife felt in the loneliness of a Florida plantation:

"May 16, 1856. . . . . Mrs. McCall's Health does not improve as yet. She suffer a gradeal at tim. She sen best wishes to Mrs. Jones.

"June 21, 1856. . . . . Mrs. McCall wishes you to remember her to Mrs. Jones and to say to her that she does not expect to live many days longer and that she is perfectly resigned to deth and all she regrets is leaving hur family and friends, she bids her far well. the Doctors have given her out."[91]

If the contact of an overseer with upper-class white persons was restricted, with slaves it was close but formal.[92] He could not work with them, lest it weaken his authority. It was necessary to keep as separate from them as possible. Phillips records an incident where an overseer "rode off in a rage, after ten days of service, because some new-coming Negroes were lodged in an unused part of his house."[93] Charles Manigault, owner of a plantation near Savannah, Georgia, discharged an overseer for many lapses, among which he named:

"Moreover, elated by a strong and very false religious feeling, he began to injure the plantation a vast deal, placing himself on a par with Negroes, by even joining with them at their prayer meetings."[94]

Slaves used "sir" when addressing, or replying to, an overseer.[95] This was formal but not intimate, for, to slaves, an overseer was "buckra," not a person of "real quality."[96] Moreover,

their respect for him was, perhaps, not enhanced by the knowledge that he was responsible to the owner, only in a lesser degree than themselves.

The slaves, perhaps, resented attempts on the part of an
overseer to play the gentleman. In one instance, John McCall,
overseer on a Florida plantation, selected a mulatto daughter of
a house slave as a "play child" for his own daughter. The slave
mother, however, disagreed with the choice, and told the daughter to refuse to serve. When the child refused, she was soundly
whipped by the overseer. Thereupon the mother herself walked
off the plantation and was only taken by officers, who lodged
her in jail.[97]

The overseer on absentee plantations, perhaps because of the
isolation, would occasionally form connections with the slave
women and thus bring about dissatisfaction in both slaves and
master. Cases of that type were numerous enough to cause discussion, both private and public. When Sturgis outlined the
qualifications of an ideal overseer, he stated that the planter
ought to encourage him "by offer of a permanent situation and
any other advantages . . . . to marry." Then, in a footnote, he
wrote: "The reasons for this are of a nature too delicate to
comment upon, but far too important to be passed over in
silence."[98]

The overseer, then, was an outsider in the plantation system.
The closeness of relation between master and slave tended to be
broken as soon as he became a factor in plantation management.
Antipathy and discord took the place of understanding and
sympathy. Moreover, the slave could scarcely fail to observe
the poorly concealed contempt in which the master held the
overseer. Then, identifying himself with the master, he also
tended to look down on the overseer. These factors, among
others, caused relations, where overseers were generally present, to be different from those on the resident plantation and
small or large farm. In general, the more the overseer was in
power, the more discordant race relations were.

CHAPTER IV

ETIQUETTE IN THE CHURCH

IN THE church and in matters of religion relations between whites and blacks, beginning, no doubt, as early as 1619, have gone through an interesting series of changes. The first Negroes to arrive in Virginia were considered "strange creatures." So strange, in fact, that they could scarcely be classified as human. Even as late as the end of the seventeenth century it was held that "the Negro was not a man but a wild beast, hardly superior to the monkey in intelligence, and with habits far more debased."[1] Hence those persons who might have been inclined to accept him as a human being still characterized him as a heathen. This classification placed him quite outside the pale of ordinary creatures.

Religion, however, was a matter of grave importance to early Virginians, who, it was said, maintained a system of religious observances quite as rigid as that of the Puritans.[2] As a reflection of these conditions, perhaps, there soon developed the practice of admitting a Negro to Christian baptism and, still later, of admitting one who had been baptized to a higher status, namely, to that of a Christian Negro.

When, however, it was found desirable and possible to reduce the Negro to slavery, a conflict occurred. A rather widespread opinion held that Christians could not righteously be enslaved. The problem then resolved itself into reconciling current religious beliefs and slavery.

Down to about 1641, while indenture for Negroes was developing into Negro slavery, baptism operated to release Negroes from slavery. But, after that time, the presumption was that baptism did not precede manumission. In 1664 the lower house of the Maryland legislature passed a law stipulating that Negroes should serve their masters *durante vita* and prohibiting freedom for Negroes even though baptized.[3] This act was calculated to reassure slaveholders who did not wish to take their slaves into the church if, by reason of that fact, they would be deprived of their services. Virginia sought, in 1670, to distinguish between servants imported by sea and by land,[4] but twelve years later dropped the distinction, repealed the previous law, and declared that all persons of non-Christian nationalities thereafter coming into the colony by sea or by land, whether or not they had been converted to Christianity after capture, should be slaves.[5]

Moreover, supporting the statutes, if not directly giving rise to them, the notion developed that bondage was a small price for the Negro to pay for the benefits of Christianity. Through the enslavement of heathen and infidels, as a precondition of becoming Christian, it was said, souls might be saved.[6] Yet, the conversion of a Negro did not raise his status, for he was still considered socially inferior. The current view of the matter was that "one might as well baptize puppies as Negroes."[7]

After admitting Negroes to baptism, the next step seemed to be to receive them into membership in the churches. Four Negroes had been accepted as members of the Dutch Reformed church of New Netherlands as early as 1674–75.[8] Yet, with the exception of the statement that "all three of the evangelical churches opened the doors wide to slaves and counted many hundreds of them among their members," during the "great awakening" in Virginia,[9] the development is impossible to trace until approximately the first decade of the nineteenth century. By 1810, however, the practice reappears to such an extent that, we may say, it had become customary.

Noah Davis was baptized, with some twenty other slaves, and admitted into the Baptist church of Fredericksburg, Virginia, in September, 1831.[10] Already that congregation counted three hundred or more colored members. In Baltimore, about 1847, Davis discovered Negroes attached to white churches and in separate organizations.[11] The Baptist, Methodist, and Presbyterian churches of North Carolina had received Negro members freely from the time that North Carolina had been recognized as a state.[12] Evidence from Kentucky indicates that slaves had been members of churches in that commonwealth throughout the period of slavery.[13] In Texas the practice had become accepted by the latter half of the nineteenth century.[14] By 1845, when the Southern Baptist Convention was organized in Alabama, there were more Negro members of that denomination than white in proportion to population. The experience of Rev. Mr. Tichenor, who had baptized over five hundred Negroes into fellowship of the First Baptist Church at Montgomery, prior to 1865, was probably unusual, for this church had six hundred Negro members to three hundred white, by the latter date.[15] In Charleston, South Carolina, the Circular Church had four hundred Negro members by 1804; while the Puritan church had three hundred by 1860.[16]

The Rev. Nehemiah Adams had personal knowledge of churches where the slave membership outnumbered the white membership one hundred to one hundred and fifty; two hundred to twenty; and four hundred to one hundred. Moreover, he cites a report from Virginia, showing that, about 1853, the Baptists of that state had forty-five thousand Negro and fifty thousand white members.[17] One commentator, after studying numerous reports from various ecclesiastical bodies,[18] remarked that "hundreds of thousands of slaves of our Southern States are fellow members of the Christian Churches with their masters."[19] Ozanne[20] assumed a large Negro membership while testifying to the essential "equality" of the slave in the church. Mrs. Sea, however, was at pains to record the relative membership of the separate denominations by 1860.[21]

Slaves were not, however, allowed complete freedom in church membership and attendance. John Brown, a slave who was born in Virginia, sold into Georgia, and had later escaped to St. Louis, Missouri, remarks that he saw Negroes going to church in the latter city—"a right denied them in other Slave States."[22] A more accurate statement is that the practice varied with communities.

The case of Henry Evans is an illustration in point. Evans, a freeborn Negro, was also a licensed Methodist preacher. Traveling from Virginia to Charleston, South Carolina, he stopped at Fayetteville, North Carolina, where he established a church among the Negroes. The town council ordered him to cease preaching within the limits of the town, whereupon he moved the church outside the corporation limits. Later, however, when it had been noted that slaves coming under his influence had become docile, the ban was removed. Still later, white persons, becoming interested, flocked to the services and increased to such numbers that the Negroes were crowded from their seats. "Then the boards were knocked from the sides of the house and sheds were built on either hand, and in these the blacks were seated."[23]

Doubtless one of the first problems to arise in the churches after Negroes were admitted to membership was the matter of seating. Since most of the early traditions of the churches of Virginia were like the established Church of England, it seems probable that the slave members and attendants of that denomination were assigned gallery seats as proper for persons of their status. On the other hand, in the Baptist and Methodist organizations,[24] slaves sat indiscriminately among white members until after the insurrection of Nat Turner, about 1831, when the laws required that they sit in separate sections.

Soon, however, race distinctions gained a foothold when slaves were seated in the rear of the smaller churches,[25] and in the galleries of larger ones, especially in the cities. The practice was somewhat general,[26] being noted in North Carolina,[27] Tennessee,[28] and South Carolina.[29] In the latter state men and women, in at least one instance, were separated among the slaves.[30] Buckingham saw slaves in the galleries of churches in Montgomery, Alabama,[31] and Norfolk[32] and Abingdon, Virginia.[33] The last was a Methodist church and shows the change brought about in the organization after 1830. The practice of seating Negroes in galleries became general in Virginia after 1860.[34] It was likewise a feature of the Presbyterian churches of Tennessee.[35] The gallery of the Circular Presbyterian Church, of Charleston, South Carolina, "as in all churches in the Southern States, was reserved for colored people."[36]

Occasionally, however, a section of a church was set aside for the slaves. In a "cathedral" at Nachitoches, Louisiana, they occupied "distinct seats from the whites."[37] In Virginia, generally, "the reserved place for Negroes" was the alternative to the gallery.[38] But in Fredericksburg, in the same state, there were separate "apartments for worship."[39] In Alabama "a certain part of every Baptist house was set apart" for slaves.[40] Among the Presbyterians of North Carolina[41] and Tennessee[42] separate sections were the rule in churches without galleries.

In general, the greater the proportion of Negroes in a given church organization, the more pronounced were distinctions in worship. If the whites were many and the Negroes few, the latter would likely be given the gallery or a separate group of pews. If the whites were few and the Negroes many, services and buildings tended to be separate, especially in the later years. Even then, however, body servants might attend the white churches. In the plantation chapel, on the other hand, the master and his family would sit in the gallery, or on a raised platform, near the front.[43] Whatever the custom, however, there was an understanding between the two groups, and appropriate sentiment supporting the arrangements effected co-operation in these matters.[44]

The minister, conducting services attended by both groups, faced a difficult task, however. If he preached to the white group, the great possibility was that the slaves would not understand; while, if he fitted the sermon to the Negro audience, it would be unsuitable for whites. Occasionally, then, he would compromise and seek to include both groups in his statements.

"The preacher told us, among other things, that God cares for all from meanest as well as the mightiest. 'He cares for that colored person,' said he,—pointing to the gallery where the people of color sit,—'as well as for the wisest and best of whites.' "[45]

As the South grew more conscious of slavery, the etiquette for ministers became more and more defined. They were not expected to indicate in any manner that slavery was un-Christian, immoral, or improper. Slaves were enjoined to obey and be subject to their masters, but otherwise they were, perhaps, not noticed. Maids might attend their mistresses to pews, and go out again, without attracting attention. Perhaps, a master would find occasion to send a slave from one part of the church to another and even into the pulpit "to restore the clergyman his pocket handkerchief, which he had let fall."[46] Formality and routine, however, eventually robbed the services of their original interest for the slaves to such an extent that one of them could remark that "da preches too much, de people is gospel harden, da don't mine it."[47]

With regard to the ordinance of the sacrament of the Lord's Supper, the general rule was that whites and blacks communed separately.[48] Goodell[49] infers, about 1855, that the custom was not universal, but the evidence of later years does not sustain him. Long noted that it was the custom of the Methodist church to administer the sacrament to Negroes after the whites had been served. This was especially true of the Presbyterian church of North Carolina.[50] Patterson comments on the observance in Tennessee,[51] while Drewry thought the practice common in Virginia.[52] Buckingham heard a minister of Abingdon, Virginia, invite his "coloured class" to the communion at three o'clock and the "white class" at four o'clock of a Sunday afternoon.[53] Only one instance was found where the two groups took the sacrament at the same time, and, as this instance occasioned no comment, it seems to have been the usual and expected thing.[54]

Negroes had been baptized since the seventeenth century and always, at first, by white ministers. Parsons remarks that a white minister baptized some seventy-five slaves at Butler's Island, Georgia.[55] The practice, as already stated, was common at Fredericksburg, Virginia, as late as 1831.[56] Slaves asked the master's permission prior to the baptizing.[57] And occasionally a Negro dignitary might perform the service.[58] Yet, the ceremony was not always without its risks. An overseer wrote his employer:

"There was forty one 41 of your Negroes Baptised Last Sunday in the Canall above the Bridge by James Page. It was the Largest Negroe meeting I ever saw. . . . . Fillis Wallis was Baptised and hur and Winter is down sick."[59]

The ceremony of christening and naming slave babies by white men was a practice in some parts of the South. It has frequently been remarked that slaves were named after biblical, historical, and mythological characters.[60] "Caesar and Cicero were often the names of Negroes in the yard more than of authors on the shelves."[61] Plato, Pompey, and McIvor out of Waverly, for men; and Flora, Florilla, Rose, Lily, and Minerva, for women, brought comment from one author.[62] Such names were doubtless given by the master or his kin. In a case mentioned by Ingraham, a slaveowner's sister had dubbed slave boys Napoleon Bonaparte, Jupiter, Apollo Belvidere, and Nicodemus; while naming the girls Victoria, Madame de Staël, Lady Jane Grey, Venus, and Vesta.[63] The christening took place in a slave chapel, where the master stood sponsor for the boys, while his sister stood for the girls. White babies, however, were not christened at the time.

After being christened the slave children might attend Sunday schools established especially for them. Teachers were generally white persons,[64] even in the instances where separate churches had become the rule. However, the law generally required white persons to be present at all Negro meetings.[65]

The ceremony of admitting slaves to membership is difficult

to trace. Frederick Douglass, however, relates how he was admitted into the church at a camp meeting:

"After the preaching was over . . . . an invitation was given for mourners to come into the pen. . . . . Master Thomas Auld was persuaded to go into the pen. I was deeply interested in this, and although colored people were not allowed either in the pen, or in front of the preacher's stand, I ventured to take my place at a sort of half-way place between the blacks and whites."[66]

The behavior of Douglass in the new situation characterizes the relations of the two races throughout their contact in matters religious. Douglass neither stood before the minister nor went into the "mourner's pen," which was reserved for whites. He did, however, stand in the halfway place, indicating that, though he was not a white man, neither was he an unconverted slave.

The camp meeting, also, had its etiquette. Inaugurated by Methodist and Baptist groups and composed largely at first of nonslaveholders and slaves, these meetings, held in the summer while the weather allowed semi-indoor services, needed but an arbor, or tabernacle, of simple construction. Later, the meetings extended throughout the inland region and became gala occasions attended by both whites and blacks. The seating arrangement of the camp meeting varied. In some instances Negroes were assigned sections at one side of the tabernacle,[67] while in others they stood behind the minister.[68] In Maryland the ministers addressed slaves "over the left" if they addressed them at all;[69] but in Arkansas, near Benton, "the servants stayed outside and set down on de logs close by."

"When de preacher git all warm up, an' had de white folks inside de shed thinkin' on what dey had ought ter know, an' on de way ter glory, he stick his haid out de window now an' den ter exhort us servan's; 'You cullud people out dar—lissen at me! De way ter make good slaves is ter obey yo' Massa an' Missis! Hyar dat! Obey 'em constant!' Den he stick his haid back in an' preach till he had some mo' words fo' us all."[70]

As slaves became members of the regularly established churches in increasing numbers, the problem of holding separate services arose. In the evangelical churches especially, each group perhaps felt "some restraint imposed on it by the presence of the other."[71] Masters were, perhaps, a little embarrassed to be converted when slaves were about. A slave might feel the urge to utter a fervent "Amen" or "Yes, Lord," but would consider such improper in the presence of whites.

The theory has been advanced that separate services for house servants originated in the cities.[72] At any rate, in the Sunday afternoon service slaves could participate to a greater extent than when they attended services with white people.[73] Moreover, these services developed over a wide rural area, as shown by evidence from Tennessee, Alabama, and North and South Carolina.[74]

Another view has it that separate services for slaves were confined to rural sections, while separate churches developed in the towns and cities.[75] It seems, however, that Negroes were first admitted to membership in churches. Later, under pressure of numbers, or desire for free and untrammeled expression, they were allowed separate services, with the regular minister officiating; and, finally, given separate churches with white ministers. It is entirely possible, however, that the development was more rapid in the cities than in the rural districts. For example, slaves on one of the plantations where Mrs. Kemble resided were not allowed to attend services given for whites but had special services with the white minister.[76] In Alabama, during the Civil War, services were separate, but "the whites attended the Negro services often, and vice versa."[77] The presbytery in which Salem, Kentucky, was included "enjoined every minister of the Presbytery who has charge of a congregation to make an arrangement for special preaching to the colored people . . . . at least once a month."[78]

Bound up with the problem of separate services was that of ordaining slaves as ministers and of determining to whom they should preach. The presbytery of Lexington, Virginia, licensed John Chavis, in 1801, "as a missionary among people of his own color."[79] The presbytery of North Middletown, Kentucky, consulted with a young slave who had felt the "call to preach"with the result that they accepted him and advised an elder to apply to the slave's mistress for his freedom in order that he might continue his education, with the presbytery responsible for his books and clothing.[80] Noah Davis was licensed by the Baptists of Fredericksburg, Virginia, to preach to Negroes, in 1831.[81] It was not unusual, in Alabama, said Tichenor, for a half-dozen slaves to be "so trained as to become voluntary missionaries to the people of their own color residing on the large plantations in the adjoining country."[82] These conditions were, perhaps, but natural outgrowths of the presence of Negro preachers since the early eighteenth century. "Uncle Jack," of Amelia County, Virginia, had held meetings and preached to slaves as early as 1734. Forbidden by law, "such was the universally acknowledged happy influence of Uncle Jack's meetings that, in his case, it was not deemed necessary to enforce the law."[83] Andrew Bryan, of Savannah, Georgia, received shorter shrift, however, and was whipped and imprisoned for preaching to Negroes in the later part of the seventeenth century.[84] Virginia, by the early part of the eighteenth century, had enacted laws prohibiting assembly of Negroes for any purpose, unless at least two white persons were present. By the fourth decade of the nineteenth century, similar laws were enacted in most of the states of the South.[85]

The Negro preacher, then, was at the same time a concession to the ambitions of slaves who had been "called to preach" and a symbol of a growing tendency to separation in religious services and ceremonials.

Some of the slave preachers acquired power and eloquence in delivery. These prodigies, usually sponsored and accompanied by white ministers, frequently preached to whites and blacks alike. Pompey, of Tennessee, a slave of Bishop McKendree's brother-in-law, enjoyed such privileges. Emanuel Mark, of Fayette County, Tennessee, "had a pass to preach anywhere"; while Silas Phillips and Simeon Hunt were extended privileges seldom granted except to prodigies.[86] Ralph Freeman, of North Carolina, traveled with the Rev. Mr. Magee and would take turns preaching with him. John Chavis, sent to Princeton to study under the renowned Dr. Witherspoon, later returned to North Carolina and preached around in the churches. He was, however, a free Negro and perhaps had no sponsor.[87] The story of Henry Evans has been related here. And John Jasper aroused so much interest, or curiosity, by his theory that "the sun do move" that he was invited to preach to whites and blacks. Details appear of his preaching to sick and wounded soldiers in a Confederate hospital during the Civil War.[88]

There were also preachers or "exhorters" on the plantations who had been self-called, licensed by the churches, or, in some cases, merely appointed by the master.[89] These preachers, of course, were orthodox and seldom, if ever, preached inflammatory doctrine. Acklen wrote in his overseer's contract:

"No Negro preachers but my own will be permitted to preach or remain on any of my places. The regularly appointed minister for my places must preach on Sundays during daylight or quit."[90]

At any rate, Negro preachers enjoyed quite a bit of freedom until the insurrection of Nat Turner, himself a preacher.[91] Thereafter, they were looked upon with suspicion. Russell found that they were not encouraged on the South Carolina Sea Islands as late as 1862.[92] Kemble records circumstances surrounding the eviction of two black preachers from a plantation in Georgia, in 1838, as one phase of a "very general panic in this part of the slave states occasioned by some injudicious missionary preaching."[93] Olmsted had heard of two instances in North Carolina where public worship had been interrupted "and the preachers—very estimable colored men—whipped publicly."[94] Yet, during the period of tension, some of the black preachers were highly esteemed and unusually privileged, though others were viewed with suspicion.[95] Relations were undergoing a change, and these were manifestations of the general current of opinion.

Separation within the church was developing from three directions: Negro preachers were being licensed or ordained to preach to Negroes; separate services for slaves within the churches were changing to separate churches for them, with white ministers; and there was a "church within a church" where the Negro members had organizations of their own, within the white church, and subordinated to it.[96]

Bishop McTyeire testified that he had preached or held more than three hundred services with Negro congregations.[97] The renowned Dr. Thornwell dedicated a church for Negroes in Charleston, South Carolina,[98] and Ferguson attended a church at the same place, which had received a white minister in 1850.[99] The establishment of churches for Negroes pastored by white men had become common in Virginia by the last decade preceding the Civil War.[100] Olmsted[101] saw many, and Hall visited the widely known "African Church" of Richmond.[102] Adams visited one such church in South Carolina.[103] while at Raleigh, North Carolina, where whites and blacks had contributed to a fund to buy a church for the blacks, there was twofold rejoicing, "by the Negroes because they had a building of their own, by the whites because the Negroes were out of the white man's church." A white minister was sent to this new congregation.[104] By 1863, one author testifies, separate churches and meeting-houses were springing up in all parts of the South, to which white ministers were being sent.[105]

"As a general rule, the Episcopal minister went to the family mansion, the Methodist minister preached to the Negroes and dined with the overseer at his house."[106] Patterson, describing the work of the Methodist minister in Tennessee in relation to the slaves, said:

"He baptized them, married them, visited them in their cabins, comforted them in distress, prayed with them when on beds
of affliction, was their counselor, friend, and spiritual guide, and
he preached their funerals when they died."[107]

As in the church where whites and blacks worshiped together,
the minister needed to observe a particular code where blacks
worshiped separately. One manual, describing the duties of
masters to slaves, suggested that the minister preach such texts
as "Servants, obey in all things your masters," or "Servants, be
subject to your own masters with all fear." If, by chance, he
preached to the masters at the same time, the minister was
urged to "unite in engaging the Christian master to do his duty
toward his servants as religious beings; remembering his interests, their happiness, and the account that must be rendered
by him to his Master in heaven."[108]

If a minister, preaching to slaves, attempted to use "Negro
language," including such words as "massa" and "buckra," he
might "even excite disgust" in his black audience.[109]

"The Negroes did not want a preacher they could understand.
Even a white preacher, if he tried to simplify his language to
suit them, would become unpopular with them. They liked
high-sounding words, and would always praise the Lord when
one was used. Rev. McNeilly tells us of a young theologian
who began his sermon to the Negroes thus—'Primarily we must
postulate the existence of a deity.' After a short pause, an old
patriarch responded fervently, 'Yes, Lord, dat's so. Bless de
Lord.' "[110]

In matters of the sacramental wine, the minister was supposed to allow free indulgence, a ten-gallon demijohn perhaps
merely sufficing for one congregation.[111] The communion service
was both duty and pleasure.

Separate churches with Negro preachers later became the
custom. An occasional white minister might grow to feel it beneath his dignity, provided Negro preachers were present, to

minister to slaves.[112] Organizations began to spring up among the slaves, utilizing slave ministers, as in Kentucky.[113]

The transition stage, however, is seen in the situation in Macon, Georgia, as related by Pollard. In that place there were, in 1858, three churches for Negroes—a Methodist, a Baptist, and a Presbyterian. Two of the churches had Negro ministers, and the third had a white minister. In the latter case the Negroes had erected and paid for their church building and were paying the minister a regular salary.[114] But the end is not yet. There were cases of separate Negro churches, served by Negro preachers, and unsubordinated to white churches.

A factor contributing to the development of the separate Negro church, with a Negro minister, was the religious training of the plantation. By this training, to a great extent, slaves were encouraged in religious practices, and persons among them who showed interest and power for leadership in religion were differentiated from the general run of slaves.

If, as it was conceded, religion made slaves more docile and, perhaps, more satisfied with their lot, personal interest of masters would dictate that they receive religious training in conformity, of course, with the inclination of masters. On the other hand, there were masters who wished to grant the boon of Christ to their slaves on principle, considering but little the ends to be gained. There were still others who felt that slavery and Christianity were incompatible, and who, sooner or later, emancipated their slaves, or at least certain favorite ones among them.[115] Gaines attributed the movement, to promote religious training, to masters who were really interested in their slaves, as well as to those who "offered religious training for its good effect on the slave order."[116]

Instances appear in which the slaves were invited to family prayer, perhaps in the master's room, but certainly with both white and black families participating.[117] Holmes recommended the practice to pious masters.[118] Mrs. Clayton recalls that the children on her plantation were taught the catechism on Sun-

days in the "big house," to which the adults were invited on
Sunday evenings to learn the Lord's Prayer, the Ten Command-
ments, and the Apostles' Creed.[119] On occasion the slaves
might even conduct these services, in which all would join.
Frequently, however, "the slaves became so religious as to
embrace their master and mistress ere the close of the service."[120]

One solution to the problem consisted in the erection of a
plantation chapel in those cases where the masters, being at a
distance from a church, would wish to have private religious
services for their slaves.[121] Ozanne visited such a chapel, where,
as would be expected, the white family took the lead in the
services.[122] Ingraham described a sumptuous chapel on a Tennessee plantation where slaves sat in the body of the house,
while the master's family, and white visitors, sat in the gallery
over the entrance. There was a white lay reader for this chapel,
and the master's daughter played the organ.[123]

Occasionally, a pious planter would wish to hear some dignitary from a near-by city; in which circumstance he would invite the minister to preach to whites and blacks in the plantation chapel.[124] For example, at "Somerset Place" in North
Carolina:

"On a Sunday morning of Ruffin's visit a lay reader in the
Collins family conducted the Episcopal service, and in the evening the Bishop of North Carolina came to deliver the address,
after which the local clergyman administered the sacrament to
the bishop, the white household, and to some thirty slaves."[125]

Complete separation ensued, however, when certain slaves,
being licensed or ordained, were appointed to conduct services
in the chapels. The planter, who had previously assumed the
function of reader, would then release that office to the slave
who had been "called to preach," and who had developed gifts
sufficient for the responsibility.[126]

A certain etiquette needed to be observed at these chapels.
After the services was visiting hour. The "uncles and aunties"

would stop just outside the door to converse with the master and his family, while the latter would make inquiry concerning their health, the state of the plantation, or merely pass the time of day.[127]

The "praise house," developed on the Sea Islands, it seems, was a chapel attended only by slaves. "About fifteen feet square, begrimed with smoke and dirt," there were few windows in it, and the pastor was likely to be a slave.[128] At Pine Grove, on St. Helena's Island, the "praise house" was merely a "rather larger and nicer hut than the others."[129] In the house the slaves, mainly field hands, prayed and sang, became "convicted" of sin, or even "got religion," without the restrictive presence of white persons. Dr. Park has, in fact, remarked that where the slave did not become converted in the praise house he was scarcely converted at all.

These praise houses were closed, as a general thing, following the tensions arising from the insurrections of Nat Turner and Denmark Vesey—when masters considered Negro assemblies prejudicial to peace and order. Nevertheless, they tended to continue as symbols of the religious emancipation of the slaves from the control and authority of the white church and churchmen.[130]

Separate churches for Negroes, then, grew up in direct response to the desires and needs of masters and slaves to adjust problems growing out of new situations and ideals. Southern thought later became articulate on this point,[131] several writers going so far as to recommend separation for one cause or another.

Richmond had an African Baptist church as early as 1780.[132] Norfolk had a church for slaves and free Negroes in 1839.[133] By 1850 the Second Presbyterian and St. Phillip's and St. Mcchael's Episcopal congregations of Charleston, South Carolina, had either organized separate Negro congregations, with a few white members for legal safety, or had built separate buildings to accommodate the Negroes.[134] Olmsted attended a Negro church in New Orleans where only a few white persons were present; and there was later in that city an African Methodist church which catered only to Negroes.[135] Baltimore had ten Negro churches by 1835, some of which had black preachers. The number increased to thirteen by 1847, with an increase in Negro ministers as well.[136] Mobile, Alabama; Nashville and Memphis, Tennessee; Richmond and Petersburg, Virginia; Charleston, South Carolina; and Savannah, Georgia, had separate churches in time.[137] Russell saw a church in Montgomery, Alabama, into which "white people rarely or never intrude."[138]

Separation was not always accomplished without disorder and tension. Negro Methodists of Charleston, South Carolina, had a separate quarterly conference prior to 1815, but the privilege was revoked in that year on grounds of abuse. Two of the Negroes, being dissatisfied with the arrangement, went to Philadelphia to consult with Richard Allen, who had previously founded a strictly Negro organization—the African Methodist Episcopal church. They were ordained by Allen and later returned to Charleston, where the dispute was renewed, this time over a burial ground for Negroes. As a consequence of the dispute, more than three-quarters of the six thousand Negro Methodists withdrew, combined, and built a new church. The city government demolished the building seven years later, making it necessary for the blacks to return:

"The bulk of the blacks returned to the white congregations where they soon overflowed the galleries and the "boxes" which were assigned them at the rear of the main floors. Some of the older Negroes, by special privileges, then took seats forward in the main body of the churches, and others, not so esteemed, followed their example in such numbers that the whites were cramped for room. After complaints on this score had failed for several years to bring a remedy, a crisis came on a Sunday in 1853, when Dr. Capers came to preach. More whites came than could be seated forward—sitting Negroes refused to vacate their seats for them; and a committee of young white members forcibly ejected the blacks. . . . . "[139]

The delicacy of the situation is attested by later action of a white minister at a love feast who criticized the conduct of the white members. These latter, feeling offended with the conduct of the Negroes, as well as with subsequent criticism, withdrew and organized the Methodist Protestant church.

The entirely separate Negro church was established as early as the third quarter of the eighteenth century, perhaps. Travelers referred to many of these in later years. Buckingham mentioned the African Baptist church of Augusta, Georgia, in 1839,[140] and "two meeting houses for colored people" at Savannah, in the same year.[141] Olmsted recorded the epitaph from the tomb of the Rev. Henry Cunningham, of Savannah, who had been the pastor of the Second African Church for thirty-nine years before his death in 1842.[142] Andrew Bryan was the first pastor of the First African Church of Savannah, beginning his work in 1788. Miss Bremer attended one of the Negro churches of Savannah and "shook hands with the powerful old Andrew Marshall" after the sermon.[143] In fact, by 1854 there were three colored churches in Savannah, each paying their pastors from eight hundred to a thousand dollars annually.[144]

Thus, the development of expected and accepted behavior in things religious, with reference to Negroes and white persons, had by the year 1860 undergone a tremendous change. Beginning with the Negro considered as a scarcely human heathen, the conception was gradually modified by situation and circumstance until it was accepted that the Negro might be a Christian. Later the admission that he might become a Christian brought up the question of membership in churches, where he should sit with reference to white persons, and whether he should, or should not, have an organization of his own within the white church. Increase in the number of Negro members, together with the natural desires of both groups, so concurred as to effect establishment of separate churches for Negroes, pastored in one case by white ministers, and later, in another case, by Negro ministers.

Meanwhile, under the influence of pious masters, family worship was instituted which later gave way to the establishment of plantation chapels. These latter organizations, although at first under control of the whites, were later given over to Negroes entirely. However, complete separation in southern denominations became possible legally only after the Civil War.

In 1866 the general conference of the Methodist Episcopal church, South, asked: "What shall be done to promote the religious interests of the colored people?" The answer was:

"When two or more Annual Conferences shall be formed, let our bishops advise and assist them in organizing a separate General Conference jurisdiction for themselves, if they so desire and the bishops deem it expedient, in accordance with the doctrine and discipline of our Church, and bearing the same relation to the General Conference as the Annual Conferences bear to each other."[145]

At the next general conference of that body, in 1870, it was reported that five conferences had been organized among the Negroes. The bishops then declared that it was their purpose:

"To call a General Conference to be holden next winter for the purpose of organizing them into an entirely separate Church, thus enabling them to become their own guides and governors."[146]

On December 15 of that same year, under the direction of Bishop Paine and a delegated group of ministers from the Methodist Episcopal church, South, the Colored Methodist Episcopal church was organized.[147] The Negro delegates then elected bishops from among their number and established an organization. And, in this wise, separation of whites and Negroes in churches of southern persuasion, while developing in the period of slavery, had crystallized into a code of comparatively complete separation after the Emancipation.

CHAPTER V

ETIQUETTE IN FORMAL AND PUBLIC RELATIONS

RELATIONS between whites and blacks during the period of slavery were not, of course, confined to the more
intimate situations that obtained on the plantations or
in such primary groups as the church. There were occasions,
for instance, where forms of address and reference were needed;
instances where the races might come into contact in trains,
theaters, or on the streets; in fact, as in the cities, wherever
under contacts, light and perhaps superficial, distances needed
to be preserved, and status to be maintained.

There is evidence that slaves used "mistis" as a title for white
women whom they had occasion to address at all in public
places.[1] To white men of apparent upper-class ranking some
military title, such as "captain" or "colonel" was generally
used. "Boss" was the title used to address persons of lower
rank than slaveholder but not so low as the "poor whites." It
would be interesting to know how the slaves addressed this
latter class; but the evidence is lacking that they addressed
them at all. Perhaps, the slaves used "mister" and "madam"
as the most formal terms of address. A letter from Port Royal
tells of an insane slave woman, who, narrating stories from the
Bible, referred to "Mr. Adam," and "Madam Eve."[2] No more
formal relation could perhaps have been conceived by Negroes
under the circumstances.

As terms of reference, "buckra" and "buckra man" were used
by the Sea Island slaves of South Carolina. In *Manuel Pereira*[3]
the term seems to refer to the nonslave-owning white man and
does not carry the contempt and scorn implied in the term
"poor buckra."[4] On the other hand, the "buckra man" must

have occupied a lowly position in the social scale. On an occasion in Charleston, where a white man was being whipped in the public square, the slaves gathered around crying, "Buckra gwine go get whip! Buckra get 'e back scratch!"[5]

In general, referring to the poorest whites, the slaves called them "poor white trash"[6] or "mean white men."[7] There is a tradition that the slaves referred to the upper classes of white persons as "quality folks," but the practice lacks verification in our sources of information. The Negroes of St. Helena's Island, South Carolina, who came under the direct supervision of the federal government during the Civil War, began to refer to the Confederate Army and soldiers and to former masters who had gone to war as "Secesh."[8]

Forms of address used by white persons to Negroes, slave or free, generally took the form of "boy," "uncle," "old man" and, in some instances, "nigger." "Boy" was perhaps the most general, "uncle" the most respectful, "old man" a bit familiar, and "nigger" the most contemptuous.

In a criminal case from Wilkes County, Georgia, in 1787, the legal reference to a slave woman, who is to be tried before a court, is "Negro Jude, the property of John Mills."[9] Wheeler has recorded a civil case given in 1796 as "Negro Mary versus the Vestry of William and Mary's Parish."[10]

Less formal terms of reference were "boy" and "girl." "Slaves, no matter how old," says Parsons, "are always *boys* and *girls*. They never become *men* or *women*."[11] Concerning a letter from an overseer to a master, in which the former refers to one Harry as a "good boy," Bassett remarks:

"The reader will observe that when Harry was thus pronounced a 'good boy' he had been a blacksmith thirty years, and was the father of at least ten, perhaps eleven, children."[12]

The slave might be referred to by his given name, but occasionally there were slaves of the same name to distinguish between; in such cases a distinction might be made by adding a parent's name (Nancy Isham or Nancy Flora), or a surname which was sometimes that of a previous owner (Prince Haber-sham, Ben Jackson), or by prefixing an adjective (Big Ben, Short-Foot Billy, Old Joe, Black Maria, Young Polly).[13]

"Wench" was a common term used with reference to slave women, when, it seems, no particular woman was meant.[14] On the other hand, "woman" and "girl" and "man" and "boy" were good commercial terms whenever it was necessary to dis-tinguish the age of slaves for sale.[15] When persons wished to refer to slaves as their possessions, they used the term "peo-ple"—such as "my people."[16] When they referred to slaves working in a company, the inclusive term became "gang"; if the number were quite small, the term was "hands"; and, if the reference to the entire working capacity of a plantation were made, the word "force" was used.[17]

The use of lower-case letters in referring to Negroes appears to have developed in the nineteenth century. St. George Tucker used the capital N in "Negroes" as early as 1796. When the book was reprinted in 1861, the same form was used.[18] Two advertisements appearing in a New Orleans newspaper about 1854 capitalized the word "Negro"; but similar advertisements in the *Richmond Enquirer* and in the *Richmond Examiner*, in 1858, put the word in lower case.[19]

There were, of course, forms to be observed in public con-tacts. A maid accompanying her mistress on shopping expe-ditions, or, on occasions, to church, usually dropped behind, sometimes a long way, or came up within a few feet if the mis-tress wished to hold a conversation.[20] In general, slaves did not walk with white persons in public, but, perhaps, free Negroes did.[21] If a Negro, man or woman, met a white person on the street in Richmond, Virginia, they were "required to 'give the wall,' and if necessary to get off the sidewalk into the street, on pain of punishment with stripes on the bare back."[22] On the other hand, even though the slaves were expected to "get off" the sidewalk, it was not expected that white persons would push them off. In Richmond, where some young white men had pushed a Negro off the sidewalk, the latter shouted:

"Can't you find anything else to do than to be knockin' quiet people 'round! You jus' come back here, will you? Here you!, don't care if you is white. You jus' come back here and I'll teach you to behave—knockin' people 'round!"[23]

In general, the two groups seemed not to shake hands in public. Buckingham, however, noticed in Athens, Georgia, in 1839 that "black slaves of both sexes shake hands with white people when they meet, and interchange friendly personal inquiries."[24] The occurrence was strange enough to cause him to mention that this was "not at all uncommon" in the town.

Whites and blacks could converse in public where the relation was known—perhaps as master and slave. Indiscriminate intercourse between them was, however, barred or reduced to a minimum. Parsons had occasion to note that a certain Mr. L., approached by a quadroon slave girl who had come to ask him to buy her at an auction sale, asked her not to "say anything about that, here," since "it was not safe for him to be seen talking with a slave, when so many were passing."[25] Moreover, a slave did not address a white person, unless first addressed:

"It was not my place to speak to a white man except when spoken to, but I omitted no opportunity of throwing myself in his way, and endeavoring in every possible manner to attract his attention."[26]

Beyond the range of the plantation and its affairs, or in relations with associates in the cities, contacts of the slave almost never reached. Although many slaves could read and write, communication by post or otherwise seemed not to have occurred among them. If, perchance, members of the family, or friends, were "sold South" or away from the immediate locality, it was almost certain that they would never be heard of again, except, perhaps, by word of mouth. This seems to be the real significance of the separation of families in slavery, whether it occurred by design or necessity.[27] The post office was, then, practically a "no-man's-land" for slaves. They had little reason to go except, perhaps, to receive mail for their masters. This situation perhaps explains why a slave at Port Royal "could not express his surprise" at the sight of Negro soldiers in the Fifty-fifth Massachusetts Regiment walking to the post office and "opening their letters to read, 'just like white men.' "[28]

Negroes frequently served as musicians at balls, and occasionally one particularly favored old slave might "call the figures" of the quadrille or "square dance."[29] On the other hand, slaves attended balls given for whites and frequently seemed as much at home there as the whites. They stood around outside at windows,[30] in some instances, or came in and mixed with the crowd. No instances were found where the slaves danced, however.[31]

Body servants, perhaps, attended the theater with their masters or mistresses. Redpath saw "playbills" indicating that theaters had conveniences for "respectable colored persons."[32] These latter were doubtless attendants of patrons, or, on occasions at least, unaccompanied house servants.

Occasionally, at funerals of prominent white persons, whites and blacks might be seen—for example, when John C. Calhoun's body was brought to Charleston.[33] The rites for a certain Judge Clayton of Athens, Georgia, were held in the University of Georgia chapel. The white population occupied the main floor—women in the center, men at the sides—while the slaves sat in the galleries—men on one side, women on the other.[34] This suggests that there was a ritual to be observed within the racial groups as well as between them.

Among the usages which are derived from ceremonial, but which nevertheless distinguish between classes, Spencer includes clothing and transportation. These serve, in public places, as symbols of difference.

Among some slaveholders it was the custom to visit some famous resort, perhaps the Hot Springs of Virginia, during the spring and to remain until fall.[35] Here a rigid etiquette of precedence obtained. The situation was more complicated than any mentioned so far since it involved not only the master and his family but also slaves of varieties in rank. MacCorkle has given a description of such a procession as follows:

"The procession was long and imposing. First came the outriders of ebon hue, each on a horse and leading another animal; then the master on his thoroughbred with one of the sons riding beside him; then the heavy traveling carriage with its splendid horses driven by the greatest dignitary of the plantation, 'the carriage driver' carrying the mother, the wife, the children, and the 'mammy.' Then came the lighter equipages bearing bright-eyed girls filled with joyous anticipation of the pleasures of the summer at The White, and behind these came the other conveyances, containing the belongings of the family and the house girls."[36]

Ingraham, describing a similar procession going to the Beaver Dam Springs in Tennessee, in 1853, noted that the master's valet came first, leading the master's horse, while the family carriage came next. After these there was the valet's understudy, then the maids, and last the coachman's page.[37]

The stagecoach was a chief mode of transportation in the South until after the fourth decade of the nineteenth century. Slaves seldom had any occasion to use such facilities except in the company of an owner, when, perhaps, they rode inside the coach. Mr. Featherstonehaugh was traveling from Abingdon, Virginia, to Blountsville, Tennessee, in 1854. The coach was very crowded, and it was necessary that someone ride outside. Since he was the last to arrive, Mr. Featherstonehaugh asked a "white man who looked like a Methodist preacher" if a servant accompanying the latter might not ride outside, whereupon the man replied, "I reckon my waiter is very well where he is."[38] On still another occasion, in the state of Virginia, an unattached Negro was asked to ride outside so that Mrs. Featherstonehaugh could ride within the coach. The Negro refused and went

outside only when threatened with bodily violence.[39] An unattached slave, probably the property of the owner of the stage
line, rode with Olmsted, near Fayetteville, North Carolina.
Later he "lay down in the bottom of the coach and slept" until
the end of the journey.[40]

Olmsted offered a seat to a white woman who entered a railway car in Virginia, whereupon the latter promptly installed
"a stout negro woman" in it, took the adjoining seat herself,
and seated the rest of the party before her. "It consisted of a
white girl, probably her daughter, and a bright and very pretty
mulatto girl."[41] As the group laughed and talked together, and
as the girls "munched confectionery out of the same paper,"
Olmsted's amazement seemed to grow. On still another occasion he observed a "fine-looking, well-dressed, and well-be-
haved colored young man" seated with a white man. He supposed that the Negro was a slave and that the white man was
his master.[42] In North Carolina he noted that a free colored
woman rode inside a stagecoach and was treated "in no way
differently from the white ladies."[43] On the other hand, when
slaves and free Negroes were unaccompanied passengers on the
trains, there was a "second-class" car for them.[44] It was the
foremost car, the latter half of which was appropriated for use
of smokers.[45] Olmsted, in fact, speaks of the "servant's car"
and shows that a trader in North Carolina had shipped some
slaves in this car.[46] Yet, in another instance related, a trader
used freight cars for slaves who were to be traded South.[47]

Stirling believed the practice of unattached Negroes riding
with white people to be common;[48] Dicey mentioned it as occurring on a journey from Maryland into Virginia;[49] and Olmsted had two slaves as fellow-travelers from Marion to Branch-
ville, South Carolina. However, in the last case, at the end of
the journey, when the white passengers went into the station,
the slaves made a fire on the ground and sat around it.[50] Perhaps there were no special station accommodations for Negroes
in this period.

For the apparent inconsistencies in travel etiquette on the railways we may look to travel conditions. Travel was light, for wealth was concentrated in the hands of a few, and the many had little occasion to travel. The statement made by Olmsted— that a majority of the trains which he saw in the South "were not paying for the fuel and wages expended in running them"— need, then, excite no surprise.[51]

Travel by way of steamboats was also a means of transportation in the period of slavery. The planters, or wealthy white persons, commonly rode on the main deck of these boats, while slaves and poorer whites commonly rode "forward of the shaft," or on a lower deck.[52] If, however, a slave attended an owner, he might sleep on the deck outside the cabin of the latter and have no bed save, perhaps, the master's luggage.[53] On the lower deck relations were more democratic. On one trip Olmsted explored after nightfall the afterdeck of a steamboat, bound from New Orleans to Shreveport, Louisiana. There he saw Negroes asleep "in all postures, upon the freight," and a "few white people— men, women and children—were lying here and there among the Negroes."[54]

The presence of free colored persons complicated the situation on the boats. Three free Negro women were on the same boat with Buckingham from Mobile to Montgomery in 1839. They slept on the cabin floor; arose "before the ladies were moving" in order to dress; but were served by white stewardesses.[55] During the day they sat in the cabin "as if on a footing of perfect equality with white passengers." Yet, when mealtime arrived, they did not dine with white passengers, or crew, or slaves, but, as already remarked, took their meals standing in the pantry.[56]

Fourteen years later, however, when Olmsted took an up-river trip in Louisiana, the forms had been better established. At this time the free Negroes dined after the white servants but before the slaves.[57] When passengers left the boat, as was found in one instance, the Negroes came after the white people.[58]

With regard to clothing as a class distinction and as a derived form of etiquette, Spencer has remarked that "the partial dress of a slave must be distinguished by shape, as well as by amount, from the complete dress of the master; and obviously, the clothing allowed to him as a slave will be relatively coarse."[59] The instances noted in this study were no exception to the rule. "Negro cloth," a coarse grey stuff, was the material of which outer garments for field hands were made.[60] In an inventory of slaves' clothing made by Olmsted, no mention is made of undergarments—perhaps none was supplied.[61] The shape of the "Negro shirt," according to Redpath, differed from that common to white men, being, as it were, "a cross between a gent's undergarment and an ordinary potato bag."[62] Even at best, perhaps, the garments "appeared as if made by contract, without regard to the size of the particular individual to whom it was allotted, like penitentiary uniforms."[63]

Perhaps the type of clothing described was issued to field hands or rural slaves. In Virginia "the greater part of the colored people on Sunday seemed to be dressed in the cast-off clothing of the white people; received as presents or purchased of Jews, whose shops show that there is considerable importation of such articles."[64]

"Among this dark gentry, the finest French clothes, embroidered waistcoats, patent-leather shoes, resplendent brooches, silk hats, kid gloves, and *eau mille fleurs*, were quite common. . . . . Many of the coloured ladies were dressed not only expensively but with good taste and effect, after the Parisian mode."[65]

Livery for servants was perhaps used in the cities, but instances discovered are few. Steward describes a scene at a famous race course in Virginia, where body servants were dressed in livery;[66] and Russell was a guest of a planter in Savannah, Georgia, who affected this type of dress for his house servants.[67]

Distinctions between the races extended to separation in

cemeteries. Redpath noted in every southern city which he had visited that white persons, free Negroes, and slaves had separate burial plots.[68] The situation has been attested to by observers in Richmond, Charleston, and Savannah.[69] In Charleston, where two plots lay side by side, the white section was inclosed by a brick wall, and the graves were marked by marble headstones. The slave plot was not inclosed, and the graves were marked by wooden crosses or diamond-shaped headboards. The stipulation that no slave should be buried in a private place "but in public cemeteries provided for the purpose" was contained in legislative enactments of Virginia as early as 1664.[70]

A slave might be given notice on a public monument, however. A theater burned in Richmond, Virginia, on the site where the Monumental Episcopal Church later stood. Eighty-odd persons lost their lives in the fire, among them slaves who had attended their owners to the exhibition. A slab was later erected on the spot, and the names of the dead inscribed thereon. The names of the slaves appeared "outside the general record, near the foot of the monument."[71]

In cities and towns persons were more mobile, relations were more impersonal, and, in attempts to maintain distances and to preserve the "front" necessary, etiquette became more rigid and meticulous. Moreover, as a response to a more or less commercial economy, as contrasted with the agricultural, it frequently happened that persons owned more slaves than they could profitably employ in their homes. As a consequence, many slaves were permitted to "hire" themselves to persons who perhaps had neither the capital nor the disposition to buy slaves for themselves, but who thought it necessary to have slaves as a sign of status.

In return for their comparative freedom, slaves who hired themselves generally paid their masters given sums at regular intervals and were allowed to keep whatever sum remained over the given amount.[72] With the residue many purchased their freedom or invested in the clothes and finery that seemed to be characteristic of city slaves. Many, however, learned trades or engaged in small businesses. As a result, the privileged city slaves often became self-supporting, accumulated money, and gained standing as substantial slave citizens. The one flaw in their happiness, perhaps, was their affluence, which excited the enmity of the poorer whites.[73]

Under these circumstances, then, we begin to look for the presence of "exceptional Negroes" in the cities, that is, slaves who were achieving independence, if not freedom. Cato, of Darien, Georgia, in defiance of law, was allowed to carry a gun.[74] Hall, traveling from Mobile to Montgomery, saw a slave who, "frequently entrusted with large sums of money and business of importance,"[75] was traveling to New Orleans on business for his master. Mrs. Royall felt herself "under particular obligation for the attentions as a servant" of a barber in Lynchburg, Virginia, who owned his own shop.[76] Moreover, when she arrived at Macon, Georgia, she met "Frank, who had become rich and was then the owner of considerable town-property— carried on a mercantile business with great success—and was respected and esteemed by everyone who knew him."[77]

City slaves were generally known to be more suave and urbane. But the exceptional slaves, perhaps, were even more sophisticated. They did not presume upon their privileged positions but continued to observe the etiquette expected of them in their contacts with white people. When Frank was presented to Mrs. Royall—and slaves were seldom presented to white women—he came to the carriage, saluted the gentleman "with great ease, took off his hat with great modesty, returned it to his head," and took Mrs. Royall's offered hand.[78] Hall described the slave who was going to New Orleans as "of dignified, gentlemanly demeanor, absolutely without ostentation."[79]

Contacts between the races in the cities and towns gave rise, however, to problems of sex relations. There had been, it is true, sex contacts between the classes as early as the seventeenth century. In fact, says Williams, the earliest prohibition against mingling of whites and blacks came in 1630, eleven years after the landing of the first Negroes in Virginia. On that occasion, one Hugh Davis was "publicly flogged before an assembly of Negroes and others for defiling himself with a Negro,"[80] and was required to confess himself the following Sunday. By 1662 Virginia had passed a law which sought "to prevent spurious issue between white and colored persons."[81] In fact, Bruce remarked that the penalties attached to prohibitions of such relations contained a "certain degree of moral punishment."[82] This was, however, a Christian morality, prohibiting sex contacts with heathen. It is not clear that the racial angle had yet been established.

It seems not to be disputed, however, that sex relations between the races continued throughout the period of slavery. Chancellor Harper, himself a chief defender of slavery, admitted it but added that it could not reach to marriage—especially of white men to Negro women.[83] The number of mulattoes increased, however; and, while many of that class were descendants of mulatto parents, "all went back to white ancestors."[84] In the later years of slavery, concubinage of Negro women with planters, their sons, and overseers became noticeable. "It was flagrantly prevalent in the Creole section of Louisiana and was at least sporadic from New England to Texas."[85] Bassett remarks that, in North Carolina, a white man who kept a Negro mistress ordinarily lost no standing on account of it and adds that "the habit, though not common, was not unusual."[86] Cases of this kind also appear to have existed in Kentucky;[87] but, perhaps, as Phillips remarked, they were, in general, sporadic.

Reuter suggests that these associations probably increased between Negroes and upper-class whites, where not only caste but also economic distinction indicated that no social equality was involved.[88] And though miscegenation seldom, if ever, reached to intermarriage in this period,[89] it nevertheless existed and was practiced more extensively in areas where white persons and Negroes were in more regular and intimate contact; that is, in the towns and cities, in the border states, and on the small plantations.[90]

On the other hand, although clandestine associations were relatively more frequent in cities, they perhaps were neither tolerated nor approved. However, they tended to become a "sub-surface type of polygamy that approached an institutional form, in New Orleans, Mobile and certain other points in the South."[91]

In Charleston, South Carolina, for one instance, there was, and still is, a large mulatto population. During slavery this class was known as "bright fellows" or, occasionally, as "free persons of color." Relations between the mulatto women and white men were by no means rare. In fact, F. C. Adams remarked that, if a white man approached the wife of one of these bright fellows, the latter would "in nineteen cases out of twenty congratulate himself on the distinguished honor." He later adds that "such attempts are so common among the social events of the day, and so well understood by the slave, that instead of being resented, they are appreciated to a large extent."[92] Three men, he says, had sold slaves twice in order that the slaves' wives might be taken as mistresses.

"These men set an example of mercantile honor and integrity, are flattered by the populace, receive the attentions of very fine and virtuous ladies, wield a potential voice in the city government, and lead in the development of internal improvements, and established custom considers their example no harm when color is modified."[93]

In New Orleans concubinage of quadroon women with white men was generally accepted. Featherstonehaugh, in 1834; Martineau, in 1835; and Olmsted, in 1853, all found occasion to refer to the system. King writes understandingly of the custom, taking her material from Gayarré.

The quadroon women were often highly educated and, as Miss Martineau described them, were "as beautiful and accomplished a set of women as can be found."[94] White men became acquainted with these women at the famous Quadroon Ball.

"When one of them attracts the attention of an admirer, and he is desirous of forming a liaison with her, he makes a bargain with the mother, agrees to pay her a sum of money, perhaps $2000, as a fund upon which she may retire when the liaison terminates. She is now called *une placée;* those of her caste who are her intimate friends give her fetes, and her lover prepares *un jolie appartment meublé.* With the sole exception of going to church, matters are conducted very much as if marriage had been celebrated; the lady is removed to her establishment, and has her little coterie of women friends."[95]

The relation thus established might continue for several years, or for life. In the former case it might terminate upon the occasion of the man marrying a white wife. It, however, appears that the woman kept her interest in the furniture and retained the title to all real estate which had previously been given to her.

This situation indicates that sex relations between white men and quadroon women in New Orleans and in Charleston could be called customary. On the other hand, there were forms to observe which maintained the distances necessary to the status of both whites and quadroons under the system. The custom was, as has been mentioned, widely known and to an extent accepted. The white women of New Orleans tolerated the practice, even if they did not accept it as part of the normal order.[96]

This tends to make clear the distinction between the mores, which make action seem right and proper, and etiquette, which enables an individual to act freely within the limits which the formal rules of personal relations impose. To the extent that the system of relations existed between white men and free women of color, they could be established and maintained so long as the parties went through the proper forms, that is, of asking for a woman's hand, establishing a domicile, and endowing the woman with real estate or money. The system was a part of the social order in so far that it was permitted, if not approved. Such relations were irregular but not regarded as inimical to public welfare. Miss King's comment on the institution, written long after, probably does not display the toleration with which it was regarded at the time. She said:

"Assuming as a merit and a distinction what is universally considered in the civilized world a shame and disgrace by their sex, their training of their daughters had but one end in view. Unscrupulous and pitiless, by nature or circumstance, as one chooses to view it, and secretly still claiming the racial license of Africa, they were, in regard to family purity, domestic peace, and household dignity, the most insidious and the deadliest foes a community ever possessed."[97]

It seems, therefore, that etiquette may regulate social relations, even within the limits of an institution it does not approve. The duello is controlled by a rigid etiquette, long after it has been outlawed as a means of settling certain kinds of personal differences.

CHAPTER VI

THE SLAVE SEES HIMSELF THROUGH HIS MASTER'S EYES

MANY persons who have had occasion to consider the adjustment of the slave to his status have come to the conclusion that, as far as the slave saw himself, the situation was far from ideal. Redpath, for example, spent two or more years in the South, before the war between the states, asking slaves whether they preferred slavery to freedom, or vice versa. His recorded opinion—which we are not certain was not fixed in advance—was that they generally preferred freedom.[1]

The Rev. Nehemiah Adams reported in a different vein:

"The slaves, so far as I had seen, were unconscious of any feeling of restraint; the natural order of life proceeded with them; they did not act like a driven, overborne people, stealing about with sulky looks, imbruted by abuse, crazed, or stupid, or melancholic."[2]

Any question as to the comparative reliability of two reports which vary so widely is probably unanswerable. However, if latitude were allowed, it might be given to Mr. Adam's report, for, in the main, he had observed slaves in the cities, where the slave population consisted largely of house servants, who lived under more or less intimate personal relations with their masters, and where conditions of life were generally better. Moreover, in such places, the etiquette was, at the same time, more complex and more rigid.

And, yet, the intention of the inquirer was, and is, to determine how far the slaves had come to accept slavery as a part of the natural order, as one accepts the weather, the climate, and the universe. We may complain about the weather, but we put up with it, or seek to improve the situation by mending the roof, and would probably be unhappy if suddenly compelled to live in another and different world—one to which we were not accustomed. What one wants to know, in short, is how far the Negro, growing up in slavery, had been assimilated to, and incorporated in, the institution. The best evidence, in such a situation, is not the slave's attempt to report on his state of mind but his actions.

Evidence of such a kind may be depended upon; for the world in which an individual lives, and in which he finds reality, is not the objective world of science, or the world in which another individual lives. It is rather "the environment by which he is influenced, and to which he adapts himself."[3]

Again, when an individual has been released from the compulsions of social life, that is to say, when he is "not at himself," or when he is off his guard, or when the thin veneer of convention wears off, we may discover his true nature. The proverb, "Scratch a Russian, and you will find a Tartar," may then be said to have a more general application.

To restate the question, then, we might inquire: How did the slave appraise his role, as a subordinate in the social order, when he was not being asked to express his opinions?[4] What opinion of himself did he derive when he saw himself through the eyes of his master and of the slaveholding class generally? What part, as an agency of control in his relations with white persons, did etiquette play, when it was considered subconsciously or, rather, when it was not considered at all? To speak of etiquette in this way is to transfer attention from the external form in which it expresses itself and to identify it with habit and the structure in which it is embodied, that is, with habits in the individual which are controlled and enforced by custom in the group.

The problem, then, shifts from a consideration of the slave's opinion about slavery—in the abstract—to his accommodation to the institution, that is, to his conduct under actual conditions which slavery imposed. With this in mind we must seek to understand his joys, hopes, expectations, sorrows, and disappointments—in short, we must seek to discover the attitudes and sentiments which eventually became the basis of a life-philosophy. For, whatever is the range of a person's interest in a given society or whatever his status, and whatever the difficulties encountered in seeking those interests or evaluating his status, the person acquires, and develops, attitudes and sentiments which make his lot endurable.[5]

The sentiment underlying the relations between master and slave, for example, may be seen in a letter written by one Harry to his master, Samuel B. Polk, about 1841. Harry had been a good slave and had become a good blacksmith as well. Consequently, his master had allowed him to "hire his time" to employers in a distant state. But Harry, far from home and the old plantation, had become so lonely that he was constrained to write his master a letter of information, incidentally assuring him of his loyalty.

Dear Master:

As a servant I want to subscribe my friendship to you and famely as I am still in Carrollton [Mississippi] yet and doing good Labour for my imploieer but tho I am filling [failing] in some degree my Eyesite is falling of me I am well treated by my imploryer he feeds me well and dont worke me Two Hard. . . . . I wish to be remembered to all of my people old mistrs esphirly Tell the old Lady Harry is hir servant until dath I would be glad to see Hir one mor I expect to come out a christ-must to see you. . . . . Dear master I have Eleven children I have been faitheful over the anvil block cen 1811 and is still old Harry. . . . .

Harry your Servant[6]

As a form of ceremonial indicating subordination comes a verbal acknowledgment of servitude.[7] The slave frequently

looked upon himself as a "nigger." The word, it seems, con
veyed a notion of low status.

"But I teels you what, Mass'r Edward, no matter how proud
de black folks hold der head up and don' love ter work, and
don' love nothin' but day ownselves, I tells you what, and I tells
'em all, I ain't nothin' but a nigger nohow; *de nigger and de
mule am de axle-tree of de world.*"[8]

When Mrs. Kemble, on her Georgia plantation, had compli-
mented a slave woman for having a clean cabin, the latter replied, "Missis no 'spect to find colored folks house clean as white
folks."[9] "Colored folks" seemed to convey the idea of lower
status. However, as late as 1862, when the Sea Islands had
come under federal rule, and the Negroes had become partially
emancipated, the attitude, nevertheless, seemed to remain. The
slaves were receiving money for their labor at this time, and one
woman had protested to the manager that she had not received
as much as others. She later apologized for her actions in these
words: "You must excuse we niggers, we no sense, and Mr.
Philbrick so patient; all Secesh on these islands couldn't make
so much as he has with we."[10] In Tennessee, Ingraham relates,
a slave had captured a son who had run away from work. Immediately he reported to the master, "Ees, masse, catch de
berry bad boy. . . . . Old Juba feel berry shame ob him. Me
gib him frashun, me git 'im home. . . . . Come long, you nigger,
ain't you shame ob you'self?"[11] "Mass' Harry"—ten months
old—had fought with a black baby who had crawled near him
and who had begun to suck "Mass' Harry's" rubber teething
ring. The "mammy," began to amuse herself by saying, "Mass'
Harry make little nigga know his place."[12]

The slave perhaps considered "nigger" as a derogatory term.
A dog, Indian by name, had spoiled a deer hunt a week previously, and for this reason the master had ordered him left
behind on a second hunt. Pete, a slave, then proceeds to scold
Indian:

"You mighty grad, Injun, ain't you? . . . . But you better

keep quiet and min'd you' business at home, or sure 'nuff massa'll hab you hanged. You ain't fit hunt deer like de gentlemen's genteel dog, you nigger you; all you do is frighten 'em away from de stan' and keep massa and oder gentlemen from gettin' shot at 'em."[13]

Perhaps the slave considered the language of white persons to be not only different from, but also superior to, his own. A maid apologized to Mrs. Kemble "with great gravity for her mispronunciation, modestly suggesting that white words were impossible to the organs of speech of black folks."[14]

If, however, the slave felt himself to occupy a subordinate position in the general society, he nevertheless felt superior to other slaves whose masters were neither so wealthy nor so prominent as his own. Steward, himself a slave, recalls that there existed among the slaves "a foolish pride which loved to boast of their master's wealth and influence."[15] Douglass relates that "when Colonel Lloyd's slaves met those of Jacob Jepson, they seldom parted without a quarrel about their masters; Colonel Lloyd's slaves contending that he was the richest, and Mr. Jepson's that he was the smartest, and the most of a man. . . . . These quarrels would almost always end in a fight."[16] "They seemed to forget all the toils and suffering of their slavery, in their admiration of the plantation built up by their labor," says Srygley.[17]

"It was, then, considered bad enough to be a slave, but to be a poor man's slave was deemed a disgrace indeed."[18] The contempt with which slaves of a prosperous family looked upon "dese yere pore folks' niggers"[19] was "only less than that with which they regarded the 'poor white trash.' "[20] Steward heard slaves object to being set to work in the fields in very small gangs, "lest some passer-by should think they belonged to a poor man who was unable to keep a large gang."[21] In general, the slaves of a relatively poor master would share about the same life as the master; but this condition created no desire to be a "poor man's slave."

The social restrictions among slaves reached even to matrimony it seems. Some slaves, it is said, considered it below them to contract matrimonial alliances—such as they were—with the "inferior" slaves.[22] Superior slaves came perhaps from Virginia. In Louisiana one William said to Mr. Olmsted, "dem's all Creole niggers ain't no Virginny niggers dah. I reckon you didn't see no such looking niggers as dem on our plantation, did you, master?"[23]

Negroes, then, tended to accept the status of subordinates, to adapt themselves to it, and to support the adaptation with the appropriate attitudes and sentiments. In Goldsboro, North Carolina, at the beginning of the Civil War, a Confederate flag was raised over a log fort. When this was done, "the people ran out, NEGROES AND ALL, and cheered."[24] In this case there was no feeling of isolation, of social ostracism. The Negroes took part in the outburst as members of the group—as subordinate members, perhaps, but members nevertheless.

Through the fabric of race relations in slavery runs a thread which gives color and contrast to the whole. This is the code of social usages practiced by the slaves among themselves. Imitation, it has been said, is the sincerest flattery. We do not know what type of imitation is meant. Yet, it is generally admitted that, when individuals adopt customs, whether consciously or unconsciously, they come, in time, to consider those customs as right and proper. To this extent, then, we may say that etiquette among slaves is, perhaps, the best index of the slaves' view of proper relations between the races.

If the Negro was sensitive to social status among the whites, he was also keenly aware of social distinction in his own world. It is true that white persons made distinctions between house and field slaves and between house and body servants. But it is probable that these distinctions arose among the slaves themselves and were later adopted by the whites. It was inevitable that white people should eventually discover and respect the distances established among the slaves.[25] For example, there is evidence that the slaves addressed older slaves as "uncle" and "auntie."[26] On the other hand, these "uncles" frequently assumed attitudes of scorn toward a field hand but recognized the superiority of a house or body servant.[27]

There was, so to speak, a caste system and caste feeling among the patrician house servants and the plebeian field hands.[28] The distinction seemed to have a physical basis. Ingraham noted that "the field servant is heavy, loutish, and slow; his features scarce elevated in expression above the mule. The domestic servant is more sprightly, better clad, more intelligent and animated, apes polite manners, and imitates the polished airs of the well bred 'white folks.' "[29] On the other hand, the superiority of the house servant seemed to be due to social selection. The masters tended to choose the more intelligent slaves for house servants, and the evidence tends to show that mulatto slaves largely composed this class. Yet, whatever the physical distinction, the house servants were more polished, urbane, and suave, due perhaps to habitual contact with their superiors. Moreover, sensing their distinction from others, they refused to engaged in "boisterous and rough amusements so common with the 'cornfield niggers,' such as wrestling, kicking, loud singing, and jib dancing."[30] Douglass testifies that the house servants on his "master's plantation were a 'sort of black aristocracy'; the distance between these favored few, and the sorrow and hunger-smitten multitudes of the quarter was immense."[31]

On the other hand, the field hands, as a compensation for their inferior status, pretended in some instances to look down on the house servants.[32] In other instances they tended to look up to, and to envy, the favored ones. The testimony of a field slave (at a slave party) is:

"House servants were, of course, the 'stars' of the party; all eyes were turned to see how they conducted, for they among slaves, are what a military man would call 'fugle men.' The field hands, and such of them as have been excluded from the dwelling of their owners, look to the house servant as a pattern of politeness and gentility. And, indeed, it is often the only method of obtaining any knowledge of the manners of what is called 'genteel society.' Such slaves are always treated with more affability than others . . . . by the master."[33]

Again, where there is a hierarchy of occupation, an etiquette springs up to preserve the distances so created. Ingraham, describing the occupational stratification on a Tennessee plantation, says:

"The carriage driver must not only have his deputy ostler, but the laundress must be waited on by a little negress, to kindle her fires, heat her irons, and do everything that the dignity of the 'lady' in question deems 'derogatorum' for her to put her hands to. The chief washer-woman has from two to four ebony maids who do the grosser work while she does the 'fancy washing.' The cook must have a strapping negress to peel and pick; a strapping lad, with feet like two copies of Mitchell's *School Atlas*, for breadth, to chop the wood, bring the water, and be at hand . . . . two or three small fry to catch the poultry, turn the spit, and steal all they can. The gardner has his aids; the marm-nurse hers to *tote* the children; the housekeeper hers; and all this army of juveniles are thus in full training to take the places, by-and-by, of those to whom they are appended. . . . . The cook never enters the house, and the nurse is never seen in the kitchen; the wash-woman is never put to ironing, nor the woman who has charge of the ironing-room ever put washing. Each one rules supreme in her wash-house, her ironing-room, her kitchen, her nursery, her housekeeper's room; and thus, none interfering with the duties of the other, a complete system of domesticdom is established."[34]

Under this system status could be preserved, friction would be diminished, and distances respected. Each slave wanted to be known for what he was, it seems. If he were "promoted," he promptly adopted the mannerisms and pretensions common to the class. Moreover, the slave children were prepared for later duties in an apprentice system. It was not merely a division of labor but the discipline of the plantation which created rank and order in what was, after all, not merely an industrial but a political system.

Precedence and rank were respected among the slaves. In Charleston Ferguson noted that the married women were "distinguished by a peculiarly-tied kerchief they wear upon their heads."[35] Wright had occasion to note that the Negro in Maryland was a "conventional person. . . . . The barbaric love of ceremony cropped out in his conduct." He stated that house servants copied the manners and mannerisms of the whites but concedes that "in some individuals, the veneer thus taken on was converted into a fair degree of refinement. Field hands and common laborers, being in a different environment, learned less of these things. In saluting white people generally, Negroes knew how to be meticulously proper and careful."[36] Thus, it seems, there was a basic etiquette, and one that was supererogatory.

It was, however, in those places where white people gathered with pomp and ceremony that we see the slave at his best. It was a custom among the wealthier planters of the South to spend a part of the year at some famous resort it seems. For example, the White Sulphur Springs, of Virginia, and the Beaver Dam Springs, of Tennessee, drew persons who wished to drink the health-giving waters, while showing their wealth or prestige. The spring itself was a center of activity. Here the white people gathered to exchange confidences or pass the time of day. After they left, the slaves came.

"If you would take your stand near the spring when they come down after pitchers of water you would witness practical politeness. The courtesy of Samuel, coachman of Dr. W——— to Mary, the maid of Mrs. Colonel———. . . . . The polite salaams of Jacob to Rachel, the dressing woman, and of Isaac, the footman to Rebecca, the nursery maid, would charm you."[37]

The author regarded this ceremoniousness as comic, and perhaps the actors themselves were not wholly unconscious of the fact that they were acting. However, evidence from another source confirms the fact that there was an etiquette of "the Springs." Featherstonehaugh saw slaves gathering at a separate spring in White Sulphur Springs, Virginia, where they drank "in imitation of their masters." This spring, however, was used for slaves and horses—although, it seems, water was dipped out for the latter.[38]

On the porch of the main building at the same resort one might, of a morning, see precedence and rank in evidence among the mammies and nurses. There they gathered, holding a baby show—airing or sunning their charges—and sitting in an order which indicated the social status of the families to which they were attached.[39]

Dining at Beaver Dam Springs, Tennessee, was a ceremony with the whites, as well as with the slaves:

"After the masters and mistresses have left the dining hall, the long table is relaid, and they who whilom served are now feasted. I have been in twice to look at them. Not less than one hundred Ethiopian and Nubian ladies and gentlemen were seated in the places occupied an hour before by their masters and mistresses. . . . . There were servants of 'de lower klass' scullions and ostlers, boot-blacks and idlers, to wait on them."[40]

We have not been able to discover who served the ostlers and scullions.

In public, especially, slaves were expected to be on their dignity in their relations one with the other. In Charleston slaves were observed going to church, dressed in their best, and referring to one another as "Sir" and "Madam," while making the "most formal and particular inquiries after each other's families."[41] In Montgomery and Richmond there were expensive "assemblies or dress balls." Tickets to these would admit "one gentleman and two ladies, $1." Cards for one of these occasions were engraved and sent not only to fashionable slaves "but to some of the more esteemed white people, who, however, took no part, except as lookers-on."[42]

The process through which the slave was assimilated to slavery was a gradual one. It came to him from childhood, especially in the later generations. The situation was defined for him, perhaps by the master.

" 'Who's yo' master?' he'd say, an' grin.

" 'You is!' We'd say. An' please him so we'd all git a nickel. "Then we'd run over to Georgetown to buy sweets with it."[43]

On the other hand, the older slaves would teach the slave children their proper place:

"When I was eight years old, I used to call old Mistis, 'grandma,' like Polly Ann; we growed up together. She was born in July and her mother died in July, and my mamma was all the mother she knew, and I called old Mistis 'grandma' like she did. One day mamma called me up to her and told me not to call old Mistis, grandma. I stuck out my mouth and pouted, and said, 'Well, I been callin' her dat.' She didn't say nothing, but one day I came to tell mamma something that old Miss said, and called her 'grandma.' Mamma said, 'I can't hear you 'way over there. Come over here, an' tell me.' I came up to her and started—'Grandma said'—mamma didn't say a word. But 'boop' she hit me in the mouth. I started crying, and she said, 'Yo' is getting older now. An' yo' is old enuf to know nigger ways.' She was putting me in a nigger's place. I never called old Mistis 'grandma' after that."[44]

So it happened that, as adults, the slaves had come to know the proper forms for their contacts with white people.

"He came daintily forward and treated us to most Chesterfieldian bows and reverences, with multitudinous inquiries after our health and well-being. I took an opportunity of offering this sable Sir Charles Grandison a trifling *backsheesh* to reward him a little for his walk to the lodge to see us (though, by the way, we were told it was no unusual thing for him, as he frequently came there); the bowing increased to almost *koo-tooing*, and he went his way rejoicing and bowing still, like a self acting Chinese mandarin, 'nid-nid-nodding.' "[45]

A slave, in case of a breach of etiquette or duty, could laugh, as a sign that no offense had been intended. Mose was a member of a fire department in a North Carolina town. One day the fire bell rang, but Mose did not respond. Upon being upbraided, he said:

" 'Why Mass' Richard, I was singin' an didn' hear de bells .... and I see twarn't in our ward, sar, so I didn't hurry myself to def. Eef eed a been in *our* ward, Mass' Richard, I'd a rallied, you knows I would. Mose would a rallied, eef eed a been in our ward—Ha! Ha! Ha!—you knows it, Mass' Richard,' and he passed on laughing comically, without further remark."[46]

We have a suspicion that Mose had no intention of "rallying"; but the laugh passed as the indication of the right attitude.

A slave, on occasion, might be impudent if he supported his impudence with a quotation from the Scriptures. A slave trader was unloading a carload of Negroes at a station in Georgia. As he stepped on the platform he asked if all the Negroes were there. Thereupon one slave replied:

" 'Yes, massa, we's all heah.' 'Do dyself no harm, foh we's all heah,' added another, quoting Saint Peter .... "[47]

" 'I reckon de Lord has 'cepted of me, and I specs I shall be saved, dough I don' look like it, ha! ho! ho! De Lord am my rock, and he shall not perwail over me. I will lie down in green pastures and take up my bed in hell, yet will not his mercy circumwent me. Got some tobaccy, massa.' "[48]

On other occasions slaves would improvise songs which were positively impudent, but which, clothed in the right forms, would pass unnoticed, or even provoke a smile or laughter.

"We raise de wheat, dey gib us de corn;
We bake de bread, dey gib us de cruss;
We sif' de meal, dey gib us de huss;
We peal de meat, dey gib us de skin;

And dat's de way dey takes us in.
We skims de pot, dey gib us de liquor,
An' say, 'Dat's good enough fer a nigger.' "[49]

Because of faithfulness and sympathy, or perhaps long service, the slave could often "get his way," with an indulgent master or mistress.

" 'Ah, dear Richard, can't you drive another street; for instance along —— Street?'

" 'No, missis. I have something to get in this street.'

" 'Ah, Richard, cannot I avoid going there?'

" 'No, missis. I want to go there, missis.'

"And in spite of renewed prayers, his mistress was obliged to yield, and we were driven the way which the obstinate Richard chose. These faithful old servants are more obstinate than ours; but their eyes beam with something so kind, with such a cordial life, that one cannot help letting them have their way sometimes."[50]

In these ways, then—conceiving himself as a "nigger" and as—shall we say?—a natural servant; taking pride in his "family connections" and looking down on other slaves of lower estate; being loyal to his community; adopting forms more or less imitative of the white masters and mistresses; laughing himself out of tight places; singing "impudent" songs; quoting Scripture to get what he wanted; relying on his known fidelity and sympathy to get some of his desires granted—in these ways, then, the slave accommodated himself to slavery. We must believe that he doubtless saw his own lot differently from others, who knew not the advantages that accrued to the thoroughly assimilated slave.

It is in his interest in imitating the manners of white persons, and in the incorporation of these forms into his own life—especially in the cities and among the house servants—that we discern the extent of the assimilation of the slave to the institution of slavery. The etiquette of race relations is, in fact, one aspect of the institution itself.

CHAPTER VII

ETIQUETTE AND THE FREE NEGRO

WHEN students and travelers sought to describe the social classes and existing conditions of the prewar South, they almost invariably neglected the free Negro. That class, however, was not of so little importance as the omission would indicate. It presented problems quite out of proportion to its numerical strength, especially in its relation with the white population. Indeed, considering the relations of free Negroes and white persons during the period, the development of etiquette between all Negroes and white persons moves into bold relief.

The first free Negroes, of course, were those who, in the seventeenth century, had served their terms of indenture, and who had consequently assumed the status of freemen. Indeed, a few of the Negro freemen had acquired other Negroes as indentured servants.[1]

Until about 1662 the free Negro class was recruited solely from released indentured servants;[2] after that time the legal development of slavery and the resulting increase of the slave population, together with the need for special controls and the discussion of legal means for manumitting slaves, all served to focus attention on Negroes, whether slave or free. Until the development of slavery, it has been said, the free Negro was "as much a part of the body politic as the white man."[3]

After the Negro had been reduced to slavery, some from the group began to acquire freedom by becoming Christians—perhaps no considerable number.[4] There was, however, an old rule that only persons taken in a just war could be made slaves. This, on the other hand, seems not to have applied to Negroes, who were considered heathen.

By the middle of the eighteenth century, as the revolution with England drew near, and as men sought to justify proposed political action with the principle that all men were created free and equal, or to support a philosophy of revolution acquired by reading Locke, Milton, and Blackstone, there grew up the notion that slavery was repugnant to the political ideals and institutions of America. Some slaveholders, unable to harmonize slavery with these views, began, as a consequence, to manumit their slaves.[5] After the Revolution broke, slaves were enlisted, with the promise of freedom, after a stipulated term of service.[6] And later, when the Revolution had succeeded, many states made legislative provision for manumission of Negro soldiers who had served in the Revolution. It has on occasion been said that the Constitutional Convention, directly after the Revolution, was opposed to slavery and hoped to see it abolished.[7]

Religious scruples, however, were among the chief causes operating to bring about manumission of Negro slaves during this and later periods. Under the conviction that slavery was contrary to the Golden Rule, for instance, many slaveholders manumitted some, if not all, of their slaves. Even before the Revolution the Methodists had begun to preach and agitate against slavery and to urge moral reform. In 1784 the Baltimore Conference of that body stated its conviction that "slavery was contrary to the Golden Law of God."[8] The sect sought generally to prevail upon its adherents to free their slaves. The Quakers of North Carolina, following somewhat the same course, progressed from the notion of "using Negroes well" to the absolute prohibition that no member of the Friends' Society could either own or buy slaves.[9] In fact, one instance is found where a certain Gloister Hunnicutt gave six slaves to a monthly meeting, "to be manumitted by such members of the said meeting, as the meeting shall appoint."[10]

Another principle operating to bring about freedom for slaves is shown in the case of a woman slaveholder who decreed that her slaves be emancipated after her death. She could not satisfy her conscience, she said, to have the slaves "separated from each other, and husbands from wives,"[11] which would most likely occur.

Still other slaves were manumitted by their masters for personal and sentimental reasons. As social distance grew less, attitudes changed. Masters felt, on occasion, that menial positions and the insecurities of the slave's condition were neither right nor proper for certain slaves. The result was that these slaves were promoted to house servants, allowed to plant little patches of land, elevated to places of responsibility, and, as in the case of the "mammy" or "uncle," given as much respect as circumstance allowed or sentiment dictated. However, to promote a slave to the status of free Negro was a more noble gesture. It raised the freed person above the conditions of a servile status at the same time that it testified to a hidden sentiment behind the act. It could not be granted to all slaves; yet, in particular instances, it might be allowed to a few of the more sensitive and loyal ones. As a matter of fact, a slaveholder might occasionally manumit one slave and leave others in slavery. In the will of one Robert Poole, he says:

" 'I give to Venie, a free mulatto woman, the half of my house in the field where she now lives, during her natural life, and after her death to go to her son George. I give to her daughter Mary, the other half of the house with the enclosed piece of ground thereto. And I give to my Negro man Andrew, in consequence of his faithful services, his freedom after my decease.' He left thirteen other slaves 'of all ages and sexes.' "[12]

In general, it is thought, manumission by will was adopted to prevent loyal slaves from coming into the hands of persons who would not treat them well.[13] In other instances, an additional bequest might be made to a faithful slave. Said Joseph Holmes:

"It is my will and desire that my Negro man Lemon shall have and enjoy his freedom after my death; and for his attention and friendship [sic] during my illness, that he shall have my sorrel horse, with a saddle and bridle and ten dollars in cash."[14]

On occasion, the fact that a female slave had borne many children, thereby increasing the master's wealth, would bring about her manumission by a grateful master. One master, indeed, promised freedom to a female slave if she bore ten living children. Another covenanted to free a woman slave when she had borne as many children as he then had—five in number.[15]

In instances where a master had cohabited with a slave woman, it occasionally happened that he would desire to manumit the woman. In Kentucky one Patton made a will to the effect that his slaves should be freed at his death. The heirs brought suit to break the will, on the grounds that Patton was insane. The evidence of insanity was that he desired to marry his slave, Grace, and, failing in this, had liberated her. The judge in the case rendered his decision to this effect:

"The fact that the deceased evinced an inclination to marry the slave, Grace, whom he liberated, is not a stronger evidence of insanity than the practice of rearing children by slaves without marriage; a practice but too common, as we all know, from the numbers of our mulatto population."[16]

It thus happened that claims of blood occasionally operated to bring freedom to the natural children of masters and slave women. One C. F. Bates wrote in his will:

"I have a daughter called Clemensa . . . . in Cumberland. I declare her to be free to every right and privilege which she can enjoy by the laws of Virginia. I most particularly direct that she be educated in the best manner that ladies are educated in Virginia."[17]

Still another type of emancipation occurred in the practice of allowing slaves to purchase their freedom. Some among them would occasionally purchase their relatives as well. The motive for such practices doubtless resulted from the conviction that "a slave who could purchase himself, was one whom it did not pay to hold as a slave."[18]

There was, however, no rule in these matters. The relationship between master and slave grew up in spite of law, religion, and formal prescription. That is to say, intimacy and closeness of contact developed forms and sentiments that, in turn, tended to give a new turn to relations.

The result of manumission, either on principle or as a result of claims, served to increase the number of free Negroes in Virginia. Tucker, in 1796, remarked that "the progress of manumission is at this time, in Virginia, continual but not rapid."[19]

When the first census was taken, in 1790, approximately 9 per cent of the Negro population was free, while the rate increased to approximately 13 per cent in 1860. The total increase from census to census had, moreover, been constant.[20]

The period from 1790 to 1810 showed the greatest rate of increase of the free Negro class for any subsequent period in the whole of the United States.[21] Under the influence of emotions and the slogans of a successful revolution, slaveholders had begun to adopt a benevolent attitude toward the slave and to deprecate the existence of slavery. Antislavery sentiment eventually became the fashion, and this fashion persisted until it was opposed by the growing conviction that slavery was, after all, the only practical scheme for securing the labor needed for the growing plantations. Thus benevolence retreated before economic interest, and principle before practical considerations. The supply of free Negroes hitherto depending upon this source was then largely cut off.

The rate of increase and the total population of free Negroes tended to vary from time to time and from state to state.[22] Yet, in the areas of the slave states, the concentration showed largely in the South Atlantic area and, by 1860, was confined largely to Maryland, Virginia, and North Carolina.[23] Washington noted that the numbers were perhaps greater than the census data showed, due to the fact that free Negroes could be enslaved and hence be counted in the census as slaves.

The problem of the free Negro, however, consisted not altogether in the increase in numbers but also in the establishment of proper relations with white people. When a Negro was emancipated, his legal status was fixed, so far as the former master was concerned. There remained, however, the definition of social status by himself and others. Accommodations made to a position of dependence were, presumably, nullified by the new status, hence new adjustments needed to be developed. Having acquired a new legal status, it was natural for the free Negro to see his own situation in a new light and to conceive his adjustment in terms of attitudes adopted by white freemen. On the other hand, the color of the freedman was a badge of servitude. It was difficult for white persons to treat him as free. Moreover, initial hostility between the free Negro class and the white group was not submerged in the customary social ritual. There was, in short, no etiquette proper to the relations of free Negroes and white persons. "Indeed," says Wright, "if any change at all resulted from the rise of the new class, it caused a more strict definition of class boundaries, a more firm repulsion of the Negro, and an outcasting of any white man who went across to the Negroes."[24]

The free Negro was, then, a misfit. White persons did not know precisely how to act toward, or with reference to, him. If, presuming that he had put away the badge of slavery with his manumission, he tried "to act like a white man," he merely excited additional hostility. Communication was hampered by the situation; co-operation was at a standstill; and the controls established in a moral order were inoperative. If, however, he was an anomaly in a society where Negroes were slaves and white men were free, so were the poor whites. Yet, if there was less sentiment in regard to the latter class, it was because it was accepted as a condition that could not be changed.

As the free Negro class increased, legal measures to control, dispose of, or to assimilate those already freed became more and more prominent. In Colonial Virginia, for example, the presence of free Negroes raised the question: What shall be done with them? One answer was provided by an enactment, in

1691, requiring that such persons should be sent out of the state within six months.[25] The hysteria of the pre- and post-Revolution periods brought enactments and re-enactments seeking to control the free Negroes if they remained in the colony, or to provide for transporting them out of the colony, or, at times, even requiring that manumission be disallowed altogether. Statutes were enacted requiring registration of all free Negroes, lest they wander about, preying on the citizens, or gather in large numbers, presumably to plot insurrection.[26]

Colonization of free Negroes in Africa was suggested by Thomas Jefferson as early as 1777. Ten years later Dr. Thornton published an address to free Negroes, offering to lead them back to Africa.[27] Judge Tucker wished to "render it their inclination to seek those privileges [of citizenship] in some other climate," and suggested Louisiana as a suitable location, especially in view of that fact that it was then under foreign control.[28] In 1800 the General Assembly of Virginia was in favor of "purchasing lands beyond the limits of Virginia for colonization purposes."[29] The plan, however, lay dormant for many years until benevolent slaveholders began to manumit their slaves for purposes of colonization. One direct outgrowth of the discussion was the organization of the African Colonization Society, which sought to solve in principle the problem raised largely by sentiment.[30] For slaveholders, by emancipating slaves for colonization, or by permitting them to buy their freedom, were constantly adding to the numbers of "free persons of color."[31]

Perhaps the basic objection to the free Negro class was that they might plunder, rob, or murder the whites,[32] or contaminate the slaves with ideas of freedom, and thus cause the latter to rise in insurrection; or, at most, to become discontented with their lot. Later defenders of the South, notably Fitzhugh,[33] Professor Dew,[34] and Judge Catron,[35] noted that free Negroes would not only corrupt the morals of slaves but would also enter into competition with white labor.

The presence of free mulattoes, in any great number, seemed to complicate the problems of relations between whites and Negroes. To know how to act toward a free Negro who was at the same time black was a sufficient task; but, when the matter was complicated with the problem of color, the solution was even more difficult. Claims of blood seemed, however, to be stronger than prudence and philosophy. And this accounts, in some measure, for the fact that a larger percentage of mulattoes was free as compared with the percentage who were slaves.[36] The mulatto population was concentrated in the eastern slave states. It was a fairly negligible quantity in the far South and Southwest, where the intimacy of the small farm-household servant relationship was replaced by the plantation, often with absentee ownership.

There were also more, and larger, cities in the seaboard states than in the newly developed Southwest. House servants were more in demand; and, since mulattoes constituted largely that class, this may account for the presence of larger numbers of mulattoes in the cities.[37] On the other hand, the possibilities for clandestine sexual relations between the races were more pronounced in the case of house servants. Hence, the presence of mulattoes in the cities was both cause and effect.[38]

Evidence, not entirely incontrovertible, indicates distinctions in the relations between white persons, blacks—slave or free— and mulattoes. The latter were generally supposed to deserve a different treatment, due to their resemblance to the master class.[39] There was an attitude of peculiar pathos toward the mulatto. But, for all that, custom unvaryingly prescribed that one drop of blood made a man otherwise white a Negro, even though there may have been exceptions to the rule.[40]

In the first three decades of the nineteenth century, "practically all of the Southern and Middle States, and a few communities in the North, began to restrict, and, in some cases, to debase the free Negro to a status next to that of a slave."[41] And the significance of the gradual debasement of the free Negro is "evidence of a steady growth of a caste system, which excluded the Negro from citizenship solely upon the basis of color."[42]

Legislation enacted in response to the revival of abolition agitation included laws forbidding immigration, and requiring the emigration, of free Negroes.[43] Under the circumstances, if a free Negro remained in a state requiring his emigration, or if he went into a state forbidding his coming in, he might sometimes be re-enslaved. Or if he lost his "free papers"—which he was required to carry—or had them taken from him, his inability to prove he was free was often an occasion for re-enslavement. Free Negroes were, then, so insecure that, it is said, some sold themselves into slavery.[44]

Thus the theoretical condition was that the free Negro had nowhere to go, even though it was frequently illegal to remain where he was. But the actual situation was that many went to the North or wandered into the slave states where laws were strict but their execution lenient.[45]

In other cases, as, for example, in the instance mentioned by Buckingham, humane owners, prevented by law from manumitting slaves, would "give them entire command of their labour, and allow them to work for themselves, and enjoy without deduction all the fruits of their industry."[46]

The passage of laws restricting and controlling free Negroes was accelerated whenever rumors of insurrection were noised abroad, and whenever any insurrection, or uprising, actually occurred. For example, in Virginia, after Gabriel's attempted insurrection in 1800, "laws concerning migration of Free Negroes into the Commonwealth were declared defective, and in need of revision,"[47] and a resolution suggesting their colonization "outside the limits of the United States" was offered.[48] They were forbidden to move from one county or town to another, and it "was thought desirable to curtail the opportunities of the free Negroes for acquiring knowledge of books which might render them propagators of seditious anti-slavery doctrines among the slaves."[49] These restrictions were enacted in face of the fact that there was little direct evidence of connection of free Negroes with Gabriel's plot.

Then, again, in the same state, after the insurrection of Nat Turner, instruction in reading or writing was forbidden. After the passage of this restrictive legislation free Negroes began sending their children to the North to be educated, thereupon the legislature declared that "any free person who should go beyond the State for education should be considered to have emigrated."[50] Having emigrated, he could not, in face of other legislation, return.

Other states and localities also indulged in excessively restrictive regulations. Witness those of Augusta, Georgia, in 1843:

"Free Negroes were forbidden to ride or drive about the towns save on business. . . . . Nor were they allowed to carry canes, clubs, or sticks, unless blind; nor smoke in public places, attend military parades; hawk beer, cake, fruit or confectionery in the streets and alleys of the town. Curfew sounded at 9:15, and all lights must be out by ten. . . . . These ordinances were typical of those of other Georgia towns."[51]

In North Carolina free persons of color gradually lost the rights and privileges which distinguished them from slaves. Taxes and road duty alone remained of all their original duties and perquisites.[52]

A classical legal statement of the position of the free Negro was perhaps rendered by Chief Justice Joseph H. Lumpkin, of the Georgia State Supreme Court, when among other things he said:

"We maintain, that the status of the African in Georgia, whether bond or free, is such that he has no civil, social, or political rights whatever, except such as are bestowed upon him by statute; that he can neither contract, nor be contracted with; that the free negro can only act by and through his guardian; that he is in a condition of perpetual pupilage or wardship; and that this condition he can never change by his own volition. It can only be done by legislation. That the fact of manumission confers no other right but that of freedom from the dominion of the master, and the limited liberty of locomotion; that it does not and cannot confer citizenship; that the social and civil degradation resulting from the taint of blood adheres to the descendants of Ham in this country, like the poisoned tunic of Nessus; that nothing but an act of the Assembly can purify, by the salt of its grace, the bitter fountain—the darkling sea.

"He, the free Negro, resides among us, and yet is a stranger. A native even, and yet not a citizen. Though not a slave, yet he is not free. Protected by law, yet enjoying none of the immunities of freedom. Though not in a condition of chattelhood, yet constantly exposed to it. He lives among us without motive and without hope. His fancied freedom is all a delusion. . . . . The great principle of self-preservation demands, on the part of the white population, unceasing vigilance and firmness, as well as uniform kindness, justice and humanity. . . . . "[53]

One inference to be gained from this legislation is that, so far as free Negroes were concerned, the control of social ritual, common to white persons and slaves, had broken down. Slaveholders, who paid lip service to policies and philosophy of slavery, while for personal and sentimental reasons they manumitted individual slaves, were largely responsible for this situation. It was to discipline these men that laws were passed and lectures from the bench delivered.

The significance of laws thus becomes apparent. They are means of social control, appearing last in the course of the evolution of institutions. Men do not enact laws when custom and etiquette prevail—but, when, under new conditions, customs fail, legislation intervenes. In the main, then, laws represent attempts to bolster up institutions that are declining. From this angle, they are symptoms of the disorganization of custom.

The constantly tightening legal restrictions imposed upon them is an evidence that free Negroes were regarded as a menace and were, therefore, never completely accepted in the

South.[54] Especially was this true when the abolition movement became aggressive and when the discussion of emancipation for all slaves became an absorbing topic in the South. Since in many cases the free Negro as a class had already been a disappointment, emancipation of the entire slave group, it was argued, would merely add to the difficulties of racial adjustment.

"I like a nigger," said a Kentuckian to Stirling, "but I hate a damned free nigger."[55] The mountain whites of Tennessee and North Carolina shared the sentiment;[56] and a white man in the upland region of Alabama suggested to Olmsted:

"They ought to get some country and put 'em whar they could be by themselves. It wouldn't do no good to free 'em and let 'em hang 'round because they is so monstrous lazy; if they hadn't got nobody to take care on 'em you see they wouldn't do nothin' but juss naturally laze 'round and steal and pilfer. . . . . Now suppose they was free, you'd see they'd think themselves just as good as we. . . . . Now just suppose you had a family of children, how would you like to hev a nigger feelin' just as good as a white man? How'd you like to hev a nigger steppin' up to your darter? Of course you wouldn't and that's the reason I wouldn't like to hev 'em free. . . . . "[57]

By the later fifties, however, unfavorable opinions of the free Negroes were not confined to specific localities and persons. Ingraham considered them "the worst possible servants."[58] A Virginian offered his opinion that they were "a miserable lot of vagabonds, drunken, vicious, worse off than those retained in slavery."[59] Another writer said they were "sad and melancholy."[60] "If any crime is committed," said Long, "and the perpetrator is not discovered, it is laid to the free Negro."[61]

Additional uneasiness, occasioned by the presence of free people of color, was traceable to the conflict of economic interests between them and working-class white people. Competition, if it had been felt at all, was not felt so keenly by white persons when Negroes were slaves. But, when free Negroes became open competitors, the whites conceived their own interests to be endangered and reacted defensively.[62] The poor whites, it is true, had moved in large numbers to the frontier. Yet, those who remained faced the problem of competing with a group considered morally and intellectually their inferior. It was generally understood that free persons of color lived on a lower standard and were expected to work for less.

The picture presented hitherto is a dismal one, to say the least. It could easily be inferred that the life of the free Negro was one long struggle against hopeless odds; or that the class, definitely criminal and irresponsible, was a social liability.

This may have been the general, or average, condition; but the lot and condition of the free Negro varied from person to person, from place to place, and from time to time. The key to this situation is perhaps found in the attitudes which the white people adopted toward the class and in the adjustments which free Negroes made as individuals.

An outstanding adjustment of free Negroes was that of occupational specialization. In Charleston, South Carolina, for example, "a large portion of the fashionable tailors, shoe manufacturers, and mantua-makers were free Negroes."[63] "A considerable number had reached a business standing recognized by the banks," and the entire free Negro population was noted for its thrift. Jehu Jones was an innkeeper and very rich, according to reports.[64] Of forty-three Negroes, of Savannah, in 1840, thirty-four were mechanics; two, butchers; five, barbers; and two, engineers and pilots.[65] Two cooks, three farmers, two blacksmiths, three washers, one barber, and a seamstress were counted among the sixteen free Negroes at Milledgeville, Georgia, in 1832; while in Washington, Georgia, one free Negro kept an "eating establishment," another a stable, and the third a shoeshop. Two thousand, eight hundred and nine free persons of color in Louisiana followed fifty-seven trades and occupations; while in New Orleans, one thousand, seven hundred and ninety-two were found in fifty-four trades and occupations.[66]

In New Bern, North Carolina, lived John Green, carpenter and contractor; Richard Hazel, "blacksmith of means"; Albert and Freeman Morris, "two nice young men"; Scipio, blacksmith and livery-stable owner; and Fellow Bragg, a tailor, to whose shop "prominent people were known to move their trade."[67] "Black Bob," of Nashville, Tennessee, kept an inn for white customers.[68] Solomon Humphries, of Macon, Georgia, had purchased his freedom, entered business—in which he employed white clerks—and, by 1839, had as large a credit as any merchant in the South.[69] In fact, free Negroes in the towns and the cities were generally engaged in personal-service occupations, or were artisans and small shopkeepers.[70]

Some among them, however, were more or less independent and had acquired positions of trust and importance in their communities. In the first decade of the nineteenth century, one Gower of Lexington, Georgia, was known for his skill in performing the most difficult surgical operations. He became the partner of a white physician and had offices in a local hotel.[71] Austin Dabney of the same state, having served with great honor in the American Revolution, was given a farm by the legislature and was "welcomed in the tavern circle of chatting lawyers, whenever his favorite Judge Dooly held court at his home village." Once, "when the formality of drawing his pension carried him to Savannah, the Governor of the State, seeing him pass, dragged him from his horse and quartered him in his house as a guest."[72]

Samuel Thomas, Harry and Andrew, founded schools for the teaching of Negroes in Charleston.[73] John Chavis, of North Carolina, taught white persons and numbered among his pupils statesmen and men of prominence.[74]

Some among the free Negroes were farmers, as, for example, in Chatham County, Georgia; on the Cane River, in Louisiana; in North Carolina; and in some sections of Virginia.[75] Others had acquired slaves and had engaged in agriculture on the scale of planters. For, while it is true that many free persons of color generally owned relatives "as a means of giving them freedom, an appreciable number of colored proprietors owned slaves purely as a productive investment."[76]

The attitudes of white men toward the slaveowners among the free Negroes varied. One author states that they were "treated as courteously as white men of the same rank, and with as much respect";[77] but another mentioned that the so-called Negro Creole slaveholders were held in low repute by white persons and slaves.[78] If the prejudice against the free persons of color was due to the fact that they were thought to be shiftless farmers, poor laborers, and incitors of slave mutinies, it could not well be based on these causes where they were thrifty, prosperous, and themselves slaveowners. The opposition to this class was doubtless based on different grounds, according as that opposition was manifest in slaveowners or poor whites. It would, therefore, be different in different places.

Still another adjustment made by free persons of color was to establish, and settle in, communities composed of their class. Noticeable among these were "Negroville" or Washington, in Louisiana; Nachitoches, in the same state; and a colony on the border between Louisiana and Texas—the Calcasieu—Jefferson County settlement.[79] On the other hand, in contrast with this isolationist policy, there was a distinct tendency for this class to settle in the towns and cities. This latter circumstance was perhaps due to the fact that they were mainly mulattoes and were more acceptable as servants than blacks, or to the fact that occupational opportunities were greater in the towns.[80]

The favorable adjustments which free Negroes made might be credited to community sentiment or to personal reactions on the part of white persons. Yet, it seems that the free Negro was not passive in his adjustments to the extent that he would allow white persons completely to mold sentiment in his favor. Successful persons among them seemed to solve problems, and to meet crises, by reverting to, or never departing from, the etiquette considered proper to the relations of all white persons and all Negroes. "They complied in all things," said Phillips, "that they might live as a third element in a system for two."[81] They conformed in their habits to the sentiment expressed in the Louisiana Black Code:

"Free people of color ought never to presume to conceive themselves equal to the white; but, on the contrary, they ought to yield to them in every occasion, and never speak or answer to them, except with respect."[82]

They knew the etiquette, had become habituated, and deemed the ritual right and proper. Moreover, they accepted their position and status and were proud of it. Again, they frequently enjoyed the confidence of the white people; and this they could not have gained had they shown any disposition to betray it. Now and then free Negroes mentioned that they "fooled" white people—or thought they did. A good deal of this "fooling" was doubtless tolerated because of the Negro's ingratiating good nature and his ability to get out of a hard place by giving the situation a humorous turn.

Cases in support of this contention, though not numerous, are frequent enough to quote. For example, John Good—"the son of his master"—when freed at his master's death, undertook to support the two white daughters of the master—but as a Negro, not as a half-brother.[83] John Stanley, of New Bern, North Carolina, had amassed a fortune of $40,000 and had been freed by his mistress.

"This lady lived until 1822, and when old and feeble could be seen on the streets, in fine weather, supported on the arm of her faithful servant,—now fourteen years a freeman. Thus she took the air, and thus she went to church on Sunday."[84]

However, when Stanley had escorted the lady to her pew in the church, he then "took his seat with his own family in the place assigned to colored people."

When Henry Evans was understood to preach no subversive doctrines to the slaves at Fayetteville, North Carolina, white persons not only came to the church but later evicted the slaves. Still later the church was admitted to the white Methodist conference, and a white minister assigned to it. Yet, Evans would preach to the white people, occasionally, and had a room in the back of the church until his death. Evans, however, "was particular to violate no law, and to all whites he showed the respect which their sense of caste superiority demanded."[85] Bishop Capers remarked:

"I have not known many preachers who appeared more conversant with the Scriptures than Evans. . . . . He seemed always deeply impressed with the responsibility of his position . . . . never speaking to a white man but with his hat under his arm, never allowing himself to be seated in their houses, and even confining himself to the kind and manner of dress proper for slaves in general, except his plain black coat in the pulpit. Henry Evans did much good, but he would have done more had his spirit been untrammeled by this sense of inferiority."[86]

In dissenting to the last statement, it might be suggested that Evans acquired the opportunity "to do good" by conforming to the etiquette expected of Negroes.

Concerning Solomon Humphries, of Macon, Georgia, Buckingham noted:

"The merchants and traders of the North, with whom he dealt and corresponded, always paid him a visit when they came South for business and pleasure; and as he kept an excellent house, with an abundance of servants and good fare, he very often entertained a large party of white persons at dinner, giving them choice dishes and excellent wines. He never ventured, however, to seat himself at the table, but waited on the guests, superintending and directing the details of the feast."[87]

Thus, when free Negroes were accommodated to their status, occasional privileges might be accorded them which seemed to violate the ritual. Yet, here again, explanation is necessary. When etiquette is rigid, it may be violated with impunity, provided that the attitudes be "conventional." That is to say, the external act—the ritual—in ceremony may be varied or discarded under certain circumstances, provided that no change of status is implied and that the parties to the act know that the instance is a special dispensation. Thus, when the Rev. James Horner testified that his father not only went to school to John Chavis but "boarded in his family,"[88] no loss of status was assumed, on the one hand, or any elevation in status, on the other.

Chavis, however, was considered a prodigy. He had been sent to Princeton Theological Seminary to test a Negro's ability to learn Greek and Latin. Upon his return he had become a celebrity and, as such, was not subjected to regulations governing Negroes in general.

"The slaves were amazed to see a Negro receive so much respect from the whites. . . . . From a source of the greatest responsibility I have learned that this Negro was received as an equal socially, and asked to the table by the most respectable people of the neighborhood."[89]

When the daughter of "Black Bob"—a tavern keeper of Nashville—was to be married, Bob sent invitations to all the prominent white people in the town. Many accepted, including General Andrew Jackson. And a certain "Dr. McNairy danced the reel with the bride."[90] Even so great a condescension on the part of Dr. McNairy effected no change in Bob's status, nor his daughter's, nor the white persons' at the wedding. Bob "stayed in his place," and etiquette, though violated in form, was adhered to in spirit and attitude. Social distance was maintained.

The assimilation of the free Negro to the etiquette of race relations is further attested to in the case of an unnamed free person of color whom Olmsted met near Marion, South Carolina. "Well I likes my country better dan dis; must say dat, master, Likes my country better dan dis. I'se a free nigger in my country, master,"[91] he said. The Negro in question was loyal to his state, to his people, and he accepted the customary status of the Negro. In addressing Mr. Olmsted as "master" and in referring to himself as a "free nigger," he showed that his changed legal status had not affected his habits and sentiments, or his conception of himself. For this reason he could make the journey from North Carolina to South Carolina alone and without apparent difficulty.

Yet, on the other hand, if the free Negro had learned to respect the superiority of the white man, and to defer to him on all occasions, he nevertheless professed to despise the slaves. Having perhaps so recently attained a higher legal status, he reacted by looking down with condescension, if not contempt, upon his recent associates of lowly status. This attitude perhaps explains why, if a free Negro could not find a woman of his class to marry and married a slave woman instead, he lost caste with his group.[92]

However, the contempt, so far as it actually existed, was mutual, for slaves also professed to despise even the ground on which a free Negro walked. Woodson offers the suggestion that the attitude was encouraged by the slaveholders, lest slaves and free Negroes conspire in insurrection.[93]

As a sidelight on slavery, then, we may see the code of relations proper to the contact of blacks and whites reflected among the free Negroes. We see also further evidence of the evolution of a caste system sustained by legislation. But we see, again, the evidence of ability in the Negro to adjust himself to circumstances and to gain a modicum of security and recognition even in the face of excessively restrictive and formal regulations. To some extent accommodation was facilitated when, and if, the free Negro retained his conception of himself—and the white man's conception of him—as subordinate in the social scale.[94]

Under the circumstances where these failed, he adopted the principle of protective coloration. That is to say, he migrated to the towns and cities, where amid the secondary contacts of urban life he might move as a symbol rather than as a person. Or he withdrew largely from contact with white persons by settling in communities made up largely of his own class. These trends were prophetic of tendencies among Negroes, after emancipation, to move to the cities—especially those Negroes of higher financial and educational standing—or to found little communities into which white men rarely, if ever, intrude.

Finally, in the confusion which resulted from attempts of white persons and free Negroes to adjust themselves to a situation where the Negro had been elevated from a slave status, we begin to arrive at a conception of the problem which later arose, when, by emancipation, all Negroes had become free; and when relations which had grown up in custom, and in the attitudes of both groups, had been changed by law.

CHAPTER VIII

ETIQUETTE DURING THE PERIOD OF THE WAR BETWEEN THE STATES

THROUGHOUT the period of slavery, and until the beginning of the war between the states, the relations of whites and blacks were, as a rule, harmonious. There were, of course, occasional disorder and discord. Kindness and brutality were intermingled; benevolence alternated with bitterness, and principle with self-interest. A system of "black laws" and slave codes which grew more repressive contrasted strangely with incidents of close association between masters and slaves, wherein all laws became dead letters.

Slavery, from the standpoint of human nature, was, on the whole, perhaps, neither a very good system nor yet a very bad one. It represented, in the main, an institution growing out of natural conditions, in which men first sought their own interests and occasionally gave some attention to the interests of others. The philosophy of slavery seldom, if ever, squared with practice. Philosophy or doctrine was a platform—a public utterance of a rule or principle to which practice was supposed to conform. Practice was, however, something else again. If the two tended to agree, it was doubtless in the regions where, due to occasional and continued absence of owners, or perhaps to extraordinary size of a resident-owner plantation, contacts between master and slave, or white and black, were restricted and formal. On the other hand, on the small-owner farms contacts of intimacy seemed to operate to counterbalance doctrine. Human nature did not meet the stipulation of principle, and relations were essentially on a human level.

Yet, the harmony existing appears as a function of the control exercised by etiquette. The code—differing in different places and at different times—comprised most, if not all, of the forms that were observed when white people and Negroes associated. The evidence that manners effected control appears in the fact that, where a code was observed, relations moved smoothly. If there were no forms established—as in the instance of relations between free Negroes and white persons—confusion resulted. Yet, understanding would be restored in these latter instances, provided that communication was renewed. When the forms that had become expected and accepted between white persons and slaves were observed between free Negroes and white people, communication actually did ensue, and control was re-established.

Among the slaves themselves forms were observed which not only reflected similar forms among the whites but also effected adjustment among the slaves. And, though the characters in this vast drama changed with the passing of time, the human nature of the participants did not change. Moreover, the code of relations which bound the cast together—and under which they were enabled to carry out a corporate existence—became crystallized by experience and fortified by habit.

Yet, when the guns of Fort Sumter announced that the war was on, embarrassing questions needed to be answered. Would the slaves remain as passive under the stress of war as they had under peace? Could they be controlled when many of their masters and most of the white men were absent at the battle front? Or would they rise to slay the wives and children of the men who had either held them in slavery or assented while others had done so?

As the war progressed, however, signs here and there indicated that the slaves, as a whole, would remain loyal to their masters and mistresses or would, at least, continue docile and submissive. Generally, the slaves gave few, if any, signs of defection. From the diary of Mrs. Chestnut,[1] kept continuously during the period when she was traveling in most of the states of the Confederacy, we are able to visualize the situation and to reconstruct the behavior of the slaves, as well as to learn of suspicions of the white people.

With her husband absent, Mrs. Chestnut had become accustomed to carry her money, in gold, in a wadded belt which she wore beneath her clothing.

"I leave it under my pillow and my maid finds it there, and hangs it over the back of the chair, in evidence as I re-enter the room after breakfast. When I forget the trunk and leave it open, Lawrence brings me the keys and tells me, 'You oughten to do so, Miss Mary.' And I fancy that the Negroes are ashamed to rob people as careless as James Chestnut."[2]

Later in the same month (July, 1861) Mrs. Chestnut remonstrated with her husband for leaving his "watch, clothes, and two or three hundred gold pieces in the tray of his trunk." "Maybe," she suggests, "he [Lawrence] will pack off to the Yankees and freedom with all that."[3] By August, Lawrence has given no sign that he is concerned with the war, or that he contemplates absconding, but his mistress writes:

"Lawrence wears the same bronze mask. No sign of anything he may think or feel. . . . . Only I know he asks for twice as much money now when he goes to buy things."[4]

Two years later Lawrence had an opportunity to relieve the suspicions of his mistress when he gave her six hundred dollars, intrusted to him by General Chestnut, for she then wrote:

"When Lawrence handed me my husband's money, I said: 'Now I am pretty sure you do not mean to go to the Yankees, for with that pile of money you must have known that there was your chance.' "[5]

Slaves, at times, actively demonstrated affection for their masters and their possessions.

"Mr. Venable said he did not see a braver thing done [at the Battle of Bull Run] than the cool performance of a Columbia Negro. He carried his master a bucket of rice, which he had cooked for him, and cried, 'You must be hungry and tired, marster, make haste and eat.' And this in the thickest of the fight, under the heaviest of the enemy's guns."[6]

Sarah, a slave woman, had been left in complete charge of a family home in East Texas during the four years of the war.

"During that time the house was occupied, on several occasions, as headquarters, by generals of our own army in command at Marshall. . . . . Sarah . . . . produced the silver and had it constantly in use. When we returned not a single piece was missing, though meantime the war had ended, and she was free to come and go as she pleased."[7]

Moreover, Sarah hid her master in the house, as he was being sought by Union soldiers, and assisted him to escape later. Of Isaac McLaughlin, another slave of the Chestnuts', on still another estate, Mrs. Chestnut wrote, "He hid and saved everything we trusted him with."[8]

Thus slaves showed a tendency to remain loyal to their masters. But they also were particular to observe the forms generally expected of them as slaves as well. While Fort Sumter was being bombarded, "old Negro maumas" went up to communion in a Charleston church, kneeling devoutly around the chancel rail, after the white people had been served.[9] When some "Yankee officers" called to visit a maid in Montgomery and, failing to find her, left their cards, the maid was called upon to explain.

" 'Oh, missis,' the maid replied, 'they come to see me, and I have been waiting to tell you. It is too hard! I cannot do it! I cannot dance with those nice gentlemen at night, at the Union balls, and then come here and be your servant the next day. I can't.' "[10]

Molly, Mrs. Chestnut's maid, did not get into such a quandary when, riding with her mistress on a crowded train, she arose to give her seat to a white woman passenger.[11] The compulsion of etiquette was too strong for her to resist. What was testified of the Chestnut slaves was generally believed to be true of most slaves, that is, they remained "circumspect, polite, orderly, and respectful."[12]

However, if all slaves were not actually loyal, the most that could be said of many was that they were indifferent. During the attack on Fort Sumter, already mentioned, Mrs. Chestnut recorded in her diary:

"Not by one word or look can we detect any change in the demeanor of these Negro servants. . . . . You could not tell that they even heard the awful roar going on. . . . . They make no sign. Are they stolidly stupid? Or wiser than we are; biding their time, silent and strong?"[13]

At Port Royal, South Carolina, where the slaves had been under government supervision for some time since the opening of the war, a federal appointee wrote of his surprise at "how little most of the people appreciate their present prospects."[14] Mrs. Chestnut wrote: "If slavery is as disagreeable to Negroes as we think it, why don't they march over the border, where they would be received with open arms?"[15]

If slaves, in the actual state of affairs, adopted a passive attitude, it must have been due to other sources than ignorance. They had come to believe that their state was similar to that of the Israelites in Egypt and that sooner or later a Moses would arise to lead them out of the land of bondage.[16] This Moses was personified in "Massa Linkum." Booker Washington said:

"I remember well a time when I was awakened one morning, before the break of day, by my mother bending over me, where I lay on a bundle of rags in the corner of my Master's kitchen, and hearing her pray that Abraham Lincoln and his soldiers might be successful, and that she and I some day might be free."[17]

Moreover, "in one way or another, many of the slaves of the plantations managed to keep pretty good track of the movements of different armies, and after a while it began to be whispered that soon all slaves were going to be free."[18] In order to spread the news of the movement of the opposing armies, or to communicate information concerning their possible emancipation, the slaves organized "intelligence departments," that is, meetings on different plantations, to which they would slip away by night.[19] As the news spread along this "grapevine telegraph" that freedom was nearer, "there was more singing than usual. It was bolder, had more ring, and lasted later into the night."[20] Slaves coined a new word—"greasy"—which referred to any slave who had news of importance, received from white people or perchance read, concerning the progress of the war.[21] Thus many, if not the majority, of the slaves knew of the war and of their chances of freedom and had, in fact, anticipated the latter. Yet, they restrained themselves.

All slaves, however, did not remain submissive under the new conditions. Some actually deserted the plantations when controls had been relaxed,[22] or grew restless and followed the Union armies whenever the latter came close to the plantations. This movement was accelerated by the edict of General Butler, who declared that Negroes were "contraband of war." Slavery generally ceased, it is said, wherever the Union soldiers passed.[23] Colonel Kinsman declared that, when Louisiana went out of the Union, "she took her black laws with her."[24] Hence, those slaves in Louisiana who were inclined to be restless tended to believe that war and freedom were synonymous terms.

The Confederate officers had sought at times to recruit slaves for menial and supply services. But later, General Joseph E. Johnston found occasion to write to Colonel Wigfall:

"The impressment of Negroes has been practiced ever since the War commenced—but we have never been able to keep the impressed Negroes with an army near the enemy. They desert."[25]

In fact, the refugees or deserters frequently made their way to a near-by town, or Union camp, where they became problems for the Union officers.[26]

Some of the slaves became actively belligerent, or perhaps

disorganized, as they conceived of the new roles they would play in a slaveless South. A barber of Baltimore expressed the conviction to Russell that the result of the war would be that "colored men would be as good as white men."[27] Mrs. Chestnut accused a coachman of being "very high and mighty," thought that Molly, her maid servant, was "full of airs," and found fault with a butler of the household when "he did not come behind the scenes as usual and have a friendly chat. Held himself so aloof, so grand and stately, we had to send him a tip."[28] Some slaves of Charleston so far forgot themselves as to be apprehended while carrying pistols.[29]

Yet, whatever the attitudes of the slaves, whether they continued to observe the forms or became disorganized, their general behavior, while natural under the conditions, was not expected by most of the white people. During the period of the war, slaves refrained from insurrection, pillage, and carnage. Desertion from the plantations was, perhaps, their most desperate stroke for freedom.

Various explanations of the docility of slaves during the war have been offered. Some writers have suggested that the trait was temperamental;[30] others, that the slaves lacked *esprit de corps*.[31] One commentator stated that slaves were contented in slavery and had already proven their inferiority by failure to revolt.[32] The slaves, it was said, were "not ripe for John Brown,"[33] and "Yankees and abolitionists" had made a mistake "in ascribing the same feelings and impulses to Negroes as if they were white men."[34]

If a new theory will throw any light on the problem, we shall advance the notion that slaves did not revolt because, during as before the war, they did not think of it. Slaves sympathized with their masters in their difficulties. Besides, the war was a white man's war, and slaves were innocent bystanders. Slavery was an institution established in the tradition and habits of both races, and institutions withstand for a long time the winds of doctrine and the gusts of opinion—even the shock of war.

Revolt was most likely probable where race relations were not cemented by intimate personal contact—that is, on the large plantations, among field hands, and among some free Negroes. Slaves of the small farms, city slaves, and personal and body servants continued to observe the etiquette which was expected of slaves before the war. They were too thoroughly adjusted to revolt. They accepted the *status quo* as a part of the natural order.

CHAPTER IX
IF ETIQUETTE FAIL

IF THE period of the Civil War was characterized generally by harmonious relationships between Negroes and white people, it also seemed to foreshadow future unrest and disorder, provided the slaves were emancipated. Hence, when Abraham Lincoln proclaimed emancipation for the slaves, a crisis[1] was precipitated in the South, and a new period of relations between the two racial groups was inaugurated. For, if the purpose back of the emancipation was to be realized, former masters and former slaves would need to learn new ways of association.

The new era represented an attempt to institute by legal procedure a system of relations different from that which had grown up in habit and in custom. It seems to have been forgotten, however, that some disorganization must, of necessity, occur in the stage of transition and that to change the status of men by executive fiat neglects the fact that the status was not originally acquired in such a way and, hence, could scarcely be so changed later. For these latter reasons, changes in the legal status of men seldom remain stable unless they have already been manifested in the social and moral order.

"Emancipation had made the Negro free, but it had not made him, in the full sense, a citizen. His status was undefined, different in some respects in every different community. Every day the Negro was compelled to face anew the problem how to be at once a Negro and a citizen. This has been, and still is, the enigma of the Negro's existence."[2]

The law stipulated that the Negro was to be a citizen, but custom had defined both the forms of behavior expected of Negroes and their place in the social system. The battle lines were thus drawn between law and custom, between principles and the mores.

In the first blush of emancipation the etiquette of slavery persisted. Many slaves had moved away from the old plantations when they heard of the Emancipation Proclamation. This was one way in which they could test their freedom. But many also returned to spend their declining days with "old marster and missus."³ Some among them, wishing perhaps to show that their inner feelings had not changed, would bring gifts—such as a loaf of bread or a basket of eggs—as tokens of their continued respect. Others, with the swift changes brought on by a reversal of circumstances, would care for their former masters and mistresses in their old age.⁴

Evidence is offered indicating that Negroes still addressed certain persons as "marster" and evinced "no inclination to drop it."⁵ Occasionally, however, younger Negroes might upbraid older ones for using the term, and "boss" became good form. "Marster" expressed a certain relationship, but "boss," while respectful, connoted no intimacy. Other terms of address used toward white men, ranging beyond the intimacy of "boss" and not reaching to that of "marster," would include the inevitable "colonel," "judge," and "major" or "cap'n."⁶

A scrape of a foot and a tug at the hat continued good form when the freedmen met white persons. Reid "passed hundreds on the road, and not a man passed without lifting, or at least touching, his hat."⁷ The women and girls tended to curtesy "like little English school-children."⁸ Even the ceremony of hand kissing appears to have continued, while pushing the hands through the hair had not entirely disappeared.⁹

If conversation were necessary, and the former slave did not know precisely how to act in the presence of a white person, he would turn his back and "mumble out his message."¹⁰ If he found occasion to dissent, he "would beg to be excused from differing verbally, and seemed to be much distressed at being required to express his opinions freely."¹¹

"If asked, 'Does this stream run up hill?' the Negro would be apt to say: 'Yes, sah, reckon it do, sah.' But if the question were put in a leading form, as 'This stream runs down hill, of course, does it not?' he would say—'Sartinly, sah.' "[12]

Some former slaves did occasionally question the acts of white men; but others occasionally remonstrated with those who showed a desire or tendency to "get out of place":

" 'Please, massa, can't you gib me a piece ob meat?' 'Massa' handed her the meat. . . . . A moment afterward, one of the girls said, as she took her flour, 'I wants meal dis time; had flour las' time.' 'You go 'long,' exclaimed an old woman, 'ef you can't take whut de white folks gib you, go widout.' "[13]

The prestige of the white man continued to be accepted in public places. Even in the lines where "destitute rations" were distributed the Negroes would be found standing at the foot, if they appeared at all.[14] Proprietors of public places had anticipated difficulty in being required to serve black customers drinks and cigars. Hotels and inns contemplated classifying their position as private houses in order to exclude possible Negro customers.[15] The theaters of Richmond, Virginia, excluded Negroes from the dress circle.[16] Negroes, generally, took it for granted, however, that they would not be admitted to public places hitherto reserved for whites. And, except for certain theater cases of the period, not a single case of civil rights has ever come to the federal Supreme Court from a southern state.[17]

The freedmen, in many cases, used the older, accepted forms to get favors which otherwise might have been refused. They learned that one way to preface a raid on a white man's pocketbook or goods was to bow, with the cap in hand, and to laugh apologetically before, and while making, a request. If this were not sufficient, continued apology throughout the request was calculated to get a desired result.

" 'Mass'r, Ise got my own 'pinion ob you,' I heard one grey-wooled fellow say to his employer, with scrape of foot and tug at his cap. . . . . 'I doesn't think you' de hardes' mass'r in de world; and all I wants is to hab you 'sidah my case. I's all alone. Ise allus been good niggah. Rain or shine, me an' my hoss am at your service. We hauls de feed for de mules to de lowah place every day; an' on Saturdays we hauls for Sunday too. Now, mass'r, I wants you to please 'sidah my case. Doesn't you think, foh de extry work on Saturdays you ought ter 'low me anodder day's wages?' And he tugged his cap again, and gave his foot an extra scrape."[18]

Occasionally, they might flatter an employer and appeal to his pride by comparing their condition with that of Negroes who worked for other persons. On one plantation the employer had paid off his hands; but the women wanted new coats. The employer mentioned that, with wages, they should buy their own coats. Yet, one woman said:

" 'But we's done tore our coats cuttin' down you' briars, and we's all rags. Why if anybody'd come along heah you'd be 'shamed ob us; 'deed you would, we looks so bad. An' all we wants is you to gib us new coats. Den we fix up Sundays, an' you be mighty proud o' you' niggers.' This last appeal was irresistible, and the girls got their coats."[19]

The explanation of continued harmony in relations with white people[20] seems to come from a consideration of the types and classes of Negroes who observed the prescribed forms of behavior. These, in general, were house servants and personal attendants, who, following their masters' fortunes, as indeed they had done in slavery, had become, to a great extent, displeased with emancipation. These house servants were predominantly mulattoes, it seems, who had come to know the forms and to practice them more perfectly than the darker field hands. Among the former "politeness seemed to be a specialty, taking on a grace which no Anglo-Saxon could hope to exceed."[21] They had learned the value of ingratiating themselves into the good graces of superiors and to use a kind of cajolery to get favors.

"At Lynchburg, we noticed that 'Charles,' one of the colored waiters . . . . made extravagant professions of his willingness to serve us, but managed to make his fellow-servant, Harry, do all the work. I therefore ventured to remark in this wise: 'It appears to me, Charles, that Harry does all the work, and you do all the talking.'

" 'Yes, sah,' he answered civilly but quickly, 'I does de talkin' an' de smokin' too, when de gemmen gives me de cigars.' "[22]

White persons also tended to perpetuate the etiquette of slavery. For example, the mistress, as in prewar days, might make a visit to the home of an especially valued servant who had removed from the plantation. In cases of sickness she might sit by the bedside or say prayers or read from the Scriptures.[23] At the same time, if hungered, she might even eat in the home—but not with the former slaves.[24] And they, according to custom, would not sit down in her presence.[25]

White persons, it is said, generally continued to believe themselves superior to labor. The women could engage in charity work for freedmen without loss of status; yet, they required servants to carry the rations received from government commissaries, in cases where they themselves needed relief.[26]

In the crisis it was to be expected that some slaves would become disorganized.[27] In some instances, even though suffering from doubts and indecision as to the correct behavior in a given situation, they would, in fact, indulge in expressions that were concomitants of the ritual, or they would use customary observances to mask hostile feelings. Said one observer of the period:

"Everywhere in this lowland region we found the Negro courteous more from habit than from desire. Even when he fell into the sullen silence which marks his supremest dissent, he was deferential and polite to an exasperating degree."[28]

The Negro, however, was beginning to form new conceptions of his role in the group, his attitudes were changing, and in response to this change he began to adopt new forms of behavior in the presence of white persons; and in this wise the ceremonial forms, so long characteristic of racial relations, were modified. This precipitated an era of misunderstanding so far-reaching in effect that the period called "Reconstruction"[29] could with much warrant be called "Misconstruction."

In general, Negroes who, in slavery, were least in contact with white people, found occasion in freedom for expression of new attitudes. For, it must be remembered, all slaves did not fare equally well under the slave regime. Those who fared poorly could then contemplate the passing of the system with less regret than those who had possessed status and some comforts. The burden of slavery and the liabilities of freedom had fallen more heavily upon the field hands. They had desired freedom, more perhaps than the houseservants, and seemed to resent the fact that it had so long been delayed; but they found it quite a disappointment when it had actually come.[30] So that, inarticulate under slavery and confused in freedom, the field hand formulated a vague notion of the wrongs done him, and sought to right the wrongs by the adoption of entirely different attitudes.[31]

To be a man the freedman required a hat—one symbol of his changed role.[32] And that the role might be comprehended by unbelieving white people, the freedman would wear the hat indoors and out; until, or unless, called to order by offended white persons.[33] Then, too, the freedman needed a name symbolizing his status.

"There was a feeling that 'John Hatcher' or 'Hatcher's John' was not the proper title by which to denominate a freeman; and in many cases John Hatcher was changed to 'John S. Sherman,' the initial S standing for no name, it being simply a part of what the colored man proudly called his 'entitles.' "[34]

One little boy, in a school for freedmen, who had recently acquired this symbol of freedom, was asked his name. He replied, "Dunno, sah, but there's a boy just gone outside that knows."[35]

With a name and a hat, the Negro occasionally demanded still higher tributes and titles.

"Florida Cantey heard an old Negro say to his master: 'When you all had de power you wuz good to me, and I'll protect you now. No niggers nor Yankees shall tech you. If you want anything call for Sambo. I mean call for Mr. Samuel; dat my name now.' "[36]

Occasionally slaves showed no disposition to address white men as "mister" but would call them "cousin" instead.[37]

However, in perhaps no other area were relations so changed, or attitudes so disorganized, as in that immediately connected with work and labor. Former slaves, in some cases indeed, remained with their former masters, working under whatever conditions were imposed or agreed upon.[38] Others, perhaps hearing of the "forty acres and a mule" that they were to receive on the following Christmas,[39] felt no call to work but moved or wandered aimlessly about and settled in large numbers in the towns.[40] As a result, then, the crops, in the year immediately following emancipation, practically all went to waste as the freedmen escaped the toil from which they had so long prayed to be relieved.[41]

Even under the conditions it was expected that a system of wage payments would guarantee sufficient labor for the farms and plantations. Yet, another obstacle remained—few masters took kindly to the notion, feeling perhaps that it showed too great a change in custom. In many cases money was scarce, and the planters were unable to pay wages, even had they been so disposed.[42] And Negroes seemed inclined to haggle about terms or questions of hire, so that confusion generally resulted. Yet, it seems, that, though frequently Negroes knew little what to demand in the way of wages, they nevertheless showed a tendency to want "something certain."[43] In case no definite earning or wage were forthcoming, the former slave might stop work altogether:

" 'I wucked Mr. C's crap on half shares, and kaze of de drouf dar warn't mo' dan a half crap rais', and Mistuh C. he say to me dat dar's no use 'sputin 'boud hit, kaze de half crap dat wuz rais' mus' sholy go fer de lan' and de mules. I done quit 'sputin wid him, an' I done quit wucking on such shares.' "[44]

In some cases the Negroes showed an active hostility to work. In Alabama they refused to go to work at the sound of the plantation bell, giving as a reason that it "was too like slavery times."[45] In South Carolina some cotton gins were destroyed, and the ironwork of the mills hidden.[46] Moreover, Negro women began also to refuse outdoor work for any reason.[47] And the men frequently refused to work merely because white men ordered it.[48]

In the disorder that ensued rumors were spread to the effect that thievery, vagabondage,[49] and starvation were rife among the freedmen. Actual facts were lacking, but the rumors, together with the economic interests of the white people, were sufficient to bring about methods of coercion. Agreements among planters appeared declaring that their policy would be to make Negroes work[50] and to set their wages.[51] A slogan was adopted and frequently heard, to the effect that "work is for niggers—not for white men."[52] If the supply of Negro labor failed, it was argued, Chinese coolies could be imported.[53]

Occasional attempts by overseers, or masters, to force the Negroes to work—by kicking or beating, as in many instances —also brought resistance from the freedmen.[54] And, again occasionally, resistance might result in murder.[55]

Some masters, seeking to allay the friction and consequent disorganization, began to use Negro overseers,[56] or to institute the now famous share-cropping system.[57] Several states adopted statutory enactments against vagrancy, provided for apprenticeships or engagement under contract, and bound the freedman to the plantation by methods strikingly similar to prewar codes.[58] These enactments held until, in some instances, they were repealed by the legislatures composed of white people and Negroes.

Disorganization was manifested when the freedmen began to settle in the towns. They engaged in seemingly endless parades[59] and rifle drills; or, taking advantage of their new freedom to move, chartered excursion trains and went from town to town celebrating. Taylor has remarked that "the Negroes of Virginia gave a new meaning to holidays and excursions."[60] Behavior of this kind aroused uneasiness among many white persons.[61] In Norfolk, Virginia, for instance, a riot resulted from one of these apparently meaningless parades.[62]

The freedmen, on occasion, adopted forms of behavior directly in contrast to those expected and accepted from them. Negro soldiers became belligerent, it was said; some Negroes adopted a style of dress quite apparently "too fine for a nigger."[63] Some became insolent and disrespectful and occasionally used insulting language to white people. When a Negro became insolent and disrespectful, it was the first and unmistakable sign that he was getting out of control.[64] Many of the "horrors" of Reconstruction, according to Dr. Park, revolved around the expression of impudence on the part of the Negro, for any evidence of the breakdown of the traditional forms of etiquette brought with it a profound sense of insecurity. The feeling was strengthened whenever there was any conscious or unconscious manifestation of lack of respect for the white man.[65]

The resentment aroused by impudence and insolence was not lessened by the flagrant infringements of the mores evidenced in interracial marriages. How extensive the practice was, is, perhaps, not known precisely; but it was sufficient to cause Mississippi, South Carolina, Alabama, and Georgia, within three years after emancipation, to enact legislation prohibiting such unions.[66] Yet the violation was apparently not one-sided, for both Negro men and women were married to members of the white caste.[67]

The notion developed that "the mixed race is the result of intercourse between the white men and the Negress"[68] and that mulattoes could not reproduce "after the third remove from original unity."[69] Interracial marriage, as was customary, was condemned on general principles.[70]

Different classes of whites showed small variation in attitudes toward Negroes who had become disorganized, or who had become disrespectful; even though all classes seemed to understand the Negro who remained loyal, submissive, and responsive to the expected and accepted forms of behavior.[71] Some saw and acknowledged that the moral order was in a stage of reorganization and called attention to the fact.[72] Others seemed to recognize change in the old order but preferred to remain indifferent.[73] While still others adopted a semitolerant attitude, as for instance, declaring:

"The death of slavery is recognized. . . . . But we don't believe that because the nigger is free he ought to be saucy; and we don't mean to have any such nonsense as letting him vote."[74]

But, perhaps, the greater portion felt the compulsions of habit and custom, as did the South Carolinian who said to a northerner:

" 'We can't feel toward them as you do; I suppose we ought to, but 'tisn't possible for us. . . . . If that's wrong we're to be pitied rather than blamed, for it's something we can't help.' "[75]

Many whites looked with scorn, hatred, and contempt on slaves who were "trying to act like white people."[76] One "Ariel," referring to the Negro as a beast, sought to prove by Scripture that inferior status was inseparably linked with kinky hair and a flat nose.[77] At least one petition was addressed to Congress, asking for the re-enslavement of the Negro on the basis of the conviction that he was subordinate to the Caucasian as the woman is to the man.[78] Occasionally, articles appeared in newspapers in which terms such as "negro city buck," "bullet-headed and brazen-faced lady of color," "asp-eyed little darkey," and the like, were freely used.[79]

Occasional statements, apparently impartial and detached, appeared. The Negro felt in his heart, said one, that he was violating the code but was being seduced by demagogues.[80] The freedmen had "disgraced themselves by lowering their own race," in aspiring to association with those whom they felt to be superior, said another.[81] Some persons "felt sorry to see them expose themselves to so much misery in making attempts that, from the outset, must be abortive."[82]

Yet, other attitudes were definitely hostile. Governor Scott of South Carolina voiced the sentiment that the dictum of Justice Taney—to the effect that the Negro has no rights that a white man is bound to respect—still held good.[83] Instances appear in which persons who felt a grievance at the emancipation of the Negro sought to express themselves with words and deeds;[84] even going so far, occasionally, as to murder a Negro who was "out of place."[85]

Any assumption of equality between the two races was, of course, rejected.[86] Association of white persons with freedmen on any level except that of difference in rank was excluded from the realm of possibilities. Even the benevolent associations characteristic of slavery came under the ban it seems. For, it was feared, recognition of, or too much tolerance toward, the change in the legal status of the Negro would be productive of familiarity and serve to make the South "absurd in the eyes of sensible people."[87]

"Nigger lovers" was a term coined to describe persons who associated with Negroes on terms of equality, or contended for their rights.[88] Under this head came "civil rights men"—represented on one occasion as those who patronized barber shops "where they shaved both blacks and whites"[89]—politicians and legislators, who in anticipation of votes might go so far as to kiss Negro babies, or to be seen shaking hands or walking on the streets with freedmen.[90] Mr. Chief Justice Chase, of the United States Supreme Court, who visited New Orleans in 1865, was declared to be "eternally disgraced for having so far forgotten his dignity as to enter a parlor filled with niggers that were trying to play lady and gentleman."[91] Missionaries from the North, being, we suppose, unfamiliar with the mores of the South, or at least violating them, were ostracized; some were whipped, or driven from communities, or even murdered.[92] A sheriff of the despised Reconstruction party, in Arkansas, was killed by the Ku Klux Klan, who, "in order to make an impressive tableau, killed Fed Reeves, an unoffending Negro, tied the white man and Negro together in the attitude of kissing and left them in the public road, where they remained for two days."[93]

The Mississippi legislature, in 1865, enacted a "vagrant law" to this effect:

"All white persons assembling themselves with freedmen, free Negroes, or mulattoes, or usually associating with freedmen, shall be deemed vagrants, and on conviction thereof shall be fined."[94]

Under the circumstances, we may say, relations between the races were strained to the breaking point. The situation was not eased by the attitudes of the poorer whites, who in certain cases associated with Negroes, but who, for the most part, hated the former slaves with a more lasting malice than they did before the war.[95]

" 'I haint nothin' agin a free nigger,' said a tall native of Mississippi bound for Texas, 'but I don't want him to say a word to me. The world's big enough for us both, I reckon. We ain't made to live together under this new style of things. Free niggers and me couldn't agree.' "[96]

Complete separation of white people and Negroes, testifies Reid, was the universal sentiment expressed among the poorer whites.

" 'How do the Negroes get along here?'

" 'What? Oh, you mean the niggahs. They's doing well enough far's I hear.'

" 'Are any of them suffering hereabouts?'

" 'Sufferin'? No more'n other folks, I reckon. . . . . I don't
see much of them, nor don't want to, the nasty black things.' "[97]
Yet, the Negro was not insensitive to the changes going on
around him. He doubtless saw the rise of the poorer whites, but
he also knew and respected white persons of the upper classes,
who, he believed, would live up to his expectations of them;
only poorer whites would arouse his contempt by low acts or
meanness.[98] For instance, when King and some companions
sought to enter a ferry at Natchez, Mississippi, they were
blocked by a drunken Negro, who was asked to stand aside.
This he did, remarking that "I'se willing to wait on you gemmen, 'cause you is gemmen; but, ef you wuz no 'count folks, I'd
go fer you. Ride in Colonel."[99] The Negro was generally convinced, it seems, that a "gentleman white man won't lose no
time to aggravate and insult, and abuse away his time with a
colored man unless he happens to be drunk."[100] And, says Pearson, even black washerwomen knew how to make distinctions
in charges for whites of different classes. One woman, for instance, asked fifty cents per dozen pieces of a man whom she
took to be "poor white" but remarked that she charged "real
gentle folks seventy-five cents."[101]

In addition to the re-establishment of old forms during this
period, new forms of association needed to be instituted. These
were, in many cases, established without too much friction but,
in other instances, were productive of discord.

Within the churches, for instance, beginning with 1865, there
was a general tendency, especially on the part of the Methodist
and Baptist groups, to state that change in political status of
Negroes would not affect relations within the church organizations.[102] Hence, as several travelers testify, separation of the
racial groups persisted whenever freedmen attended white
churches,[103] or whenever white persons attended the separate
Negro churches.[104] A few Negroes remained in the smaller and
more radical sects, such as the Shakers;[105] a white preacher
might occasionally be found in a Negro church,[106] or white

teachers in Negro Sunday schools,[107] or white churches with mixed congregations, and white churchmen standing for the principle of nonseparation.[108]

Gradual changes began to appear, however. In 1866 the General Conference of the Methodist Episcopal Church, South, provided separate quarterly conferences, licensed and ordained Negro ministers, appointed presiding elders and districts, and declared that even annual conferences of Negro churches might be organized if wished.[109] The Presbyterians of Virginia made "provisions to ordain colored men to preach the Gospel" in 1868.

The bi-racial character of the church organization was not wholly due to the attitudes of white people. Some Negro preachers in Virginia, it is reported, considered any continuance of the prewar church etiquette and organization to be an indication of dependency and inferiority. They were not content with agitation for separate churches but went so far as to insist on admission to the University of Virginia upon the same terms as whites. They insisted on being called "mister" and declared that "nothing short of the absolute equality with the whites in all things would satisfy them."[110] The agitation may account for the fact that, when Negroes generally remained as part of the ecclesiastical organization of white people, they were found in churches of northern persuasion and customs.[111]

It happened, however, that a basis of understanding remained in spite of unexpected events. Negro churchmen could receive a measure of respect even under the new conditions; and the benevolence which is characteristic of religion was frequently maintained, without assumption of equality in social relations.[112]

The church problems were not solved during the period. Yet, the significant fact seems to be that, whatever the solution offered, adjustment was made, generally without friction.[113] Within a few years after the war, "practically all of the Negroes had withdrawn from all the white ecclesiastical organizations, and formed numerous denominations entirely independent of white control or direct influence."[114]

Adjustments were no less necessary and desirable with reference to the public carriers. Phillips has remarked that, during the period of slavery, with the exception of the constant transit of the slave traders and migrating planters with their squads of slaves for the Southwest, "it was as if the trains did not run" for Negroes.[115] But, this, in the light of what has been previously said, was not true of the Reconstruction period.

During the period of slavery personal and body servants traveled in the coaches with their masters or mistresses; but unattached slaves went in separate coaches, if they traveled at all. This practice continued into the period of Reconstruction. The "ladies' car" was reserved for white persons and personal servants, and the smoker's car was set aside for unattached Negroes and for white men who wished to smoke.[116] Hence, the entrance of a Negro into the "ladies' car" was generally a signal for the forcible ejection of the offender.[117]

Occasionally, however, a Negro, would resent such separation and declare for, if not actually demand, equal accommodations. Instances came to notice in which Negroes, of Louisiana and South Carolina, created disturbances when their presence was objected to in the trains. But the situation was, perhaps, better described by King, who said that "the Negroes, as a mass, have not been difficult to manage in the matter."[118]

When the freedmen had occasion to travel on the river boats, they generally rode on the deck, "with the firewood, cotton and sugar, horses and pigs."[119] In 1866 a freedman, near Vicksburg, asked for a stateroom aboard a river steamer. For his temerity he received a "God damn your soul" from the captain and a "Kick the nigger! He ought to have his neck broke! He ought to be hung!" from the passengers. Eight years later, however, a similar situation, near the same city, seemed to be taken as a matter of course; at least, it did not bring violent emotional reaction.[120]

Street railways were generally a much later development in the South, and then only a few cities were provided with them. In Virginia, prior to 1867, Negroes were not allowed to ride on the streetcars. And afterward, upon bringing suit to establish their right so to ride, they were separated from the white people by the "ladies' car" arrangement, similar to that on the railways.[121] Customs differed however. As late as 1875 Negroes were accepted as passengers on the street railways in Augusta and Atlanta but were prohibited from riding in Savannah, Georgia.[122]

Yet, among the new problems set by the Reconstruction, none was perhaps more vital than that of educating the freedmen. There had been education of Negroes, both formal and informal, during slavery,[123] it is true; yet, it seems, the majority had been denied access to book knowledge. On the other hand, the practical value of being able to read and write had been demonstrated by those slaves who had learned to calculate, or to keep accounts for their masters, and even in some instances to forge passes, which allowed them to remain out of quarters after curfew.[124] Moreover, Greek and Latin, symbols of leisure and refinement among the white people, seemed desirable also to the slaves.

Thus, when emancipation became an accomplished fact, the freedmen evinced a general desire to obtain an education. Perhaps, as Washington has remarked, this was due to a natural curiosity to discover what, in the books, was so dangerous as to be forbidden during slavery.[125] Perhaps, the idea, and frequent statement, that Negroes were incapable of education served to stir the more ambitious ones to prove the falsity of the assumption. At any rate, there sprang up a "craze for Greek and Latin," as the Negroes sought to test their ability to learn as difficult subject matter as white persons learned.[126]

On the other hand, northern persons attached to the various organizations for the relief of freedmen, and others who came as missionaries, also felt that education for Negroes was a decided necessity. Hence it happened that, by the close of 1865, in Virginia alone, there were ninety schools for freedmen, with one hundred and ninety-five teachers, and eleven thousand, five hundred pupils.[127] The subsequent five years witnessed an increase of private schools and colleges for freedmen—supported largely by the Freedmen's Bureau—and the adoption of a public-school system by fourteen of the southern states.[128] The private schools were established mainly for Negroes.[129] The public-school system tended to include Negro and white children but in separate schools.

Yet, if the Negroes were interested in education for themselves, the white people, at times, were actively antagonistic. They considered the public-school system a northern institution, assumed that the burdens of taxation in their support would become oppressive, and feared above all that it would lead to mixed schools in direct violation of the mores.[130] Moreover, it was argued, since God intended Negroes to be slaves, the best that can be done in the situation of emancipation is to "keep them as near the state of bondage as possible."[131]

The activities of the Yankee "schoolma'ams," as they were called, contributed little toward a peaceful solution of the problem. It was thought that they were "continuing hostilities against the vanquished South, and was so regarded on both sides."[132] It was objected that they acted on the principle of social equality and extended social courtesies to Negroes that were not in keeping with the mores of the South.[133] As a direct consequence, northern teachers were ostracized, or subjected to intimidation by the Ku Klux Klan,[134] or even to mob violence. A minister of North Carolina said that "the work may be good in itself, but for good or bad, we don't want the Yankees among us."[135]

Then, in direct response to the attitudes of white persons, the Negroes felt that the South was oppressing them since it treated their saviors—as they regarded the northern teachers—with so much contempt. Thus the situation indicates the state of race relations as well as of the mores. There was no common ground on which the groups—southern whites, northern whites, and freedmen—seemed to be able to meet; no ground on which understanding might be established.

The solution of the problem might have come in the volunteering of southern whites to teach the freedmen. Yet, in the traditions of the South, a teacher of white persons did not occupy a very high social position, and a teacher of freedmen would necessarily occupy a lower.[136] Even in the cases where local tradition would warrant teaching one's own former slaves, the promiscuous inclusion of any and all freedmen was quite out of reason.[137]

Yet, in occasional instances, southern white people did establish schools for Negroes of their own religious denomination, or perchance of their own political persuasion.[138] The practice became more respectable,[139] in later years, when the theory was advanced that southern teachers would give the type of instruction thought best for former slaves; hence more and more southern white people were found instructing freedmen.[140] There were, in fact, instances where the latter asked for southern teachers, preferring them to strangers.[141]

With respect to the effect of problems of education of freedmen during Reconstruction, two theories have been offered. The first is that education probably increased the distance between the two racial groups of the South. Negroes, it was contended, not only became disorganized, as they sought education to the exclusion of more pressing business and important problems,[142] but they also changed their conceptions of themselves and of their status in southern society. For example, on the Sea Islands, it was remarked:

"The schools have improved the children, their manners have improved, as have the grown people's,—less cringing and subservient, but more respectful and manly. Tim does not pull his forelock at every word he speaks, as he did last year, looking like a whipped dog, but looks you full in the face and speaks out as if he were not ashamed of himself, and is perfectly respectful withal."[143]

On the other hand, as Booker T. Washington remarked, perhaps education served to effect adjustment in race relations during this period. He, among others, had a premonition that "there was something in the situation into which the course of events had pushed the Negro people that was unstable and could not last." This group, composed largely of field hands and house servants, as he notes, became more interested in education than in politics. Lewis Adams, a slave of Tuskegee, who had "never had a day's formal schooling," but who could, nevertheless, read and write, and who was an expert shoe- and harness-maker, felt that the trades provided an outlet for Negroes. "It was he who first urged the establishment of a normal school for his race in the town"—the school that was later to become Tuskegee Institute.[144]

In the face of these opposing views, then, conclusions concerning the effect of education upon Negroes during this period may be reserved. If education brought disorganization among the former slaves, it may be counted as a liability. If, on the other hand, it served as an outlet for feelings that might otherwise have been directed into politics, where discord might have resulted, it may be counted as an asset. The situation doubtless varied in different places at different times—assisting or retarding adjustment in areas where the one effect or the other, already mentioned, preponderated.

Another problem of adjustment appearing in the period of Reconstruction concerned the freedman in politics and his position before the law. With this subject few, if any, writers have dealt in terms of etiquette and social control.

Before the Civil War had fairly ended incidents occurred indicating that, if freedom came to Negroes as a result of the war, it would be resisted by southern whites, who would advocate a "return to compulsory labor which will make the Negro useful to society and subordinate to the white race."[145] Immediately following the cessation of the conflict, a judge, known for his benevolent attitude toward his slaves, suggested that the white people "secure the services of the Negroes, teach them their places and how to keep them, and convince them that we are their best friends."[146] In Texas "public attention was engaged solely with the measure of freedom to be accorded the late slave and the best method of securing his labor."[147]

In the three years directly following the issuance of the Emancipation Proclamation, then, the South turned its attention to the problems of defining and determining the precise legal and political status of the freedmen. The several states enacted civil rights laws, repealed provisions that had become inoperative— such as curfew and patrol laws—regulated the right to vote or to sit on juries, decided problems concerning school facilities, and arranged provisions for legal marriage and disposition and control of property.[148] In general, voting, jury duty, intermarriage, and "mixed schools" were interdicted. In some localities the municipal ordinances were such exact counterparts of the slave laws that they received the name of "black codes."[149]

In response to this situation, the Freedmen's Bureau—an agency instituted under northern auspices—sought to centralize control, and to prevent overriding, of rights just granted to Negroes. In some instances Union leaders ruthlessly disposed of old slave laws, placed blacks in authority over whites, and tended to reopen old sores of discord.[150]

In 1866 Congress passed the Civil Rights Bill; followed it in 1868 with the Fourteenth Amendment, making Negroes citizens; later revised enforcement acts;[151] and declared, with the Fifteenth Amendment,[152] that denial of the vote to Negroes was unconstitutional. This activity, on the part of the North, brought the freedman into politics, convinced the South that it could expect no quarter from the North, and continued the "white man's quarrel," according to Washington, "in which the Negro was the tennis ball, batted backward and forward by the opposing parties."[153]

As a matter of fact, the Negro did not know which way to turn. In spite of the harsh enactments of the southern legislatures, he looked forward, in many instances, to leadership from the southern white people.[154] Thus, friction occurring in political matters was not wholly due to the fact that the Negro refused to be led by southern whites. Southern white people generally refused to lead the Negroes. They could not play such roles in the Reconstruction drama.

The Democratic party refused to accept Negroes as members and adopted a generally hostile attitude.[155] Under the circumstances the Negro naturally gravitated to the party and to those people under whose aegis he might receive some protection, a minimum of recognition, and an opportunity for self-expression.

Into this impasse the Freedmen's Bureau stepped to give to a large number of ambitious Negroes opportunities to become prominent in the field of politics.[156] As Washington says:

"One of the surprising results of the Reconstruction Period was that there should spring from among the members of a race that had been held so long in slavery so large a number of shrewd, resolute, resourceful, and even brilliant men, who became, during this brief period of storm and stress, the political leaders of a newly enfranchised race. And that from this group should arise so many sons of white planters by colored mothers (such as J. M. Langston, P. B. S. Pinchback, Josiah T. Settle, B. K. Bruce, and others)."[157]

It must be remembered, however, that the Freedmen's Bureau, and the other organizations which served to bring the Negro into southern politics, were Republican organizations. This same party had been in power when emancipation came to the Negro. Rebuffed by southerners and Democrats, the Negro then assumed that the Republicans were responsible both for freedom from slavery and for opportunity after freedom. Politics became a religion with some freedmen, and republicanism a political sect. The affiliation they said, was a matter of principle. Said one Negro, "Some wote straight, and some don't;

some is 'suaded, and some is paid; but I wote according to my
principles and my principles is Republican."[158] A nursery
rhyme, says Taylor, was changed to meet the situation:

> "Now I lay me down to sleep,
> I want to be a Republican.
> I pray the Lord my soul to keep,
> Because I am a Republican.
> If I should die before I wake,
> I want to be a Republican,
> I pray the Lord my soul to take,
> Because I am a Republican.
> And this I ask for Jesus' sake,
> If I have been a Republican."[159]

Since, then, most, if not all, of the southern white people
were Democrats, Negroes perceived them as political enemies.
One Negro testified to this effect:

"We watches de white man, an' we keeps watching him till
we find out which way de white man's going to vote; and when
we finds out which way de white man's going to vote, den we
vote 'xactly de other way. Den we knows we's right."[160]

In order, then, to cement the bonds of party loyalty among
the Negroes, the Union League—a secret society, in the interests of the Republican party—was organized. The activity of
this league was in a measure directed toward recalcitrant Negroes who dared to vote the Democratic ticket, or who showed
any disposition to accept Democratic programs and principles.[161]
A Negro Democrat became anathema—his father and mother
disowned him, his wife expected to leave him, his church ex-
pelled him, and the preachers "consigned him to a lake which
burneth with fire," while even the children would call him a
"demercrat nigger."[162]

However, one direct result of the alignment of Negroes with
the Republicans was their accession to office in the states,
counties, and municipalities. County officers—such as sheriffs,

constables, prosecuting attorneys, coroners, and other officials
—might be seen in towns where there were Negro policemen,
postmasters, aldermen, street supervisors, and magistrates.[163]
Negroes, pushed forward by Union men, held seats in the constitutional conventions, or legislatures, of South Carolina, Virginia, Alabama, Mississippi, Louisiana, and Texas.[164] These,
in given cases, were both blacks and mulattoes.[165] State officials
—such as superintendent of public instruction, commissioner of
state lands, warden of penitentiaries, commissioner of emigration, and secretaries of state—were appointed from the ranks
of the freedmen.[166]

The most significant index to the disorganization which ensued after the entrance of Negroes into the political field is
doubtless found in the legislation enacted by bodies of which
both whites and blacks were members. Perhaps, the greatest
single aim of Negro legislators was to secure the results for
which, they assumed, the war had been fought. Legal and political, if not social, equality was their battle cry.[167] Some among
them, impressed with a sense of responsibility, assumed an antagonistic spirit, frequently singing:

> "De bottom rail's on top
> An' we's gwine to keep it dar."[168]

Yet, to a great extent, under the circumstances, the freedmen
remained becomingly docile and deferred to the leadership of
white men. One assemblyman, of Mississippi, wrote to the
governor to this effect:

I was a slave of Colonel W. G. Henderson . . . . in the relation of body-servant. . . . . Now, Governor, I, by the mysteri-
ous providence of God, am a member of the Legislature. I want
no office, no honor save that of standing here in my place of
duty to my race. But I believe that I have a claim upon your
patronage, and I now place, without reservation, all the credit
of that claim to the account of my earnest prayer that you
appoint to the judgeship, the playmate of my boyhood, the

companion of my manhood, the generous friend of my whole life, my former master, Colonel W. G. Henderson.

[*signed*] Ambrose Henderson[169]

This letter suggests that the Negro was looking for leadership and still felt kindly toward his former masters. Yet, it also indicates to what extent he could be imposed upon by "carpet-baggers" and "scalawags," who, in their endeavor to prosecute the war after its close, merely used the Negro to draw their own chestnuts from the fire, or to profit personally by the Negro's ignorance. For, after all, the activity of the carpetbaggers and scalawags in the period—to the extent that they pushed Negroes into positions over white people, or used the situation of disorganization to continue the war—could only have served, as it did, to widen the breach which had already been opened between southern white people and Negroes.[170]

The entire political situation, so far as southern white men were concerned, was a violation of the most sacred customs of the South. They regarded the Negro "as an inferior race, unqualified to take a leading part in government."[171] The sight of Negroes in the halls of legislatures was unbearable.[172]

"Seven years ago [said one man] these men were raising corn and cotton under the whip of an overseer. Today they are raising points of order and questions of privilege. They find that they can raise one as well as the other. They prefer the latter; it is easier, and better paid."[173]

The *Van Buren* (Ark.) *Press*, referring to the constitutional convention of that state, in 1868, said:

" 'This will be a rich congregation. We sincerely pity the decent people of Little Rock whose sense of smell is sensitive.' The convention was referred to as a 'menagerie,' 'the bastard collection,' 'the mongrel assemblage,' and 'a compound of villainy and indecency.' "[174]

The *Raleigh North Carolinian*, reporting the constitutional convention in that state, "headed its daily report with the title—

BONES AND BANJO CONVENTION; and .... added 'nigger' to the name of every colored delegate .... thus, 'Jim Harris (nigger).' "[175] A Richmond (Va.) newspaper referred to a visit of General Butler, and to a subsequent speech, as follows: "Butler spoke, chairman Wardwell smiled, mob applauded. Sublime occasion! Hen-roost and pig-stye thieves forgot their avocation, and chickens and pigs slept in undisturbed security, while the petty pliers of small trades vied with each other in doing homage to the more successful rascal."[176]

Under the circumstances, it may be seen, governmental participation on the part of Negroes—comprising all functions from voting up to office-holding—was borne with when inescapable but abolished when opportunity offered.[177]

The issue soon became clearly drawn—that is, get the Negro out of politics and re-establish a government of white persons in which the superiority of the white man, and his right to rule, is recognized and admitted.[178] As the issue became clarified, class lines, within the white group, began to vanish, especially when the issue of equal rights or the so-called "social equality" legislation came to the fore.[179] The cry of "Negro domination" brought about a solidarity among the whites, and "white leagues" were promoted as counterirritants to the Union League.[180] The Ku Klux Klan was established as an agency to secure the return of government to the white South and to assist in a re-establishment of customs which had been undermined.[181]

The South, described by Trowbridge in 1868 as "in the condition of a man recovering from a dangerous malady,"[182] had been so restored by 1874 that King, remarking that the races were drifting farther apart, could nevertheless note convalescence.[183] Between 1874 and 1876 the southern whites returned to power in Alabama, Arkansas, Florida, Louisiana, South Carolina and Texas.[184] By 1883 the decision of the federal Supreme Court—declaring the Third Civil Rights Bill unconstitutional—was accepted as a virtual declaration that the North would thereafter leave the South to solve its own political problems.[185]

Reconstruction had been followed by restoration of government to the South, but it had brought a wider rift in racial relations than had, perhaps, hitherto been known. The animosities kindled by the political antagonisms, occasioned largely by the introduction of former slaves into political life as opponents of their masters, had not then—if indeed they have ever—died out.[186] The kindly relations between the freedmen and their former masters had, of course, not been wholly destroyed. Yet, the germs of a society, divided vertically, had been planted, and the etiquette determined by such a condition was in the formative stage.

From thenceforth, according to the best light of the South, the two races might walk in the same direction, but they must walk separately. The superiority of the white man was to be admitted by the Negro whenever the latter found it necessary to associate with white people. Moreover, it was expected that the Negro would adopt the old forms—the etiquette of slavery —as proper to his station in life and as sanctioned by custom and tradition.[187]

Under the circumstances, then, though a presidential proclamation had changed the legal status of the Negro in the South, his social status remained inferior. The control of the mores proved to be stronger than legal enactments. The habits of the white South, as was to be expected, proved stronger than principles. The Negro might cling to his new legal status, but the penalty for so doing was exclusion from harmonious association with white people—for laws do not create mores.

Meanwhile, the Negroes, who in the early days of freedom had felt that it was scarcely possible for colored people to become their own masters,[188] had become disillusioned with freedom.[189] They had been forced out of politics. The promised, or expected, forty acres and a mule had not materialized. Freedom, so long desired, became as dust in their mouths.

Race consciousness began to show itself among the freedmen. The old conflict between blacks and mulattoes was buried
formally, if not actually.[190] The entire group set out to find an
acceptable name.[191] Freedmen began to discuss race solidarity,
asked for their own churches and schools, and even protested,
in given cases, the employment of white persons as teachers in
their schools.[192]

" 'What we want,' said one Negro, 'is to protect the virtue
of our girls. That is the rights we want. I don't want no social
equality with the white people, and I don't want them to have
none with me. . . . . Give a nigger a chance to till the white
man's soil, and he is going to keep out of his house too.' "[193]

Negroes began to buy land,[194] to organize provident and
building and loan associations,[195] and to establish businesses of
their own,[196] so that, when he visited the United States in 1878,
Sir George Campbell was able to write:

"Now the whites assert their superiority by social exclusion;
and the blacks, not willing to accept the old situation in social
matters, have much withdrawn to themselves, and now refrain
from associating with the whites on occasions that formerly
brought them together."[197]

The separation which was then distinguishable between the
races by the end of the period of Reconstruction had been established in the natural course of events by agreement of both
racial groups. The basis of understanding which had existed
during the period of slavery had largely disappeared. Some Negroes, it is true, accepted the old code of relations and had adjusted themselves to it. Others, however, were inclined to cast
aside the reminders of their former status and had, as a result,
become disorganized or had brought about friction in relations.
Yet, to the white people, no code of relations was acceptable
save that of inferiority for Negroes; and sufficient time had not
passed to establish a new code of etiquette. That was the task
of the next period in race relations.

CHAPTER X

ETIQUETTE RESTORED

A NEW period in race relations was inaugurated in the early eighties by the restoration of southern whites to political power and by the establishment of a hands-off policy adopted by the North and the Republicans with regard to the so-called "race problem" in the South.[1] At the same time, however, the South was faced with the grave problem of re-establishing peace and harmony between the races. Contacts between the groups no longer, except in rare instances, existed on the basis characteristic of slavery. Yet, co-operation had to be maintained if the two races were to live together in security. In other words, social control needed to be re-established in the new order.

It was natural, and hence not unexpected, that the South would revert to the ante-bellum code as far as possible.[2] For patterns of behavior, hitherto regulating the contacts of the races, had been fixed in habit and custom, and persons had come to expect and to accept those observances as just, right, and proper. Hence, even though the basis of ceremonial control underlying the relative peace of slavery was, perhaps, not at the time understood, it was nevertheless felt that the ante-bellum system of relations was a good one.

Moreover, the racial code was bound up with the bitter political struggle, in which the North, through the Civil Rights bills, had sought to impose its own mores upon the South. It was at least logical to assume that, if the moral order of the South had been disturbed by political action and legislative enactment, it could by these same means be re-established. Hence, when the South realized that political power was actually restored, a veritable deluge of legislation ensued looking to regulation of contacts between white and colored persons. It was the characteristic of this legislation that it ignored, more or less completely, the changed political status of the Negro.[3] In other words, laws were passed to enforce what had, prior to emancipation, enforced itself, namely, a code of etiquette in race relations.

To a great extent the status of race relations in the period since about 1883 might well be included in the phrase "solving the race problem by politics and politicians." There were, and are, of course, other phases. Yet, to some extent, they have been blotted out in welter of cross-purposes originated in the period of Reconstruction.

Moreover, by the early twentieth century, the poorer whites had risen to power politically. The destruction of the planters and upper middle classes had given this class an opportunity to force themselves into places of power and influence.

".... Capitalizing upon the temporary ineptitudes of the sturdy middle class and Bourbon groups, the political demagogues found easy sailings. They inveighed against the helpless Negroes and almost non-existent Catholics; supposedly moral grounds offered an excellent basis for the populist revolt throughout most of the Southern States."[4]

There are, of course, many threads, woven into the fabric of race relations, which ran back to previous periods. In the two or three decades immediately preceding the Civil War, many overseers had risen to the status of planters or large slaveholders. If they had become immune to the sentiments which close association with slaves would naturally inspire, they would not be expected to deal liberally with emancipated slaves. Then, too, in the ranks of the freedmen were also found individuals who had become disorganized. It would, then, occur to the whites in power to suppress these Negroes, as far as possible, in the interests of a social order which the white people sought to maintain, but with which, before the war, many of them had been scarcely concerned. Perhaps, then, the descendants of the Negro field hand, of the rural blacks, of the overseer class, and of the poor whites, feeling at a loss in the new conditions, were the classes from whom the ensuing disorder largely came.

"The strangest point in the new code," said Sumner, "seems to be that any white man is boycotted and despised if he associates with Negroes."[5] Under the circumstance we may understand why a citizen of Orangeburg, South Carolina, felt constrained to apologize publicly for acceding to the request of a Negro teacher that he address a few words to little Negro pupils.[6] Likewise, the action of an attorney—in the trial of Gastonia, North Carolina, strikers—is understandable when it is shown that he sought to impeach the character of a defense witness on the grounds of speaking from the same platform with a Negro and advocating social equality.[7]

Negroes early learned to respect, and to defer to, white persons who acted "in character," that is, who were dignified and had no fear for their status. On the other hand, they tended to have nothing but contempt for white people who acted "out of character." In an instance related by Ralph, a Negro on a steamboat was heard to remark: "Guess dem gemmen nevah been steamboatin' befoh. Nevah seen white folks lay 'round de freight dat way. Seen niggers do it though."[8]

To a great extent, then, the racial code is breaking down. Negroes, and the descendants of the poorer whites, for whom slaves never had any respect, have so far not arrived at any code in which emotions might become economized; hence, conflict between them occasionally occurs. For example, when two prominent Negroes were in a train wreck near Memphis, Tennessee, they were kept seven hours waiting for relief. Finally, a trainman deigned to notice them and wrote a pass—"Take two niggers to Memphis."[9] The implication underlying this instance is scarcely less subtle than that occasionally found in writings which refer to white "women" and Negro "females."[10]

This, then, was the situation prior to, and during the first decade of, the twentieth century—i.e., laws to enforce social distances and insistence on separation of the races, mainly by those who prior to emancipation occupied a lower social standing.

The laws, requiring separation of the races in schools, public places, railroads and streetcars, theaters and parks, and other places of amusement, or in whatever type of public contact which is interdicted, have been mainly passed since 1883.[11] They have doubtless assisted, in many instances, in defining distances and in preventing racial conflict. Yet, in others, they have been direct stimulations to conflicts and have brought about attempts to solve by political action many problems which arise in the cultural process. For Negroes have not been slow to reason that problems raised by one set of laws may be solved by recourse to other laws.

Likewise, the politicians have seen their opportunity to gain access to office by arousing slumbering prejudices. Harking back to the Reconstruction, they have sought to keep in the foreground the threat of "Negro domination." The cure to this, they say, is white supremacy. The method of establishing this supremacy is by exclusion of Negroes from the ballot. And this, in one form or another, has been done in most of the southern states.[12]

Occasionally, when the furore has apparently died down, spasmodic attempts occur purporting to extend suffrage to the Negro. Yet, again, politicians arise and almost invariably, by crying "white supremacy," are able to thwart such a movement.[13]

There is, however, a contradiction in the situation. The flaw in the viewpoint of the white man who would exclude Negroes from the ballot, or in the viewpoint of those Negroes who would extend suffrage to the entire race, is that the Negro masses are, in general, not interested. The situation serves as an illustration to draw the distinction between the controls established by laws and formal regulation and those fixed in custom and habit. The Negro masses look on the white man as chosen to rule and on the ballot as a means to that end. They feel out of place participating in such. They accept their status as nonvoters and expect to be guided thereby. They would much prefer that "quality" white people govern them; but, even in other instances, they exhibit a lack of interest. From this standpoint the battle for and against Negro suffrage, on principle, or on a platform of the enforcement of the fourteenth and fifteenth amendments of the Constitution, is hampered by the underlying sentiments and habits of the Negroes themselves. Voting and participation in governmental affairs seem not to be in the mores of the Negro group.

By a peculiar twist of logic, support is brought to the political slogans of white supremacy in the doctrine that the Negro is biologically and socially inferior. The argument proceeds from doctrines of white supremacy to Negro inferiority and, finally, to the tabooed social equality. One author writes:

"Since then [the Reconstruction] 'White supremacy' has become with us as cardinal a principle as any in science or religion. The casual observer is apt to classify the principle as a political one only; but the warp of it is social in substance and strength. Constitutional and legal and political equality of the races are now normal acceptances by Southern whites. But anything tending to set up any form of social equality of the races arouses elementary resistance, and that resistance can be forced even unto blood."[14]

Southern white people consider "the race as an organic whole," says Cooley, "and believe it is practically necessary to recognize this in dealing with race questions."[15] A Georgia senator, and former judge of the Supreme Court, pronounces the dictum that "no statutory law, no organic law, no military law supersedes the law of social necessity and racial identity."[16] Social necessity means subordination of the Negro, and racial identity means no social equality.[17] Yet, by far the most cogent statement of the southern credo, if not indeed its most extreme viewpoint, is put forth by Bailey, when he says, in fifteen conclusions:

"1. Blood will tell. 2. The white race must dominate. 3. The
Teutonic peoples stand for race purity. 4. The Negro is inferior
and will remain so. 5. This is a white man's country. 6. There
must be no social equality. 7. There must be no political equality. 8. In matters of civil rights and legal adjustment, give the
white man, as opposed to the colored man, the benefit of the
doubt; and under no circumstances interfere with the prestige
of the white race. 9. In the educational policy let the Negro
have the crumbs that fall from the white man's table. 10. Let
there be such industrial education of the Negro as will fit him
to serve the white man. 11. Only Southerners understand the
Negro question. 12. The status of peasantry is all the Negro
may hope for, if the races live together in peace. 13. Let the
South settle the Negro question. 14. Let the lowest white man
count for more than the highest Negro. 15. The above statements indicate the leadings of Providence."[18]

This, then, has been, and still largely is, the situation in race
relations in the present period regarded from the standpoint
of laws and the mores of the South. However, the description
is not therewith complete. Laws have been increased, and the
mores have been extended, to cover practically every situation
in which the two races meet and come into contact. And yet,
in the South, except where antagonisms flare into conflict, relations move smoothly and, to a great extent, harmoniously.

"In the main, the millions in the South live at peace with their
white neighbors. The masses of Negroes, just one generation
[now two] out of slavery and thousands of them still largely
controlled by its influences, accept the superiority of the white
race as a race, whatever may be the private opinion of some of
its members. And furthermore, they accept this relation of
superior and inferior as a mere matter of course—as a part of
their lives—as something neither to be questioned, wondered
at, or worried over."[19]

The peace of the South, said Dunning, was due to the fact
that the Negro "goes more or less cheerfully about his affairs,

evincing little interest in his 'rights' or 'wrongs.' "[20] Dr. Park noted the disposition of white men to treat all Negroes familiarly and of "every Negro to treat every white man respectfully."[21] Perhaps the actual reason for the relative peace is that, beneath the surface of the laws declaring what the races must do in association and contact, and within the limits of the mores determining actions as right and proper, a system of relations has grown up enabling individuals to act freely within the limits imposed by formal rules of personal relations. In short, if there is comparatively little friction between races, as the case seems to be, it is perhaps due to the fact that there is a code of etiquette in race relations.[22]

The etiquette defining the forms to be observed by white and colored people comprises those observed in personal and private relations; in public relations and situations in which reference is made to persons of either group; in railways, streetcars, and other modes of transportation; in education, religion, and amusements; and, in short, in most, if not all, of the circumstances under which the two races must come into contact.

Negroes normally greet white men with the title "Mister."

"When we stopped at a crossroads store for information, my guide was quick to doff his hat and preface his every sentence with 'Mister' and to end his every interrogation with 'Sir.' If one has occasion to say 'yes' or 'no,' the monosyllables must always be followed with the respectful 'sir.' "[23]

Occasionally, however, "cap" or "cap'n"[24] or even the round term "boss" may be substituted for "mister," or even just "white folks" may be used. If white persons are well known, Negroes may address them by the intimate "Mr. John" or "Miss Mary," as the case may be. If, however, formality is required, the forms may be changed to "Mr. So-and-so" or "Miz [never Mistress] So-and-so."[25] When persons of the two groups meet, varying with locality, the Negro is expected to speak first and, perhaps, "bow with the greatest deference."[26]

On the other hand, white persons are not expected to address

Negroes as "mister"; but "boy" is still good usage as a term to address Negro males of all ages.[27] Even "nigger" is occasionally used, though Moton remarks that the term is rarely heard in public on the lips of white people.[28] This term does not strictly conform to what is accepted, for Negroes resent it occasionally.[29] Where these terms are not used, the ubiquitous "Jack" and—as on Pullman cars—"George" and "boy" are in good form.

The rule is that shaking hands, walking together, and otherwise associating in public, except on terms of superior and inferior, are not done.[30] The rule is, however, honored in the breach occasionally.

In hotels, offices, restaurants, or in public places that are reserved for white people, the Negro is expected to remove his hat, whether others have done so or not, and whether or not he is engaged in conversing with white persons. Outside of such places, Negroes commonly do not, and are perhaps not expected to, remove their hats; yet, they find frequent occasions to scratch their heads, which necessitates removing the hat. This is, perhaps, a gesture of respect, or a holdover from the forelock pulling of slavery. It may even be a compromise between habit and conception of new status.

It is apparently not etiquette for a white man to remove his hat in either public or private places reserved for Negroes. The insurance collector and the instalment collector—known in some sections as "muddy-foots"—come into Negro homes without removing their head covering; and messengers, salesmen, and occasionally even beggars come into offices of Negro business houses, schools, and the like, seldom offering to show this bit of courtesy. One place in which white men do remove their hats, however, and they are seldom found there, is in a Negro church.[31]

Titles of "Mister" and "Mistress" or "Miss" are seldom used by white persons with reference to Negroes. This is especially true of the white press. The title "Mrs." for Negro women is especially taboo. Negroes themselves, says Moton, would regard it as a good joke if a proofreader let the title slip by when referring to a Negro woman.[32]

"Europeans will hear about the highly publicized Scottsboro case through the lectures of Ada Wright, mother of two Negro defendants in the case. . . . . The Alabama Negro sailed Wednesday. . . . . One of Ada's sons is under death sentence. . . . ."[33]

Newspapers referring to the death of Mrs. Booker T. Washington recalled her as "the widow of Booker T. Washington" or "a noted Negress"—however, with a lower-case *n*. This last statement serves to introduce the tradition that a lower-case *n*, except where variations have been introduced consciously, is the rule in spelling "Negro."[34]

Occasionally—more frequently than Moton is inclined to believe[35]—"nigger" as a term of reference is heard. A concession is made when "Negro," "darky" or "colored person" is substituted. In fact, ranged in order of acceptability, as Negroes view it, "nigger" is lowest in the scale, "darky" next, and "colored people" just on the verge of respectability.[36] But the "limit of contumely," says Moton, "is reached in the term 'Negress.' "[37]

"There's a colored lady out on the porch who wants to speak to you," said a small white child to her grandmother. "Colored lady!" expostulated the grandmother, "say 'that nigger.' "[38] "Lady" seems to be a term only occasionally used by white persons in referring to a Negro woman, but Negroes commonly speak of white women as "white ladies." The incident taken from Bailey, then, may be discounted the slightest bit. He says:

"When one of your servants announces that a 'gentleman' or a 'lady' wishes to see you. . . . . We all know perfectly well it means a Negro man or woman; but if they said simply instead 'man' or 'woman' we are never in doubt as to *color*, that always designates a white person, not a black."[39]

"Negro" is seldom qualified as a term of reference—for example, "American Negro"—unless a Negro uses it;[40] "American" without the term "Negro" is almost never used in referring to members of the Negro group. A Negro boy, man, girl, woman, or baby is just "Negro." Newspapers referring to a train wreck, for example, may say that "two men and two women were killed, and four Negroes."

Thus, in the present period, the forms of the old code, in many instances, have been preserved after they have no longer conformed to actual race relations. Before the granting of a Doctor's degree to Booker T. Washington served to release white persons from the necessity of calling him "mister,"[41] he had generally been addressed as "Professor" Washington[42] and, on occasion, even "mister." However, the deep-seated nature of the habit of not addressing Negroes by such a title is revealed in Washington's own statement to the effect that it was a matter of interest to him "to note the number of people who have come to shake hands with me after an address, who say that this is the first time they have ever called a Negro 'Mister' "[43] The incident is significant in showing that, as Negroes rise to places and positions of importance, white persons become self-conscious when they realize the break required in the habit of not addressing such persons as "mister." Hence, "where some consideration is to be shown the position of public distinction of an individual Negro, recourse is had to the titles "Professor" and "Doctor."[44]

Perhaps new forms are developing, as in the instance where medicine sent to the wife of a prominent Negro instructor in a southern college was addressed to "the wife of Professor So-and-so";[45] or, for example, in the recent practice on the part of one of the oldest newspapers in the South of conceding a portion of its paper each day to "Negro News" but, at the same time, referring to Negroes as "Messieurs, Mesdames, and Mademoiselles."[46] No justification for employing the French forms of address was perhaps deemed necessary under the circumstances.

Sufficient concession had already been made when "personals" and "society items" about Negroes were included at all.

With reference to the use of the term "nigger":

"Colored people are often amused at the effort of some of their white friends to give consideration to their wishes in this matter [i.e., in not referring to them as "niggers"] without at the same time appearing in the eyes of their own set to be straining for effect. In these circles the term 'niggra' is used as a compromise between 'nigger' and 'Negro.' They know plain 'nigger' is offensive to colored people. They also probably feel that 'Negro' is pretentious. . . . . They save their faces by the compromise 'niggra'; but they are not aware of the amused contempt that the effort inspires in the colored audience."[47]

Legal prescriptions for separation of the races in hotels, inns, streetcars, railroads, schools, and public institutions are incorporated, in some form, in statutory law or ordinances of all the southern states.[48] And yet, these laws are merely formal rules and generalizations. For both white and colored people resort to devices that define the ways by which separation, under the law and mores, is to be maintained. That is to say, the practices and customs of the people go on, not necessarily because of the laws but often in spite of them.

Occasional laws are found prohibiting association of white and Negro in public eating places.[49] This means that they must not eat together. Negroes are not, and do not expect to be, served in white restaurants, hotels, or drug or department-store lunch counters. Yet, they frequently buy food from those places. In such instances they may stand—they do not expect to sit—at the rear of the counter; in some instances they wait at the cigar counter until food is handed to them. In most cases, however, they take the food outside before eating it, although they may occasionally eat in the kitchen. One Negro traveler, upon entering an eating place where his presence was frowned upon, hastened to remark that he wanted some sandwiches "in a paper sack." A Negro may not drink Coca-Cola at a soda fountain for white people, but he may present a tin bucket—in which, by the way, he frequently gets more than the amount given a white customer for the same money. He, of course, drinks his Coca-Cola outside.

The effectiveness of the customs and etiquette, as contrasted with the effect of law in bringing about the desired separation in dining, is seen in the instance reported by Johnson, who quotes from a conversation with a southern white man:

" 'And yet the President of the United States had a nigger to dine with him! The South never got a worse shock than that. Up to then we'd thought a heap of Roosevelt down hyer. Why, we'd named all our dogs after him and his family; but we've changed the dogs' names since that dinner.' "[50]

Laws generally prescribe the separation of the races in theaters, playhouses, and places of amusement. The interpretation is often made that exclusion of negroes is meant. Negroes, however, do attend white playhouses, and, so long as the custom of separation is met, almost any variation may be found. For example, they commonly enter white amusement places from the side, or rear, or, if in the front, by a separate door.[51] A side entrance may be down an alley or on a side street, and the approach may be by the fire escape. Once within the theater, or playhouse, "Negroes never sit downstairs, but the galleries are black with them." In fact, the second balcony, or gallery, is known as "nigger heaven" and, less generally, as the "buzzard roost."

If parks are separate by law, custom decides whether Negroes may pass through them,[52] be admitted on certain days,[53] or be excluded altogether with the notice given upon a sign at the entrance—"Negroes and dogs not allowed."[54] There is not, Schuyler remarks, "a single amusement park in the late Confederacy in which Negroes are admitted."[55]

In the larger southern cities, which boast streetcars, the races are generally separated. This separation, accomplished by statute or ordinance, and frequently by both, is generally interpreted to mean within the same vehicle but may, however, be accomplished in any way deemed necessary locally.[56] Custom, on the other hand, determines whether Negroes will sit in the front or rear portion of the cars[57] and by what doors they shall enter or leave. Except in instances where one-man cars are used, and in others where Negroes sit in the front part of the cars, Negroes generally board the cars at the rear. They also leave by separate exits, as a rule, but the exit is more generally the rear one. Yet, even these customs are frequently complex.

"In Nashville, Negroes may enter from the front or rear of certain cars. In some instances they enter from the front and leave by the rear; in others they enter from the front and leave by the front. In still others they both enter and leave by the rear; occasionally—on lines which serve Negro sections—they enter from the front and leave by either rear or front."[58]

If a number of persons of both races is awaiting the arrival of a car, the white persons will generally board the car first, regardless of the portion of the car assigned to them.[59] Meanwhile, the motorman or conductor may assist white women passengers; but to assist a colored woman, says Moton, "just isn't being done."[60] Once inside the car, signs and notices tell where each race should sit; the boundaries being definite in some instances but quite hazy and ill defined in others. Signs may read "White—Negroes," defining boundaries; may require that white people be seated from the front toward the rear, while Negroes be seated from the rear toward the front; or may make subtle distinctions in status, while, at the same time, leaving boundaries unclear by stating "this part of the car for white *people;* this part of the car for the colored *race*."[61]

To an extent this situation allows generalization on the system of race relations in the South and the function of etiquette in controlling relations. Referring to the streetcars in Atlanta, Baker remarks that "the color line is drawn, but neither race knows just where it is. Indeed it can hardly be drawn in many relationships, because it is changing"[62] Thus where racial boundaries are not clear and defined, conflict is likely to ensue if, and when, persons of either group are ignorant of what is proper under the conditions. If a Negro sits too far front when he is expected to sit in the rear of the car, or vice versa, he may, as in a case reported from a Tennessee city, arouse the indignation of white passengers[63] to the extent that bloodshed may ensue; or he may be asked or told to move by white passengers.[64] If, on the other hand, the color line is definite, he goes beyond it only after due thought; and, meanwhile, he expects that no white person will intrude upon the section assigned to him. It may be stated, then, that, as a rule, relations in the South are less strained when the expected and accepted forms, common to contact and association of the races, are very precise and clearly drawn; and that, on the other hand, racial antagonism and conflict ensue when, even within the limits of what is deemed right and proper, individuals do not know precisely how to act.

The southern states generally have statutes requiring separation of the races in railway cars and depots.[65] While these are, in general, explicit, the adjustments which have grown up in, and around, these formal requirements are many and varied. For example, even the law does not require that entrances to the separate waiting-rooms in the depots be on different sides of the building. Yet is it not uncommon to see the white entrance on the front of the depot, and the Negro entrance on the side or rear.[66] The law does not require that ticket agents serve white customers first, but it is an accepted fact that this will be done. And occasionally, even when there are no white customers to serve, a Negro may stand at the ticket window for many minutes before being served. If he is in a hurry, he may clear his throat, scratch on the window, or even call.[67] Even these acts, however, are not guaranteed to gain attention.

"What you see on the railroad is characteristic of the whole structure of the Southern States. The Negro occupies a position of inferiority and servility, of which he is constantly reminded when traveling, by restriction, by discriminating laws, and by the attitude of his white neighbors."[68]

In a railroad station at Memphis, Tennessee, a sign in the white waiting-room reads "Passengers will please wait in the station until trains are called." The notice in the Negro section, calling attention to the same request reads "No loafing. Stay in the waiting-room until trains are called."[69] The peremptory nature of the latter notice serves to "maintain more effectively social distances and the rank and order of individuals and classes."[70]

"It is practically impossible for the average Negro to go to the ticket window and secure Pullman accommodations of any sort."[71]

". . . . A colored nurse may ride, without objection, if she has a white baby in her arms. On the other hand, if a white nurse would appear in the same car with a colored baby, no one knows what would happen. There is no provision in the social ritual for the unprecedented."[72]

On the other hand, if a Negro does secure a berth, upon boarding the train, he may occasionally—if he asks, or if the conductor suggests—be placed in the drawing-room, without an extra charge. Or, if there is a sufficient number of Negroes to fill an entire car, they may charter a special Pullman—subject, of course, to the customs of the particular locality.[73]

Generally, Negroes do not eat in the dining cars on the trains. Yet "aboard some trains this has been remedied to the extent of permitting Negro passengers to enter the dining car after all white passengers have been served, or, on some lines on the third call.[74] This situation, however, is not confined to dining cars. The custom of white and colored people eating together is taboo in the South.

"The colored people all love me where I live. Some would almost give their right hands to help me if I asked them. But I would starve to death before I would eat a crust of bread at a table with one of them."[75]

"I am from Mississippi, and I just can't eat with you niggers," said a traveling salesman who, in the little Negro town of Boley, Oklahoma, where white people seldom go, found it necessary to ask a Negro hotel owner for food.

Southern laws and custom require separation of the races in the public schools. The law generally implies, if it does not state, that children should be instructed by persons of their own racial group. Hence, Negroes never teach white children; and, if any white person teaches Negroes, except under local custom and in occasional private schools, ostracism is a result.[76] It is generally not customary for Negroes to receive the same salaries for teaching as white persons.[77]

Yet no law requires, as is practiced in some southern towns, that the Negro schools open and close at different hours; or that white and colored children walk on different sides of the street while coming or going to school.[78] Again, the law usually states that "separate but equal accommodation" be provided even in cases of schools. But it is a notorious fact that Negro schools are generally inferior in structure and equipment in most of the South. Some are nondescript buildings, perhaps previously used by white people, and occasionally furnished with equipment discarded by the white schools.

Public hospitals, in the instances where they occur at all, have separate wards for whites and blacks according to law; but private hospitals are provided only for separate groups. In some instances, if a Negro should require ambulance service to remove him to a hospital, he would need an ambulance owned by a Negro, for the white ambulance may refuse service.

"A Negro switchman .... lay bleeding to death by the Bellevue viaduct in Memphis. His foot had slipped, and he had fallen beneath a switch engine. His right arm and leg were severed. Ambulances rushed to the man's aid. They took one look, saw that he was a Negro, and backed away."[79]

If by some circumstance he is accommodated in a public hospital and happens to die, the body will be placed in the corner of the "dead house" away from the white corpses.[80] The corpse of a Negro will be carried to a separate cemetery.[81] If a white undertaker is in charge of the funeral, he will generally, but not always, have a separate hearse for Negro patrons. Otherwise, a Negro undertaker will have charge.[82]

In perhaps no other instance is the complexity and noticeable contradiction in race relations more apparent than in the customs practiced in courts, police stations, and jails. If the law were all-powerful to control relations, the force would certainly appear when the Negro comes into actual contact with the law. But, as Spencer says, ceremonial precedes, goes along with, and continues after laws are enacted. For example, a Negro if arrested will be conveyed to jail in the same patrol wagon as that used for white people. When he gets to jail, he is thrown into a separate portion from the whites, according to law. When he appears for trial, although the law makes no mention of it, he will on occasion enter the courtroom by a separate door from the white prisoners; Negro or white witnesses for his trial will be seated on opposite sides of the courtroom, or perhaps in separate sections, according to custom.[83] "Afterwards, when he comes to trial, two Bibles are provided; he may take his oath on one; the other is for white men."[84] If he is convicted, he finds that according to law he will be separated in the chain gang, jail, reformatory, or penitentiary from the white prisoners.[85]

As a citizen rather than as a prisoner, the federal law states that he must not be excluded from jury duty because of race or color. Again, however, custom is stronger than law. For, though Negroes do occasionally appear on juries, the event is sufficiently rare to provoke comment[86] whenever it does occur.

Statutes and constitutional provisions of fifteen southern states prohibit intermarriage between white and colored persons.[87] But the mores supporting the law seem to be even more effective than the law. In fact, the taboo against such marriage is so great that, it might be said, intermarriage would occur in but few cases regardless of statutory regulation to the contrary.[88] Negroes, perhaps, as much as white persons regard such intermarriages with suspicion and distrust.[89]

"We hear much of 'social equality' these days, and white and black speakers tell the world that the Negro does not desire 'social equality.' That depends upon what is meant by the term. If the white man means 'social intermingling' or mongrelization of the white group, or any approach by either side toward miscegenation, the black man utters 'Amen.' "[90]

Kelly Miller says that "the Negro does not hope and dream of amalgamation." That is to say, it seems to be etiquette for Negroes to deny that they wish "social equality."[91]

In relations that are not touched by legislation, but which, on the other hand, are deemed to come under control of the mores, etiquette has also sprung up to preserve the rank and order of white and colored people. Commercial relations, generally conceded to be those least affected by the mores, have in the South not been entirely able, however, to free themselves from the incubus of taboo. In the stores white customers are all waited upon, in general, before any Negro patron is served. Negro men commonly try on hats in haberdasheries, but a rule, occasionally honored in the breach, is that a Negro woman may not try on either hat or gloves. If a colored woman desires to purchase a certain hat, the saleswoman tries the hat on herself in order to show its style and becomingness. Separate sections for white and colored customers are the rule in shoe and clothing stores, where a try-on is necessary. In shoe stores, however, the Negro is frequently in a quandary to know whether the clerk will fit a shoe, or whether he, or she, will be required to fit it in person.[92] Stores have been known to state that their policy is not to serve Negroes under any circumstances.

In a large southern city, a prominent bank, where, if anywhere, relations are expected to be impersonal, has provided a separate window and teller for Negro patrons.[93]

Laws have likewise not regulated contacts necessary in

situations where the two races work on the same job, but an etiquette of precedence has nevertheless arisen. If white and colored persons are employed together, they do not engage in the same tasks, generally, and certainly not as equals.[94] The superintendent, foreman, leader, or "straw boss" is generally a white person; the Negroes make up the rank and file of workers.[95] That is to say, Negroes are seldom, if ever, put into authority over white persons.[96] Moreover, the Negro expects to remain in the lower ranks; rising, if at all, only over other Negroes.

"The humblest employee knows that the better he does his work the more chance there is for him to rise in the business. The black employee knows that the better he does his work, the longer he may do it; he cannot often hope for promotion."[97]

Then, too, in the cases where the two races do work on the same job, a division of labor appears which effectively shows distinctions. A Negro may become a locomotive fireman but never an engineer.[98] In Chattanooga, Ralph reported, Negroes dug the ore and worked in the furnaces of the iron foundries; while the white men dug the coal.[99] In a Georgia town the postmen were once all Negroes; but the residents of a Texas city refused to receive mail from a Negro postman.[100] At one time, Miami, Florida, would not tolerate Negro chauffeurs; Atlanta, Georgia, refused to license Negroes to operate motion-picture machines.[101] A Negro buyer, who had risen to the position in a white department store, was frequently intimidated and insulted by white people, who considered him out of place.[102] Another Negro, who had been made head of the shipping department of a large store, experienced the situation where a white salesman refused to talk to him.[103]

There must, then, be a division of labor where the two races are employed,[104] and menial labor is commonly supposed to be that division assigned to Negroes. At any rate, a Negro may occasionally be reminded that his status in the South is generally as a menial and that he must look and act the part.

"A friend of mine, during vacation period, visited a young woman of his acquaintance, in my home town. One day he had occasion to go down to the square. There he met some white men who forced him to procure overalls, saying he was 'too dressed up for a week day.' "[105]

Moreover, in order that the status of menial be preserved, Negroes who do not work for white people are occasionally intimidated.

"The wife of a respectable colored man was sitting on her porch one afternoon, paring potatoes for her husband's supper, and waiting for him to come home from work. An officer saw her, asked if she was working, and on being told that her home duties required all her time, arrested her for vagrancy and took her to the county jail."[106]

Custom thus assigns the Negro his place in the South, and racial antagonisms are excited if it seems that he is getting out of place. The state of Tennessee, at one time, established a board for registering nurses; but the white members of the board refused to register Negro nurses, even with the required training and experience.[107] In one of the larger cities of the same state, colored nurses were employed to attend colored patients in the city hospital. Thereupon the white nurses walked out on strike.[108]

The generalization which might be advanced, considering the evidence so far given, is that the South, in the late modern period, shows a society divided into halves, with the white people on one side of an imaginary line and the Negroes on the other. Yet, even if the line is imaginary, the acts which allow us to make the inference are nevertheless very real. For example, if water wagons are ordered to sprinkle the streets of a city, the drivers know that they are expected to stop at the Negro section. It is, perhaps, a common experience with automobile tourists to pass through a southern town part way upon pavement, part way upon dirt roads; and then to arrive at the pavement again. They have also doubtless learned that the dirt section of the road is generally confined to the Negro section.

When a bond issue is voted for pavement, or schools, or public improvements, it is generally accepted that the pavement is not for Negro sections, that new schools are not for Negroes, and that public improvements are commonly confined to white sections. If an orator addresses an audience as "fellow-citizens," Negroes, if any are present, know they are not included in the gesture. A prominent southern newspaper, printing weekly notices of church services and, in the fall, football scores, classifies the former into "denominations" and "Negro churches"; the latter into western, eastern, southern, and Negro football.[109]

This situation is, however, "in the mores." In fact, within the limits set by the doctrine of white superiority and separation of the races, local sentiment and habit will generally determine the forms and observances proper to association and contact of the races in a given area. For this reason, then, the codes not only vary but also show exceeding complexity.

"How a colored man, or a white man either, for the matter, can be expected to know all the intricacies of segregation as he travels in different parts of the country is beyond explanation. The truth of the matter is, he is expected to find out as best he can.[110]

However, both white and colored people do discover and observe the forms expected and accepted in a given locality. They do this not only because it is a relatively easy method of adjustment but also because they believe, not necessarily consciously, that the moral order in which their actions are judged is the best under the circumstances and because they have sentimental attachments for the order and expect it to be continued.

It is generally accepted that the white man wishes a continuance of the situation in which, because of his racial identity, he dominates. It is perhaps not so generally assumed that Negroes accept, in general, the position of inferiority. However, it seems to be true that Negroes do accept the evaluation of events and circumstances made by white people and that they adopt the customs and ideas of white people as far as possible. Moreover, in ways both formal and informal, and at times both consciously and unconsciously, they criticize themselves for failing to understand or to live up to the standards thus idealized.[111] "The Aframerican would rather be proper and unhappy, than naturally himself and in Paradise. If he is improper, the white man ridicules him, and ridicule hurts."[112] The clue to the interpretation is that the Negro considers proper or improper those acts, thoughts, or forms of behavior which are so considered by white people. To the extent, then, that both agree upon this, we may say that the sentiments of both white and colored people support the mores and social ritual. Tradition thus assigns the Negro his status in the South, law defines it, sentiments support it, custom and habit continue it, and prejudice maintains it in those instances where it seems to be breaking down.

The movement for segregation of the races, as described here, has to a great extent broken up the old intimacies upon which the traditional code of race relations rested. It has, moreover, increased the distances between the two groups and, consciously or unconsciously, has effected noticeable changes in the sentiments underlying the code of etiquette.

"Few white persons ever visit the home of their cook or butler or nurse, unless it be in case of emergency, such as serious illness or death, perhaps. Or if otherwise, they do come to the street where the servant lives, they must be directed to the particular house they seek, and usually remain without while some accommodating passer-by calls to the door the man, woman, boy or girl. Very often they are not encouraged to enter. Such a Negro servant would hesitate to invite her mistress into the home, lest it be counted a presumption."[113]

Wherever the sentiment of the Negro supports the situations described, it is rather a prejudice in favor of an order in which, with all its disabilities, he has been able to gain a livelihood without constant disharmony. It is not, as he sees it, a prejudice in favor of an order in which he defers to superiors because they have shown traits of superiority but one in which the race and possible economic status of a man determine whether deference shall be paid. The Negro does, however, look to the white man for traits of character which call forth spontaneous expressions of respect. One of the problems of his existence has recently been, perhaps with the rise of the poor white to power, to learn how to look up to a white man who does not in some way seem to merit respect.[114] When the lamb, standing on the roof, cursed a wolf, the wolf replied, "Not you, but the roof curses me." In this fable, as with the Negro, circumstances and accident, not natural superiority, seem to determine adjustment as well as sentiment.

Likewise, the white man must occasionally feel that the constant deference of the Negro is not spontaneous but formal and even cynical. He would much rather be respected for himself; but, failing in this, he wants to be respected for his race. Hence those who have the least personal standing insist upon their racial status as a basis of adjustment, for only in this way may they be deferred to at all. Moreover, it is in relations with this class that the Negro makes use of supererogatory flourishes and embellishments of behavior. He has learned that such persons will pay, in one way or another, for deference. In such circumstances he will emphasize the ritual and the external forms, although sentiment may occasionally be lacking. They speak publicly, says Schuyler, of how they love the white people, "but privately, the majority of them sing another tune."[115]

On the other hand, there are still white men who merit respect personally. In an order where men counted for their own worth, they would normally receive deference from Negroes. But these white men feel that such an order has passed and that the Negroes of today are, in general, acting out of character, either when they strive to attain a new status or when they defer ritualistically but not wholeheartedly to white people. In his more lucid moments the Negro does, in fact, have much respect for this class. He refers to them as "our best white people" and would much rather, as in slavery, have them govern and control. But the odds are overwhelming, and he must meanwhile live. He firmly believes that if peace is to come to the South, in the ways that it formerly existed, it will come through the efforts of this class. Meanwhile, he moves in a world of forms; he cannot take the time to determine the class and character of every white man with whom he comes into contact; he can only observe those forms which are calculated to allow him to go his way with the least expenditure of thought and energy. And in this way, if perhaps in no other, the etiquette of race relations exerts its most effective control.

CHAPTER XI

THE NEGRO GETS BY

IT HAPPENS, then, that in the welter and chaos of codes, and amid the changes which have been forced upon him by circumstance, the Negro gets along and occasionally "gets by." One of the ways by which he gets along is by maintaining his faith in "the best white people." He cultivates their acquaintance and good will and, as evidence of it, will occasionally invite them to some special event as a gesture of respect. Moreover, he will go even farther than that:

"White people have attended Negro functions. They know that they have always been given, if not 'special' seats, places where they could enjoy the affair, and seats arranged where all the white folks would be together. When they walk in a function that is apt to be attended by mixed races, they always pause to see where the white people are sitting. This the Negroes know as well as the white people. . . . . The white people know that they will get reserved seats; it is our time-worn custom, and as long as we want them we are going to give them, and contribute every courtesy and comfort of entertainment while they are with us.[1]

In general, whenever a Negro convention, or conference, or association, or lodge meets in a city, white officials are invited to give addresses of welcome, or to "extend the keys of the city." Negroes know that the extended key will only unlock such places as those to which they normally go; but they also know that the gesture, by showing respect is effective in building up good will. On such occasions Negroes will invariably treat such persons with extreme courtesy but will feel at a disadvantage until the visitors have gone.

"Not that anything will transpire that has not already

occurred, but there is a reserve which Negroes maintain in the presence of whites, partly to refute the charge that they are seeking social equality, and partly to conserve a dignity that refuses to be made a spectacle to the curious."[2]

And partly, we add, because in the existing state of conditions, they are not always certain that officials are really and truly "our best white folks."

In cases of conflict that break out between the races, Negroes generally utter a stereotyped remark, to the effect that the conflict did not occur in the ranks of the "best white people." Moreover, in an effort to subdue the disorder, they often send emissaries to representatives of this class, whose opinions they respect, to ask them what to do under the circumstances. If a new movement is attempted, the effect of which is unknown because it departs from the expected, they will consult the "best white people"—whose sanction, if given, will cause all to be well.[3]

This is the real significance of such organizations as the Inter-racial Commission and all those numerous associations in the South, in which white and colored persons meet and discuss their common problems. It preserves intact the communication between the Negro and the white people whose opinions he respects and whose standing he regards. It keeps open the channel of good will, which the Negro believes will finally assist in, if it does not complete, the solution of many vexing aspects of race relations.

The Negro also "gets along" because, when in doubt as to what is expected of him, he will ask what is customary—not what is the law. He seems subconsciously to feel that custom is more powerful than law. And yet there are instances where no one can tell him just what is the custom or what will be accepted. In this case he falls back on old habits. If these habits are not accepted, the Negro merely "turns on his personality" and, by apology, ingratiation, or laughter, will be able to turn even this hard corner.[4]

The Negro gets along, to some extent, because in some cases he appeals to law to right conditions which seem to him intolerable. He appeals to law, in fact, only as a last resort. Perhaps subconsciously he then reasons that, if his status is defined by law, it may be changed or even supported by the same means. Organizations have, indeed, been established among Negroes which seek, by process of law, to change the system of relations now existing. Some, for example, the National Association for the Advancement of Colored People, have been militant enough to attempt to change the forms which are observed between the races, in face of the fact that feeling and sentiment have not changed. These organizations do undoubtedly attain and preserve gains that otherwise would, perhaps, be impossible. They do not always bring peace. In fact, they almost never do so. The significance of the agitation for rights and equality, as exemplified in, say, Mr. DuBois, formerly a guiding spirit in the National Association for the Advancement of Colored People, was that under his scheme the races were not to be allowed to come to terms, and race relations were not again to be fixed in custom and formulated in codes before the Negro had fully experienced his freedom. Resistance to compromise has, then, helped to keep the racial situation in a state of flux and has tended to serve notice on the white man that weaker peoples expect him to live up to the principles established in his laws—those laws to which he proclaims loyalty.[5]

In perhaps no other respect is the change in relations made clearer than in the development of what has been called "biracial organization." This has seemingly resulted from the destruction of the old intimacies upon which the racial code traditionally rested. The movement for complete segregation of the races not only destroyed those intimacies but also destroyed the system by which the white man was limited to one set of occupations and the Negro to another. As a result, a professional class of physicians, ministers, lawyers, teachers, and small business men has sprung up to provide services for mem-

bers of the Negro race who are unacceptable to white profes-
sionals as patients, parishioners, clients, pupils, and customers.
In some instances they do, indeed, serve both races. But the
common expectation is that they will confine their services to
Negroes.[6] A Negro undertaker, says Murphy, does not bury
white persons in any discovered instance.[7]

Churches, following the trends begun in slavery and continued throughout the Reconstruction, have become definitely
racial in organization. An old Negro may occasionally be found
who is a member of a white church. "But with due regard, however delicately managed, for the sacred traditions which demand
a distinction between black and white; no new members of the
Negro race are received."[8] In some instances, however, a white
evangelist will hold services in a white church, and Negroes will
be invited as special subjects for his ministrations. The service
for Negroes may, then, be held in a Negro church; or Negroes
may attend a special service; or they may sit in a special section,
at the same service with white people, in the white church. It
is not entirely proper for a Negro to "get religion" under the
circumstances, however.

"Some years ago there was a great revival in one of the
churches of my own city. The evangelist was fervently inviting
all kinds of people to come to the 'anxious seat.' Tramps,
beggars, and drunkards were among the number. At last it was
announced to the officials that a Negro, upon one of the back
seats, was under conviction. Here was a problem of serious
import. The officials held an anxious consultation, and it was
finally announced that the Negro might receive salvation provided he remained in the inconspicuous pew."[9]

No instance is found where a white person "got religion" in a
Negro church; but the expectation is that the evangelist, the
minister, and the congregation would all feel highly honored.

The question of segregation of the races has occurred also in
the labor unions. It has finally been reduced to the problem of
accepting the principle of affiliation of laborers or of separating

the races. The original solution was to exclude Negroes altogether from membership, but "in places where the Negro has shown his ability to compete, and has managed to gain a sufficient foothold to compel recognition, labor unions have made earnest efforts to bring Negroes into the unions."[10] The unions, so far as discovered, are separate for white and black; and the latter seldom have affiliation with the national and international organizations.[11]

To continue the list of institutions which show this biracial organization would have small value. A generalization covering the situation may be made:

"The Negro at the present time has separate churches, schools, libraries,[12] hospitals, Y.M.C.A. associations, and even separate towns. In general, it may be said that where the Negro schools, churches, and Y.M.C.A. associations are not separate they do not exist."[13]

Separation of the races, with reference to residences, "exists in some form in all American cities."[14] And, though the line is indistinct in many cases, it is doubtless exceptional when the two groups appear together in a given block.[15] The phenomenon is perhaps economic; yet it is so widely observed and understood that violations of the expected have brought legal and extralegal attempts at enforcement.[16] Within this Negro residential area the traits of the Negro are almost wholly uncontaminated by white traditions and customs. The inhabitants are almost completely shut off from the white world. Indeed some of them have become so race conscious that they resent the presence of white persons within the areas.

The extension of this feeling has doubtless brought about the establishment of Negro towns. To some extent this is a form of protective coloration, for in towns where all residents, as well as all officials, are Negroes, white persons seldom intrude.[17]

Along with the development of biracial organization has gone also the increase of race consciousness among Negroes. The motive to this type of solidarity, says Dr. Park, has come from an increasing sensibility of the Negro to pressure and prejudice from without his own group.[18] These responses represent accommodations to changing internal and external relations and typify what Moton has called the "defense mechanism."

For our purposes, however, whatever the stimulus or motive, the biracial organization and development of race consciousness tend to perpetuate the state of affairs in which the two races meet and associate as though across a great chasm. Under such circumstances communication and co-operation do proceed, but the chief effect is to maintain proper social distance. Race-conscious Negroes thus insist on a rigid observance of forms which preserve distance and protect personal reserves; but they decry those forms which seem to remind them of dependency or of inferiority.

White people also tend to realize that forms appropriate for use, when Negroes are considered as members of a lower social status, are not suitable when individual Negroes have risen to professional ranking. The mores may indeed prohibit absolute equality, but they do not completely prevent recognition of worth as Negroes arise to a higher status. Booker T. Washington testifies, for example, that in all his personal contact with the white people of the South, he "never received a single personal insult." Not long since, the city of Richmond, Virginia, Moton relates:

". . . . without hesitancy or solicitation, and quite spontaneously, officially set aside its segregation ordinances and opened street cars, taxis, restaurants, and soda fountains, and even the porches of private houses on the line of march, to the unrestricted use of visiting delegates to the annual convention of a great Negro fraternal organization."[19]

An instance has come to our attention where a Negro woman in a small Texas town is, by the upper class of business and professional persons, commonly addressed as "Mrs. X," even though the title is given to no other woman in her group. Dr. Park relates that a clergyman resolved to address a "colored woman, recently married, as 'Mrs.'—out of respect for the holy estate of matrimony."[20] Ralph tells of two mulatto sons of a white farmer, who inherited their father's property:

"When they went to town, the bankers enjoyed conversing with them. . . . . The best men of the countryside bowed to them, even conversed with them in passing on the roads. But no white man ever visited their beautiful home . . . . except an Episcopal bishop, who dined with one. . . . . The bishop died before many white men knew of his daring."[21]

Not long since, a daily newspaper reported that, when opponents of a Negro baseball team failed to appear for a scheduled game, white amateurs from the city league volunteered to play instead.[22] In this instance, as in others that have appeared, and will continue to appear, "the individual's ability to get results gives him an interest and a status independent of, and quite overshadowing, the superficial marks of personality."[23]

In many instances where the races meet daily, "boss" has supplanted both "mister" for white men and "George" for Negroes as a term of address.[24] "Conversation is introduced with common salutations about the day, or the state of one's health, and individuals are addressed in the second person."[25] "Even the asperities of segregation are sometimes accompanied by a smile of deprecation, that deplores its necessity and ridicules its absurdity."[26] One enthusiast writes:

"In no case are these discriminatory and segregational laws carried out to the letter. In many instances they are only half-heartedly applied. We often see Negroes on street cars riding in front of the whites. Only recently I was shown into a toilet in a theatre marked "For whites only." . . . . The segregation laws are becoming noticeably weak in certain phases of community life. Nobody seems to care whether the letter of the law is lived up to or not, although in some cases very positive gestures are made by officious whites."[27]

In the field of commerce there is a growing realization that the Negro group controls a vast purchasing power.[28] The growth of the chain store, with its emphasis upon turnover and its impersonal contacts, has brought about the situation where Negroes "get in line" to be served as customers; where as in most other stores they wait, as Negroes, for white people to be served first.

Yet changes and infractions of the code to allow for association on the level of economic, matrimonial, professional, or social status do not imply absence of social distances. In fact, "the distances which separate the races are maintained, but the attitudes involved are different. The races no longer look up and down; they look across."[29]

Racial conflict and friction exist, on the other hand, where tradition and racial prejudice are breaking down, and the social order which they supported seems to be going to pieces;[30] that is to say, in the instances where the Negro is "getting out of his place." The Negro in his place is a smiling menial, like the stereotypes carried in advertisements of Cream of Wheat, or of Swift's hams;[31] or is a low-comedy character like Florian Slappey of Octavius Roy Cohen fame. These Negroes will, while feeling their inferiority, "do the dirty work and not fuss about it."[32] On the other hand, a Negro who is acquiring property, approaching the standard of the white men, becoming educated, showing prosperity in a way to be seen by white people, or seeking to improve his status rather than his condition, is definitely out of place.[33] He stimulates, to an extent, the apprehension that the South may eventually be dominated by the Negro.[34]

Conflict may also arise where the Negro who conceives his status as not in the nature of things subordinate, or who, because he has not felt the superiority of the white group, resents his treatment as a subordinate. He makes small attempt to ingratiate himself into the good will of white people and is classed as bumptious or as a "smart nigger." Writers have noted that this class has changed manners, rarely using "ma'am" or "sir" when conversing with white people, seldom touching or removing their hats as a sign of respect; and even on occasion monopolizing the inner side of the sidewalk, which is the "white man's right of way."[35] Negroes of this class try to reach the highest point of achievement and want no more nor any less than equal opportunity, says Moton.[36] It is perhaps needless to state that this conception does not fit in with the traditional one held in the South.

"'You used to could tell a nigger something, and they'd listen to you, but that time's gone by. She as much as said she knew more than I did, and I'd rather be called the meanest name there is than have a nigger tell me that.' "[37]

However, it seems that there are no racial antagonisms that cannot be overcome by scrupulous adherence to etiquette.[38] When a new situation arises that produces racial conflict, it may generally be changed to bring about harmony if only the groups will revert to the etiquette of race relations. A corollary of this statement would be, then, that conflict is relatively greater either where the observances expected and accepted between the races have not been regularized and codified or where they are neglected.

There remains still one other potential source of conflict. A Negro will occasionally find great cause for merriment in contemplating the existing codes of etiquette.[39] It might be assumed that, if the person found such a source of joy, he would subscribe to the situation quite wholeheartedly. The attitude seems, however, to be one of contempt rather than one of cheerfulness. The expectation is that the individual will neglect the code since it seems to have no real significance. The person, however, has detached himself from the situation, has evaluated it critically, and needs to spend small emotional energy either in defending or decrying existing conditions. He may, or may not, be called upon to use the traditional forms. If he does use the forms, he plays at the practice, as at an amusing game. He feels no inferiority or superiority. And this, in the broadest sense, is the true emancipation of the Negro.

Summarizing, then, and comparing the period of slavery with the one beginning in the early eighties and continuing to the present, we find a remarkable resemblance in the forms and observances that have been, and still are, common to the contact and association of the two races. Separation of the races is relatively more prominent in this latter period, and the intimacy which was characteristic of the relations in slavery has seemingly vanished. Relations, that is to say, have changed. They have, however, changed so gradually that only here and there are differences made obvious.

However, the comparative peace of the South, which also was characteristic of the period of slavery and of relations between the races, still to a great extent continues, even though conditions have changed. The situation seems not necessarily to be due to the laws and enactments which seek to define the circumstances and conditions under which the races meet, for those laws may or may not be observed, and yet relative harmony will continue. The peace which exists is, perhaps, not due to the formal changes in the political status of the Negro, for these have not everywhere, or by all Negroes, been attained. Moreover, if they had been attained, it is possible that they would have provoked more discord than harmony. The mores, requiring separation of white and colored persons, may be held accountable for the present conditions; but they have made communication and reciprocal exchange of influence between the races more difficult.

Perhaps the explanation of the situation may be found in the generalization that, under the laws which define the status of the Negro, and within the limits of the mores which tend to segregate the races more and more, the Negro still moves freely. This is accomplished by expressing himself in the ways, and by observing the forms in personal relations, which have become expected and accepted.

He has learned, through two hundred odd years of slavery, to accept the superior status of, and to defer to, white people in most situations. Moreover, he has withal gained a livelihood, some comforts, and a status, even if a lowly one, in the social order. He has a sentimental attachment for the *status quo*, and, in general, expects no cataclysm to change conditions overnight, if indeed he thinks of such things at all.

To the present situation he brings the assets of personal and racial adaptability gained under the harsh regime of slavery. He has learned to smile, to be pleasant, and to select from the situation such elements of adjustment as he can from among those which are available. Moreover, he has learned that the surest method of retreating from a difficult position is to express himself in ways that show he meant no offense.

The tempo of latter-day American society is such, however, that changes are inaugurated rapidly and extensively. As the Negro is forced into competition with white people new situations arise which demand new adjustments. Under the circumstances animosities are released, opposition of action, or antagonism develops, and conflict too frequently ensues. The Negro is conceived as "out of place"—that is to say, prejudice appears. And the prejudice, says Dr. Park, is reinforced by apparently natural contrarieties in feeling.

The two races, however, are part of the same social order, articulated with and supplementing each other in many and diverse ways. Conflict prevents the co-operation which is necessary, even if at all times it seems not to be desired. Co-operation is, however, only possible when conflict ceases and accommodation occurs. In most cases, then, accommodation ensues when the Negro assumes the status generally assigned to him and when he adopts the forms of behavior commonly expected of him. That is to say, a reversion to the code of expected and accepted forms of behavior is generally calculated to solve situations where conflict exists in racial relations. For, by preserving the rank and precedence of persons, etiquette makes effective social action possible.

In still other situations where contact and competition with white people is prohibited or tabooed, the Negro is compelled to seek expression in his own group. As a consequence he then tends to acquire status higher in type but separate and apart from the white people. He may, indeed, be considered by white people as a superior person, but he must keep his distance from them. Under these conditions, when members of the two races meet, the etiquette of racial relations is again reverted to, but it then preserves distance rather than rank and precedence.

If, however, as the Negro rises to a higher status in financial, academic, professional, or social life, he begins to see himself in a new light, and to adopt forms calculated to express the new sentiment, the circumstance may release latent animosities and may start the cycle of conflict-accommodation all over again. This latter situation may result in a return to the old code of etiquette, or, as seldom happens, it may end in extermination of the offending Negro. In most cases it will cut the Negro off from association with white persons, for they will not understand his conduct.

Occasionally, however, under the same conditions, white people may also see the Negro in a new light and see themselves in a new relation to him. They will then express themselves in such ways as to convey this change of sentiment, and the Negro will respond fittingly. In this way new forms, new observances, and new codes of etiquette will arise. Yet, since the mores require separation of the races, the new forms will preserve and maintain distances between the races.

"This is the significance of the ceremonial and social ritual so rigidly enforced in the South, by which racial distinctions are preserved amid all the inevitable changes and promiscuity of an expanding industrial and democractic society. While etiquette and ceremonial are at once a convenience and a necessity in facilitating human intercourse, they serve even more effectively to preserve the rank and order of individuals and classes, which seems to be essential to social organization and effective collective action."[40]

Considering, then, the relations of white and colored persons during the period of slavery, through the manifold changes of the Reconstruction, and into the more extensive changes of the present-day scene, we find that etiquette of race relations has been the earliest kind of government, the most general kind of government, and the government which is ever spontaneously recommencing in the contact and association of the two races. Moreover, besides preceding all other kinds of control, and besides having in all places and times where the races have associated approached nearer to universality of influence, the etiquette of race relations has ever had, and continues to have, the largest share in regulating their lives.

BIBLIOGRAPHY

GENERAL SOURCES

STATISTICAL AND DOCUMENTARY

BAKER, O. E., and STINE, O. C. *Atlas of American Agriculture*, Part V: "The Crops"; Sec. A: "October." Washington: Government Printing Office, 1918.

CENSUS BUREAU. *A Century of Population Growth*. Washington: Government Printing Office.

——. *Negroes in the United States*. Washington: Government Printing Office, 1904.

——. *Negro Population in the United States, 1790–1915*. Washington: Government Printing Office, 1918.

COLBY, CHARLES C. *Source Book for Economic Geography of North America*. Chicago: University of Chicago Press, 1926.

MACDONALD, WILLIAM. *Select Statutes and Other Documents Illustrative of the History of the United States, 1861–1898*. New York: Macmillan, 1922.

PHILLIPS, ULRICH BONNELL. *Plantation and Frontier Documents; 1649–1863*. (Documentary History of American Industrial Society.) 2 vols. Cleveland: A. H. Clark, 1902.

Statistical Abstract of the United States. Washington: Government Printing Office, 1901.

WORK, MONROE N. (ed.). *The Negro Year Book* (1925–26, 1931–32). Tuskegee, Ala.: Tuskegee Institute, 1927.

LOGIC AND THEORY OF CEREMONY, ETIQUETTE AND RACE RELATIONS

COOLEY, CHARLES HORTON. *Social Organization*. New York: Scribner's, 1914.

DEWEY, JOHN. *Human Nature and Conduct*. New York: Henry Holt, 1922.

DEWEY, JOHN, and TUFTS, JAMES H. *Ethics*. New York: Henry Holt, 1908.

DURKHEIM, EMILE. *The Elementary Forms of the Religious Life*. Translation by JOSEPH WARD SWAIN. London: Allen & Unwin, 1915.

——. *Les Règles de la méthode sociologique*. 2d ed. Paris: Alcan, 1895.

FARIS, ELLSWORTH. "The Concept of Imitation," *American Journal of Sociology*, XXXII, No. 3 (1926–27), 367–78.

FOLLETT, MARY. *Creative Experience*. New York: Longmans, Green, 1924.

HOBHOUSE, LEONARD T. *Morals in Evolution*. New York: Henry Holt, 1925.

MAINE, SIR HENRY SUMNER. *Ancient Law: Its Connection with the Early History of Society, and Its Relation to Modern Ideas*. 3d American ed. from the 5th London ed. New York: Henry Holt, 1888.

MEAD, GEORGE HERBERT. "Social Psychology as Counterpart to Physiological Psychology," *Psychological Bulletin*, VI, No. 12 (1909), 401–8.
———. "The Genesis of the Self and Social Control," *International Journal of Ethics*, XXXV, No. 3 (1915), 251–77.
PARK, ROBERT E. "The Bases of Race Prejudice," *Annals of the American Academy of Political and Social Science*, CXXXX (November, 1928), 11–20.
———. "Negro Race Consciousness as Reflected in Race Literature," *American Review*, I, No. 5 (September–October, 1923), 505–17.
———. "Human Nature and Collective Behavior," *American Journal of Sociology*, XXXII, No. 5 (1926–27), 733–42.
PARK, ROBERT E., and MILLER, HERBERT A. *Old World Traits Transplanted.* Chicago: Society of Social Research, 1925.
SPENCER, HERBERT. *Principles of Sociology.* 2 vols. London: Williams & Norgate, 1882.
STEINER, JESSE F. *The Japanese Invasion.* Chicago: A. C. McClurg, 1917.
SUMNER, WILLIAM GRAHAM. *Folkways.* New York: Ginn & Co., 1910.
THOMAS, WILLIAM I., and ZNANIECKI, FLORIAN. *The Polish Peasant in Europe and America.* 2 vols. New York: A. A. Knopf, Inc., 1927.
THOMAS, WILLIAM I. "The Psychology of Race Prejudice," *American Journal of Sociology*, IX (1903–4), 593–611.
———. *Source Book for Social Origins: Ethnological Materials, Psychological Standpoint, Classified and Annotated Bibliographies for the Interpretation of Savage Society.* 6th ed. Boston: Badger, 1909.
YOUNG, KIMBALL. *Source Book for Social Psychology.* New York: A. A. Knopf, Inc., 1927.

SECONDARY AUTHORITIES

HISTORIES, ETC.

ALEXANDER, WILLIAM T. *History of the Colored Race in America.* Kansas City, Mo.: Palmetto Publishing Co., 1887.
BROWN, WILLIAM WELLS. *The Rising Sun: Or the Antecedents and Advancement of the Colored Race.* Boston: A. G. Brown & Co., 1874.
COMMONS, JOHN R. *Races and Immigrants in America.* New York: Macmillan, 1924.
COUCH, W T. (ed.). *Culture in the South.* Chapel Hill, N.C.: University of North Carolina Press, 1934.
GILLIN, JOHN L. *Criminology and Penology.* New York: Century Co., 1926.
JENNINGS, WALTER W. *A History of Economic Progress in the United States.* New York: Crowell, 1926.
KELSEY, CARL. *The Physical Basis of Society.* New York: Appleton, 1928.
KING, GRACE. *New Orleans, the Place and the People.* New York: Macmillan, 1895.
LIPPINCOTT, ISAAC. *Economic Development of the United States.* New York: Appleton, 1930.

MOORE, JOHN TROTWOOD, and FOSTER, AUSTIN P. *Tennessee, the Volunteer State; 1769–1923.* 3 vols. Chicago.: S J. Clark Publishing Co., 1923.

PARK, ROBERT, and BURGESS, ERNEST W. *Introduction to the Science of Sociology.* 2d ed. Chicago: University of Chicago Press, 1926.

RHODES, JAMES FORD. *History of the United States from the Compromise of 1850,* Vol. I: *1850–1854.* New York: Macmillan, 1902.

SIMONS, A. M. *Social Forces in American History.* New York: Macmillan, 1925.

SUTHERLAND, EDWIN H. *Criminology.* Philadelphia: Lippincott, 1924.

THOMAS, WILLIAM HANNIBAL. *The American Negro: What He Was, What He Is, and What He May Become.* New York: Macmillan, 1901.

THOMPSON, HOLLAND. *The New South: A Chronicle of Social and Industrial Evolution.* ("Chronicles of America," Vol. XLII.) New Haven: Yale University Press, 1921.

WHITBECK, RAY H., and THOMAS, OLIVE J. *The Geographic Factor: Its Role in Life and Civilization.* New York: Century Co., 1932.

WILLIAMS, GEORGE WASHINGTON *A History of the Negro Race in America.* New York: Publisher unknown, 1882.

WILSON, WOODROW. *A History of the American People.* 5 vols. New York: Harper & Bros., 1902.

WOODSON, CARTER G. *The Negro in Our History.* Washington: Associated Publishers, 1927.

SPECIAL STUDIES

BANCROFT, HUBERT H. *Popular Tribunals,* Vol. XXXVI: *The Works of Hubert H. Bancroft.* San Francisco: History Co., 1887.

BELL, WILLIAM A. "Missions and Co-operation of the Methodist Episcopal Church, South, with the Colored Methodist Episcopal Church" (mimeographed). Nashville: Board of Missions, M.E. Church, South, 1933.

CASON, CLARENCE E. "Middle Class and Bourbon," in *Culture in the South.* Chapel Hill, N.C.: University of North Carolina Press, 1934.

DOYLE, BERTRAM W. "Racial Traits of Negroes as They Assign Traits to Themselves." M.A. thesis, University of Chicago, 1924.

DUNNING, WILLIAM ARCHIBALD. *Studies in Southern History and Politics.* (Inscribed to him by his former pupils and students.) New York: Columbia University Press, 1914.

LEE, E. FRANKLIN. *Social Solidarity and Race Inequalities in the South.* Ph.D. dissertation, Columbia University, 1911. Privately printed.

NORDHOFF, CHARLES. *The Communistic Societies of the United States.* New York: Harper & Bros., 1875.

PARK, ROBERT E. "Negro Home Life and Standards of Living," *Annals of the American Academy of Political and Social Science,* XLIX (1913), 147–63.

———. "Racial Assimilation in Secondary Groups with Especial Reference to the Negro," *American Journal of Sociology,* XIX, No. 5 (1913–14), 606–23.

PARK, ROBERT E., and BURGESS, ERNEST W. *The City*. Chicago: University of Chicago Press, 1925.

PORTER, KIRK H. *A History of Suffrage in the United States*. Chicago: University of Chicago Press, 1918.

REUTER, EDWARD BYRON. *The American Race Problem*. New York: Crowell, 1927.

———. *The Mulatto in the United States; Including a Study of the Role of Mixed-Blood Races throughout the World*. Boston: Badger, 1918.

———. *Race Mixture: Studies in Intermarriage and Miscegenation*. New York: McGraw-Hill, 1931.

STEPHENSON, GILBERT T. *Racial Distinctions in American Law*. New York: Appleton, 1910.

STONE, ALFRED H. "Is Race Friction between Blacks and Whites in the United States Growing and Inevitable?" *American Journal of Sociology*, XIII, No. 5 (1907–8), 677–96.

ESSAYS, CONTROVERSIES, AND REVIEWS

BAILEY, THOMAS PEARCE. *Racial Orthodoxy in the South; and Other Aspects of the Negro Question*. New York: Neale Publishing Co., 1914.

CRAVEN, AVERY O. "The South in American History," *Historical Outlook*, XXI, No. 3 (1930), 105–9.

DuBOIS, W. E. BURGHARDT. *Souls of Black Folk; Essays and Sketches*. Chicago: A. C. McClurg, 1903.

KIRBYE, J. EDWARD. *Puritanism in the South*. Boston: Pilgrim Press, 1908.

STONE, ALFRED H. "Recent Race Problem Literature" (review) *Southern History Association Publications*, VIII (1904), 451.

THE PERIOD OF SLAVERY

STATISTICAL AND DOCUMENTARY SOURCES

American Annual Encyclopedia, and Register of Important Events (1861–1902), Vol. VI. New York: Appleton, 1866.

CALLENDER, GUY STEVENS. *Selections from the Economic History of the United States, 1765–1860*. Boston: Ginn & Co., 1909.

CATTERALL, HELEN TUNNICLIFF. *Judicial Cases concerning American Slavery and the Negro*. 2 vols. Washington: Carnegie Institution, 1926.

DeBow, J. D. B. *Statistical Review of the United States; Being a Compendium of the Seventh Census*. Washington: O. P. Nicholson, 1854.

DUMOND, DWIGHT LOWELL. *Southern Editorials on Secession*. New York: Century Co., 1931.

KENNEDY, JOSEPH C. G. *The Eighth Census of the United States, Agriculture*. Washington: Government Printing Office, 1864.

NEVINS, ALLAN (ed.). *American History as Recorded by British Travellers*. New York: Henry Holt, 1923.

PHILLIPS, ULRICH B., and GLUNT, JAMES D. *Florida Plantation Records: From the Papers of George Noble Jones.* St. Louis: Publications of the Missouri Historical Society, 1927.

STROUD, GEORGE MCDOWELL. *A Sketch of the Laws Relating to Slavery in the Several States.* Philadelphia: Kimber & Sharpless, 1827.

WHEELER, JACOB D. *A Practical Treatise on the Laws of Slavery.* New York: A. Pollock, 1837.

WOODBURY, LEVI (secretary of the treasury). *House Documents,* No. 146. 24th Congress, 1st session, 1836.

WOODSON, CARTER G. *The Mind of the Negro as Reflected in Letters during the Crisis, 1800–1860.* Washington: Associated Publishers, 1926.

JOURNALS, DIARIES, LETTERS OF TRAVELERS
MEMOIRS, AND REMINISCENCES

ADAMS, NEHEMIAH. *A South-Side View of Slavery.* Boston: Marvin & Mussey, 1854.

AVIRETT, JAMES BATTLE. *The Old Plantation: How We Lived in the Great House and Cabin before the War.* New York: F. T. Neeley, 1901.

BREMER, FREDERIKA. *Homes in the New World.* 2 vols. New York: Harper & Bros., 1853.

[BROWN, DAVID.] *The Planter: Or, Thirteen Years in the South.* Philadelphia: H. Hooker, 1853.

BUCKINGHAM, J. S. *The Slave States of America.* 2 vols. London: Fisher & Son, 1842.

CHESTNUT, MARY BOYKIN. *A Diary from Dixie.* New York: Appleton, 1905.

CLAYTON, VICTORIA V. *White and Black under the Old Regime.* Milwaukee: Young Churchman Co., 1899.

CREVECOEUR, ST. JOHN DE. *Sketches of Eighteenth Century America; More Letters from an American Farmer.* Ed. HENRI L. BOURDIN, RALPH H. GABRIEL, AND STANLEY WILLIAMS. New Haven: Yale University Press, 1925.

DAVIS, VARINA. *Jefferson Davis, Ex-president of the Confederate States.* 2 vols. New York: Belford & Co., 1890.

DETOCQUEVILLE, ALEXIS. *Democracy in America.* Edited by FRANCIS BOWEN. 2 vols. Boston: John Allyn, 1876.

DOUGLASS, FREDERICK. *My Bondage and Freedom.* New York: Miller, Orton & Mulligan, 1855.

FEATHERSTONEHAUGH, G. W. *Excursion through the Slave States; from Washington on the Potomac to the Frontier of Mexico, with Sketches of Popular Manners and Geological Notes.* New York: Harper & Bros., 1844.

FERGUSON, WILLIAM. *America by River and Rail.* London: Nisbet & Co., 1856.

FITZPATRIC, JOHN C. *The Diaries of George Washington.* 4 vols. Boston: Houghton Mifflin, 1925.

FLEMING, WALTER L. "Home Life in Alabama during the Civil War," *Publications of the Southern History Association*, VIII, No. 2 (1904), 81–103.
HALL, BASIL. *Travels in North America in the Years 1827 and 1828.* 3 vols. Edinburgh, 1829.
HALL, MARSHALL. *The Two-Fold Slavery of the United States; with a Project of Self-Emancipation.* London: Adam Scott, 1854.
HIGGINSON, THOMAS WENTWORTH. *Army Life in a Black Regiment.* Boston: Fields & Osgood, 1870.
———. *Travellers and Outlaws.* Boston: Lee & Shephard, 1889.
HUNDLEY, D. R. *Social Relations in Our Southern States.* New York: H. B. Price, 1860.
JEFFERSON, THOMAS. *Notes on the State of Virginia; with an Appendix Relative to the Murder of Logan's Family.* Trenton, N.J.: Wilson & Blackwell, 1803.
KEMBLE, FRANCES ANNE. *A Journal of Residence on a Georgia Plantation in 1838–1839.* New York: Harper & Bros., 1863.
LONG, JOHN DIXON. *Pictures of Slavery in Church and State.* Philadelphia: Privately printed, 1857.
LYELL, CHARLES. *A Second Visit to the United States of North America.* 2 vols. New York, 1849.
McDONALD, JAMES J. *Life in Old Virginia.* Ed. J. A. C. CHANDLER. Norfolk, Va.: Old Virginia Publishing Co., 1907.
MARRYAT, C. B. *A Diary in America; with Remarks on Its Institutions.* Paris: Crepelet, 1839.
MARTINEAU, HARRIET. *Society in America.* 2 vols. New York: Saunders & Otley, 1837.
MELISH, JOHN. *Travels in the United States of America, in the Years 1806 and 1807 and 1809, 1810, and 1811; Including an Account of Passages between America and Britain, and Travels through Various Parts of Great Britain, Ireland and Upper Canada.* Philadelphia, 1812.
NASON, D. (a citizen of Cambridgeport). *Journal of a Tour from Boston to Savannah.* Cambridge: Privately published, 1849.
A NORTHERN MAN. *The Planter or Thirteen Years in the South.* Philadelphia: H. Hooker, 1853. *See* David Brown.
OLMSTED, FREDERICK LAW. *The Cotton Kingdom; a Traveler's Observations on Cotton and Slavery in the American Southern States.* 2 vols. New York: Mason Bros., 1861.
———. *A Journey in the Back Country; in the Winter of 1853–1854.* New York: Mason Bros., 1860.
———. *A Journey through the Seaboard Slave States; with Remarks on Their Economy.* 2 vols. New York: Dix & Edwards, 1856.
———. *A Journey through Texas; or a Saddle-Trip on the Southwestern Frontier.* New York: Dix & Edwards, 1857.
OWEN, NICHOLAS. *Journal of a Slave-Dealer—a View of Some Remarkable Axcedents in the Life of Nics. Owen on the Coast of Africa and America from the Year 1746 to the Year 1757.* Ed. EVELINE MARTIN. London: Routledge & Son, 1930.

PARSONS, C. G. *An Inside View of Slavery; or a Tour among the Planters.* Boston: J. P. Jewett, 1855.
PEARSON, ELIZABETH WARE (ed.). *Letters from Port Royal; Written at the Time of the Civil War.* Boston: W. B. Clarke, 1906.
REDPATH, JAMES. *The Roving Editor: Or Talks with Slaves in the Southern States.* New York: A. B. Burdick, 1859.
ROYALL, ANNE. *Mrs. Royall's Southern Tour, or Second Series of the Black Book.* 3 vols. Washington: Privately printed, 1830, 1831.
RUFFIN, EDWARD. "Extracts from the Diary of Edward Ruffin, on the Conduct of Negroes during the War, 1861–1865," *William and Mary Quarterly,* XXIII (1913), 258–63.
RUSSELL, WILLIAM H. *My Diary, North and South.* Boston: Burnham, 1863.
SINGLETON, ARTHUR. *Letters from the South and West.* Boston: Richardson & Lord, 1824.
SMYTH, J. F. D. *A Tour in the United States of America.* 2 vols. London, 1784.
SRYGLEY, F. D. *Seventy Years in Dixie: Recollections, Sermons, and Sayings of T. W. Caskey and Others.* Nashville: Gospel Advocate Co., 1891.
STIRLING, JAMES. *Letters from the Slave States.* London: Parker & Sons, 1857.
WASHINGTON, BOOKER T. *Up from Slavery.* New York: A. L. Burt Co., 1901.
WORTLEY, LADY EMMELINE. *Travels in the United States during 1849–1850.* New York: Harper & Bros., 1851.
WRIGHT, MRS. D. GIRAUD. *A Southern Girl in '61; the War-Time Memories of a Confederate Senator's Daughter.* New York: Doubleday, Page, 1905.

SLAVE AUTOBIOGRAPHIES

BALL, CHARLES. *Slavery in the United States: A Narrative of the Life and Adventures of Charles Ball, a Black Man.* Lewiston, Pa.: John Shugert, 1836.
BROWN, JOHN. *Slave Life in Georgia: A Narrative of the Life, Sufferings, and Escape of John Brown, a Fugitive Slave.* London: Chamerovzow, 1855.
CLARKE, LEWIS AND MILTON. *Narratives of the Sufferings of Lewis and Milton Clarke; Sons of a Soldier of the Revolution, during a Captivity of More than Twenty Years among the Slaveholders of Kentucky, One of the So-called Christian States of North America. Dictated by Themselves to J. C. Lovejoy.* Boston: Bela Marsh, 1846.
DAVIS, NOAH. *Narrative of a Colored Man.* Baltimore: J. F. Weishampel, 1859.
DOUGLASS, FREDERICK. *Narrative of the Life of Frederick Douglass, an American Slave; Written by Himself.* Boston: Anti-Slavery Office, 1849.
LOGUEN, J. W. *As a Slave and as a Freeman: A Narrative of Real Life.* Syracuse, N.Y.: J. G. K. Truair, 1859.
NORTHUP, SOLOMON. *Twelve Years a Slave: Narrative of Solomon Northup, a Citizen of New York: Kidnapped in Washington City in 1841 and Rescued from a Cotton Plantation near the Red River in Louisiana, in 1853.* Auburn, N.Y.: Derby & Miller, 1853.
STEWARD, AUSTIN. *Twenty-two Years a Slave, and Forty Years a Freeman.* Rochester, N.Y.: William Alling, 1857.

IMPRESSIONISTIC MEMOIRS, FICTION, NOVELS

ADAMS, F. C. *Manuel Pereira: Or the Sovereign State of South Carolina.* Washington: Buell & Blanchard, 1853.

MacCORKLE, W. ALEXANDER. *White Sulphur Springs.* New York: Neale Publishing Co., 1916.

ARMSTRONG, ORLAND KAY. *Old Massa's People.* Indianapolis: Bobbs-Merrill Co., 1931.

HARRISON, W. S. *Sam Williams: A Tale of the Old South.* Nashville: Barbee & Smith, 1894.

INGRAHAM, JOSEPH HOLT. *The Sunny South: Or the Southerner at Home.* Philadelphia: C. G. Evans, 1860.

ROBERTS, ELIZABETH MADOX. *The Green Meadow.* New York: Literary Guild, 1930.

WARNER, CHARLES DUDLEY. *Their Pilgrimage.* New York: Harper & Bros., 1886.

SECONDARY AUTHORITIES

HISTORIES, GENERAL STUDIES, ETC.

ABERNETHY, THOMAS PERKINS. *From Frontier to Plantation in Tennessee: A Study in Frontier Democracy.* Chapel Hill, N.C.: University of North North Carolina Press, 1932.

ADAMS, JAMES TRUSLOW. *Provincial Society, 1690–1763.* ("History of American Life Series," Vol. III.) New York: Macmillan, 1928.

ANDREWS, CHARLES M. *Colonial Folkways: A Chronicle of American Life in the Reign of the Georges.* ("Chronicles of America" series, Vol. IX.) New Haven: Yale University Press, 1921.

FISKE, JOHN. *Old Virginia and Her Neighbours.* 2 vols. Boston: Houghton Mifflin, 1901.

GAYARRÉ, CHARLES. *History of Louisiana: The French Domination.* 2 vols. New York: William Widdleton, 1866.

GOODELL, WILLIAM. *Slavery and Anti-slavery: A History of the Great Question in Both Hemispheres, with a View of the Slavery in the United States.* New York, Privately published, 1855.

HART, ALBERT BUSHNELL. *The American Nation: A History,* Vol. XVI: *Slavery and Abolition, 1831–1841.* New York: Harper & Bros., 1906.

INGLE, EDWARD. *Southern Sidelights: A Picture of Social and Economic Life in the South, a Generation before the War.* New York: Crowell, 1896.

JERNEGAN, MARCUS WILSON. *The American Colonies, 1492–1750: A Study of Their Economic and Social Development.* ("Epochs of American History" series.) New York: Longmans, Green, 1929.

NIEBOER, H. J. *Slavery as an Industrial System.* The Hague: Martinus Nijhoff, 1910.

PAXSON, FREDERIC L. *History of the American Frontier, 1763–1793.* Boston: Houghton Mifflin, 1924.

PHILLIPS, ULRICH BONNELL. *American Negro Slavery.* New York: Appleton, 1918.
————. *Life and Labor in the Old South.* Boston: Little, Brown, 1929.
————. *The South in the Building of the Nation,* Vol. IV: *Racial Problems, Adjustments, and Disturbances.* Richmond, Va.: Southern Publication Society, 1909.
TURNER, NAT. "Nat Turner's Insurrection," *Atlantic Monthly,* VIII, No. 46 (August, 1861), 173–87.
VESEY, DENMARK. "Denmark Vesey," *Atlantic Monthly,* VII, No. 44 (June, 1861), 728–44.
WASHINGTON, BOOKER T. *The Story of the Negro.* 2 vols. New York: Doubleday, Page, 1909.
WERTENBAKER, THOMAS J. *History of American Life,* Vol. II: *The First Americans: 1607–1690.* New York: Macmillan, 1929.

SPECIAL STUDIES

BALLAGH, JAMES CURTIS. *A History of Slavery in Virginia.* Baltimore: Johns Hopkins University Press, 1902.
BANCROFT, FREDERIC. *Slave-trading in the Old South.* Baltimore: J. H. Furst, 1931.
BASSETT, JOHN SPENCER. *Slavery and Servitude in the Colony of North Carolina.* ("Johns Hopkins University Studies in Political Science," Ser. XIV, Nos. 4–5.) Baltimore: Johns Hopkins University Press, 1896.
————. *Slavery in the State of North Carolina.* ("Johns Hopkins University Studies in Political Science," Ser. XVII, Nos. 7–8.) Baltimore: Johns Hopkins University Press, 1899.
————. *The Southern Plantation Overseer; as Revealed in His Letters.* (Smith College Fiftieth Anniversary Publication.) Northampton, Mass.: Smith College, 1925.
BIRNIE, C. W. "The Education of the Negro in Charleston, South Carolina, before the Civil War," *Journal of Negro History,* XII (January, 1927), 13–21.
BLACKNALL, O. W. (DAVID DODGE, pseudonym). "Free Negroes of North Carolina," *Atlantic Monthly,* LVII (January, 1886), 20–30.
BOYD, MINNIE CLAIRE. *Alabama in the Fifties: A Social Study.* ("Columbia University Studies in History, Economics, and Public Law," No. 353.) New York, 1931. Author's copyright.
BRACKETT, JEFFERY R. *The Negro in Maryland.* ("Johns Hopkins University Studies.") Baltimore: N. Murray, 1889.
BRUCE, PHILLIP ALEXANDER. *An Economic History of Virginia in the Seventeenth Century: An Inquiry into the Material Condition of the People Based on Original and Contemporary Records.* 2 vols. New York: Macmillan, 1896.
————. *Institutional History of Virginia in the Seventeenth Century.* 2 vols. New York: G. P. Putnam's Sons, 1910.

CURLEE, ABIGAIL. "The History of a Texas Slave Plantation, 1832–1863," *Southwestern Historical Quarterly*, XXVI, 79–127. (Also reprinted in E. C. BARKER, *Texas History*. Dallas: Southwest Press, 1929.)

DREWRY, WILLIAM SIDNEY. *Slave Insurrections in Virginia*. (Ph.D. Dissertation, Johns Hopkins University.) Washington: Neale Publishing Co., 1900.

DuBOIS, WILLIAM E. B. *The Suppression of the Slave Trade to the United States of America, 1638–1870*. New York: Longmans, Green, 1904.

DYER, G. W. *Democracy in the South before the Civil War*. Nashville: M.E. South Publishing Co., 1905.

EVJEN, JOHN. *Scandinavian Immigrants in New York, 1630–1674*. Minneapolis: K. C. Holter, 1916.

FLANDERS, RALPH BETTS. *Plantation Slavery in Georgia*. Chapel Hill, N.C.: University of North Carolina Press, 1933.

———. "The Free Negro in Ante-bellum Georgia," *North Carolina Historical Review*, IX, No. 3 (July, 1932), 250–72.

GAINES, FRANCIS PENDLETON. *The Southern Plantation*. New York: Columbia University Press, 1925.

GEWEHR, WESLEY M. *The Great Aawkening in Virginia, 1740–1790*. Durham, N.C.: Duke University Press, 1930.

JACKSON, LUTHER P. "Negro Religious Development in Virginia," *Journal of Negro History*, XVI, No. 2 (April, 1931), 168–239.

JOHNSON, FRANKLIN. *The Development of State Legislation concerning the Free Negro*. New York: Arbor Press, 1918.

JOHNSON, GUION GRIFFIS. *A Social History of the Sea Islands*. Chapel Hill, N.C.: University of North Carolina Press, 1930.

JOHNSTON, JAMES HUGO. "The Participation of White Men in Virginia in Negro Insurrections," *Journal of History*, XVI, No. 2 (April, 1931), 158–67.

LIVERMORE, GEORGE. *Historical Research Respecting the Opinions of the Founders of the Republic on Negroes as Slaves, as Citizens, and as Soldiers*. Boston: Wilson & Son, 1862.

MUMFORD, BEVERLEY B. *Virginia's Attitude toward Slavery and Secession*. New York: Longmans, Green, 1909.

PATTERSON, CALEB PERRY. *The Negro in Tennessee, 1790–1865*. (University of Texas Bull. 2205 [February, 1922]) Austin, Tex., 1922. Author's copyright.

PHILLIPS, ULRICH BONNELL. *A History of Transportation in the Eastern Cotton Belt to 1860*. New York: Columbia University Press, 1908.

———. "The Origin and Growth of the Southern Black Belts," *American Historical Review*, XI (July, 1906), 798–816.

———. "Slave Crime in Virginia," *American Historical Review*, XX (January, 1915), 336–40.

RUSSELL, JOHN HENDERSON. *The Free Negro in Virginia, 1619–1865*. Baltimore: Johns Hopkins University Press, 1913.

SCOTT, ARTHUR P. *Criminal Law in Colonial Virginia*. Chicago: University of Chicago Press, 1930.

SHANKS, CAROLINE E. "The Biblical Anti-slavery Argument of the Decade 1830–1840," *Journal of Negro History*, XVI, No. 2 (April, 1931), 132–57.
STARKE, W. PINCKNEY. "Account of John C. Calhoun's Early Life" (abridged from the manuscript), *Report of the American Historical Association*, Vol. II (1899).
TUCKER, ST. GEORGE. *A Dissertation on Slavery; with a Proposal for the Gradual Abolition of It in the State of Virginia*. Philadelphia: Matthew Carey, 1796. 2d ed. New York, 1861.
VANCE, WILLIAM REYNOLDS. *Slavery in Kentucky*. Ph.D. dissertation, Washington and Lee University: Privately printed, 1895.
WERTENBAKER, THOMAS J. *The Planters of Colonial Virginia*. Princeton, N.J.: Princeton University, 1922.
WHITFIELD, THEODORE M. *Slavery Agitation in Virginia, 1829–1832*. Baltimore: Johns Hopkins University Press, 1930.
WOODSON, CARTER G. "Beginnings of the Miscegenation of the Whites and Blacks," *Journal of Negro History*, III (October, 1918), 335–53.
———. *The Education of the Negro prior to 1861: A History of the Education of the Colored People of the United States from the Beginning of Slavery to the Civil War*. New York: G. P. Putnam's Sons, 1915.
———. *Free Negro Heads of Families in the United States in 1830*. Washington: Associated Publishers, 1925.
WRIGHT, JAMES M. *The Free Negro in Maryland*. ("Columbia University Studies in History, Economics, and Public Law," Vol. XCVII, No. 3, Whole No. 222.) New York: Columbia University Press, 1921. Author's copyright.

ESSAYS IN PROPAGANDA AND CONTROVERSY

BOOKS

BLEDSOE, ALBERT TAYLOR. *Liberty and Slavery*. Philadelphia: Lippincott, 1857.
FITZHUGH, GEORGE. *Sociology for the South: Or the Failure of Free Society*. Richmond, Va.: A. Morris, 1854.
GOODELL, WILLIAM. *The American Slave Code*. New York: American and Foreign Anti-Slavery Society, 1853.
HAMMOND, JAMES H. "Letters on Slavery," in the *Pro-slavery Argument*. Charleston, S.C.: Walker Richards Co., 1852.
HARPER, CHANCELLOR, *Memoir on Slavery*. (Read before the Society for the Advancement of Learning, Columbia, S.C., 1837.) Charleston, S.C.: James S. Burgess, 1838.
HARPER, CHANCELLOR, et al. *The Pro-slavery Argument*. Charleston, S.C.: Walker Richards Co., 1852.
HELPER, HINTON. *The Impending Crisis*. New York: A. B. Burdick, 1859.
McTYEIRE, H. N., STURGIS, C. F., and HOLMES, A. T., REVS. *Duties of Masters to Servants: Three Premium Essays*. Charleston, S.C.: Southern Baptist Publishing Society, 1851.

MAYO, REV. A. C. "The Third Estate of the South," *New England Magazine*, November, 1890, pp. 299–311.

OZANNE, REV. T. D. *The South as It Is: Or Twenty-one Years' Experience in the Southern States.* London: Saunders & Otley, 1863.

PAGE, THOMAS NELSON. *The Old South: Essays Social and Political.* New York: Scribner's, 1892.

POLLARD, EDWARD A. (signer of Preface). *The Southern Spy: Or Curiosities of Negro Slavery in the South.* Washington: Henry Polkinhorn, 1859.

SEABURY, SAMUEL. *American Slavery Distinguished from the Slavery of British Theorists, etc.* New York: Mason Bros., 1861.

STUDENTS OF A VIRGINIA COLLEGE. *Studies of the old South.* (A collection of essays to which have been awarded the George W. Bagby Prize.) Hampden-Sidney College, 1916.

WALKER, DAVID. *Walker's Appeal; with a Brief Sketch.* New York: J. H. Tobitt, 1848.

PAMPHLETS

ALLEN, REV. HEMAN H. *The General Assembly and Its Accusers: Being a Compilation from Official Records of the Deliverances of the Church (Presbyterian) on Civil Affairs and Slavery.* Louisville: Hill & Bros., 1867.

ARIEL (pseudonym). *See* Buckner H. Payne.

BLANCHARD, REV. J. *Sermon on Slave-Holding.* (Preached at Mount Pleasant, Ohio, October 20, 1841.) Cincinnati, Privately printed, 1842.

BROWN, WILLIAM W. *A Lecture Delivered before the Female Anti-Slavery Society of Salem, at Lyceum Hall, November 14, 1847.* Boston: Anti-Slavery Society, 1847.

CAMPBELL, A. (of Bethany, Va.). *A Tract for the People of Kentucky*, Louisville: Courier Office, n.d.

CHANNING, WILLIAM E. *Letter to the Honorable Henry Clay on the Annexation of Texas to the United States. S.l.:* Privately printed, 1837.

CHILD, LYDIA MARIE (or MARIA). *Anti-slavery Catechism.* Newburyport, Mass.: C. Whipple, 1836.

A CITIZEN. *See* Benjamin Lundy.

COLLINS, ROBERT (of Macon, Ga.). *An Essay on the Management of Slaves.* Boston: Eastburn's Press, 1852.

HOSS, REV. E. E. *Elihu Embree, Abolitionist.* ("Publications of Vanderbilt Southern Historical Society," No. 2.) Nashville: Vanderbilt University, 1897.

(LUNDY, BENJAMIN.) *A Citizen of the United States. The War in Texas: A Review of Facts and Circumstances Showing That This Is a War against Mexico . . . . and To Perpetuate Slavery.* Philadelphia: Merrihew & Gunn, 1837.

PALFREY, JOHN G. *Papers on the Slave Power.* (First published in the *Boston Whig.*) Boston: Merrill & Cobb, 1846.

PAYNE, BUCKNER H. (ARIEL, pseudonym). *The Negro: What Is His Ethnological Status?* Cincinnati: 1867. Privately published.

POWELL, THE HONORABLE L. W. *Speech on the Bill—"To Confiscate the Property and Free the Slaves of the Rebels," United States Senate, April 16, 1862.* Washington: L. Towers, 1862.

QUINN, DAVID. *Petition and Memorial of David Quinn Addressed to the United States Congress Asking for Re-establishment of Slavery in the United States.* Chicago, 1866 (No publisher).

SEA, MRS. SOPHIE FOX. *Slavery in the United States: A Brief Synoptical Review.* Louisville: A. S. Johnston Chapter of the U.D.C. (n.d.).

SEDGWICK, THEODORE. *Thoughts on the Proposed Annexation of Texas.* New York: D. Fanshaw, 1844.

WILSON, REV. JOSHUA LACY. *Relation and Duties of Servants and Masters.* (Two sermons.) Cincinnati: Isaac Hefley, 1839.

THE PERIOD OF RECONSTRUCTION

DOCUMENTARY AND LEGAL SOURCES

FLEMING, WALTER L. *A Documentary History of the Reconstruction.* 2 vols. Cleveland: Arthur Clarke, 1907.

———. *Laws Relating to Freedmen, 1865–1866.* Morgantown, W.Va.: West Virginia University, 1904.

Joint Committee on Reconstruction, The Report of. See United States Congress.

UNITED STATES CONGRESS. *The Report of the Joint Committee on Reconstruction.* (39th Cong., 1st sess.) Washington: Government Printing Office, 1866.

JOURNALS, DIARIES, LETTERS OF TRAVELERS
MEMOIRS, AND REMINISCENCES

CAMPBELL, (SIR) GEORGE. *White and Black: Outcome of a Trip to the United States.* London: Chatto & Windus, 1879.

CLAYTON, POWELL. *The Aftermath of the Civil War in Arkansas.* New York: Neale Publishing Co., 1915.

DICEY, EDWARD. *Six Months in the Federal States, in 1862.* 2 vols. London: Macmillan, 1863.

FERGUSON, ROBERT. *America—during and after the War.* London: Longmans, Green, 1866.

KING, EDWARD. *The Great South.* Hartford, Conn.: American Publishing Co., 1875.

LATHAM, HENRY. *Black and White: A Journal of a Three Month's Tour in the United States.* London: Macmillan, 1867.

MACRAE, DAVID. *Americans at Home.* 2 vols. Edinburgh: Edmondston & Douglas, 1870.

NORDHOFF, CHARLES. *The Cotton States in the Spring, and Summer of 1875.* New York: Appleton, 1876.

REID, WHITELAW. *After the War: A Southern Tour from May, 1865, to May, 1866.* London: Lampson, Lowe & Morriston, 1866.

SOMERS, ROBERT. *The Southern States since the War.* New York: Macmillan, 1871.

TROWBRIDGE, J. T. *A Picture of the Desolated States and the Work of Restoration, 1865–1868.* Hartford: L. Stebbins, 1868.

ZINCKE, F. BARHAM. *Last Winter in the United States.* London: John Murray, 1868.

SECONDARY AUTHORITIES

GENERAL

BROWN, WILLIAM GARROTT. *The Lower South in American History.* New York: Macmillan, 1902.

DUNNING, WILLIAM A. *The American Nation: A History,* Vol. XXII: *Reconstruction: Political and Economic.* New York: Harper & Bros., 1907.

FLEMING, WALTER LYNWOOD. *The Sequel of Appomattox: A Chronicle of the Re-union of the States.* ("Chronicles of America series," Vol. XXXII.) New Haven: Yale University Press, 1921.

SPECIAL

McCONNELL, JOHN PRESTON. *Negroes and Their Treatment in Virginia from 1865 to 1867.* Pulaski, Va.: B. D. Smith & Bros., 1910.

PIKE, JAMES S. *The Prostrate State: South Carolina under Negro Government.* New York: Appleton, 1874.

RAMSDELL, CHARLES WILLIAM. *Reconstruction in Texas.* ("Columbia University Studies in History, Economics, and Public Law," Vol. XXXVI, No. 1.) New York: Columbia University Press, 1910. Author's copyright.

SIMKINS, FRANCIS BUTLER, and WOODY, ROBERT HILLIARD. *South Carolina during Reconstruction.* Chapel Hill, N.C.: University of North Carolina Press, 1932.

STAPLES, THOMAS S. *Reconstruction in Arkansas; 1862–1874.* ("Columbia University Studies in History, Economics, and Public Law," Vol. CIX, Whole No. 245.) New York: Columbia University Press, 1923. Author's copyright.

TAYLOR, ALRUTHEUS A. *The Negro in the Reconstruction of Virginia.* Washington: Associated Publishers, 1926.

———. *The Negro in South Carolina during the Reconstruction.* Washington: Associated Publishers, 1924.

WALLACE, JOHN. *Carpet-Bag Rule in Florida.* Jacksonville, Fla.: Da Costa Co., 1888.

WOOLLEY, EDWIN C. *The Reconstruction of Georgia.* ("Columbia University Studies in History, Economics, and Public Law," Vol. XIII, No. 3.) New York: Columbia University Press, 1901. Author's copyright.

THE PERIOD SINCE RECONSTRUCTION—
OR THE MODERN PERIOD

DOCUMENTARY SOURCES

Documents from persons living in—Birmingham, Eufaula, Huntsville, Selma, Alabama; Fort Smith, Arkansas; Savannah, Brunswick, Georgia; Georgetown, Owensboro, Kentucky; Oklahoma City, Oklahoma; Charleston, South Carolina; Chattanooga, Gibson County, Memphis, Nashville, Tennessee; Dallas, Fort Worth, Texarkana, Texas.

RECORDS OF TRAVELS AND OBSERVATION

BAKER, RAY STANNARD. *Following the Color Line: An Account of Negro Citizenship in the American Democracy.* New York: Doubleday, Page, 1908.

EVANS, MAURICE S. *Black and White in the Southern States.* London: Longmans, Green, 1915

JOHNSON, CLIFTON. *Highways and Byways of the South.* New York: Macmillan, 1895.

MOTON, ROBERT RUSSA. *What the Negro Thinks.* Garden City, N.Y.: Doubleday, Doran, 1929.

RALPH, JULIAN. *Dixie: Or Other Southern Scenes and Sketches.* New York: Harper & Bros., 1895

SECONDARY AUTHORITIES—SPECIAL STUDIES

BROUGH, CHARLES HILLMAN. "Work of the Commission of Southern Universities on the Race Question," *Annals of the American Academy of Political and Social Science,* XLIX (September, 1913), 47–57.

BRUNNER, EDMUND DES. *Immigrant Farmers and Their Children.* Garden City, N.Y.: Doubleday, Doran, 1929.

BURGESS, ERNEST WATSON. "Residential Segregation in American Cities," *Annals of the American Academy of Political and Social Science,* CXL (November, 1928), 105–14.

DETWEILER, FREDERICK G. "The Rise of Modern Race Antagonisms," *American Journal of Sociology,* XXXVII, No. 5 (March, 1932), 738–47.

DuBOIS, W. E. BURGHARDT. *The Philadelphia Negro: A Social Study.* ("Publications of the University of Pennsylvania, Series in Political Economy and Public Law," Vol. XIV.) Philadelphia: University of Pennsylvania, 1899.

EDWARDS, PAUL K. *The Southern Urban Negro as a Consumer.* New York: Prentice-Hall, 1932.

FISHER, ISAAC. "Black and White in Certain Parts of West Africa," *Annals of the American Academy of Political and Social Science.* CXXXX (November, 1928), 319–30.

HOLMES, GEORGE K. "The Peons of the South," *Annals of the American Academy of Political and Social Science,* IV (September, 1893), 265–74.

JOHNSON, JAMES W., and SELIGMANN, HERBERT. "Legal Aspects of the Negro Problem," *Annals of the American Academy of Political and Social Science,* CXXXX (November, 1928), 90–97.

MILLER, KELLY. "Government and the Negro," *Annals of the American Academy of Political and Social Science,* CXXXX (November, 1928), 98–104.

NEGRO WELFARE SURVEY COMMITTEE, THE REPORT OF. *The Negro in Richmond, Virginia.* Richmond: Council of Social Agencies, 1929.

REID, IRA DEA. *Negro Membership in American Labor Unions.* New York: National Urban League, 1930.

WEATHERFORD, W. D. "Race Relationship in the South," *Annals of the American Academy of Political and Social Science,* XLIX (September, 1913), pp. 164–72.

WOODSON, CARTER G. *The Rural Negro.* Washington: Associated Publishers, 1930.

WOOFTER, T. J. *Negro Problems in Cities.* Garden City, N.Y.: Doubleday, Doran, 1928.

YOUNG, DONALD. *American Minority Peoples: A Study in Racial and Cultural Conflicts in the United States.* New York: Harper & Bros., 1932.

ESSAYS AND ARTICLES OF OPINION AND CONTROVERSY

BOOKS

LOCKE, ALAIN LEROY (ed.). *The New Negro.* New York: A. & C. Boni, 1925.

MILLER, KELLY. *Race Adjustment: Essays on the Negro in America.* Washington: Neale Publishing Co., 1908.

MURPHY, EDGAR GARDNER. *Problems of the Present South.* New York: Macmillan, 1905.

TANNENBAUM, FRANK. *Darker Phases of the South.* New York: G. P. Putnam Son's, 1924.

TILLINGHAST, JOSEPH ALEXANDER. *The Negro in Africa and America.* Published for the American Economic Association. New York: Macmillan, 1902.

WASHINGTON, BOOKER T., and DUBOIS, W. E. B. *The Negro in the South: His Economic Progress in Relation to His Moral and Religious Development.* Philadelphia: George Jacobs, 1907.

NEWSPAPERS AND MAGAZINES

BOND, HORACE MANN. "A Negro Looks at His South," *Harper's,* CLXIII (June, 1931), 98–108.

CABLE, G. W. "The Freedman's Case in Equity," *Century Magazine,* XXIX, No. 3 (January, 1885), 409–18.

EWING, QUINCY. "The Heart of the Race Problem," *Atlantic Monthly,* CIII (April, 1909), 389–97.

FLANAGAN, THOMAS. "From My Window," *The Nashville* (Tenn.) *World,* September 16, 1932.

FRAZIER, E. FRANKLIN. "The Pathology of Race Prejudice," *Forum*, LXXVII (June, 1927), 856–62.

GORDON, EUGENE. "The Negro's Inhibitions," *American Mercury*, XIII, No. 50 (February, 1928), 159–65.

GRADY, HENRY W. "In Plain Black and White," *Century*, XXIX, No. 6 (April, 1885), 909–17.

HARRIS, CORRA. "Black and White," *Saturday Evening Post*, CCIII, No. 22 (November 29, 1930), 21.

JONES, ESTHER BALDERSTON. "Where Should a Negro Get Hurt?" *Christian Index*, LXI, No. 33 (August 25, 1932), 9–10.

MILLER, KELLY. "Negro Leadership," *Baltimore Afro-American*, October 23, 1923.

NORTH, SUE. "Damyankees in Negro Schools," *American Mercury*, XXXV, No. 138 (June, 1935), 198–209.

REBOUX, PAUL. "Le nouveau savoir-vivre," *American Weekly*, May 31, 1931.

SCHUYLER, GEORGE S. "A Negro Looks Ahead," *American Mercury*, XIX, No. 74 (February, 1930), 212–2c.

———. "Keeping the Negro in His Place," *American Mercury*, XVII, No. 68 (August, 1929), 469–76.

———. "Our White Folks," *American Mercury*, XII, No. 48 (December, 1927), 385–92.

SIMPSON, JOSEPHUS. "The Best Negroes in the World," *Opportunity*, IX, No. 9 (September, 1931), 283–84.

SMALL, SAM. "A Statement to the Forum Magazine concerning Southern Race Prejudice," *Atlanta* (Ga.) *Constitution*, Vol. LX, No. 75 (1927).

THOMAS, JESSE O. "Social Work among Negroes in the South," *Opportunity*, Vol. I, No. 1 (January, 1923).

VILLARD, OSWALD GARRISON. "The Crumbling Color Line," *Harper's*, CLIX (July, 1929), 156–67

NEWS ITEMS, COMMENT, ETC.

NEWSPAPERS AND PERIODICALS

Atlanta (Ga.) *Independent*, October 24, 1929.

Baltimore (Md.) *Afro-American*, November 24, 1928.

Chicago (Ill.) *Defender*, November 14, 1931; March 21, 1931.

Houston (Tex.) *Defender*, May 14, 1932.

Jacksonville (Fla.) *Sentinel*, October 8, 1929.

Kansas City (Mo.) *Call*, August 8, 1933.

Nashville (Tenn.) *Banner*, April 21, 1932.

Nashville (Tenn.) *Evening Tennesseean*, June 9, 1932.

Nashville (Tenn.) *Independent*, June 11, July 9, July 16, 1932.

Norfolk (Va.) *Journal and Guide*, October 18, 1929.

Oklahoma City (Okla.) *Black Dispatch*, October 20, 1929.

Philadelphia (Pa.) *Tribune*, October 24, 1929.

MAGAZINES

Crisis, The. February, April, December, 1911; January, March, 1912; January, July, 1913; July, 1917; November, 1918; June, 1919; January, June, 1920; September, 1925; April, 1927.
Opportunity: A Journal of Opinion, October, 1929.

LETTERS AND PAMPHLETS

TAYLOR, C. H. J. *Whites and Blacks: Or the Question Settled.* Atlanta: J. P. Harrison & Co., 1889.
WOODSON, CARTER G. "An Open Letter to G. D. Eaton," *Journal of Negro History,* XII (April, 1927), 332–34.
————. "Letter to Miss Carrie Gleed," *Journal of Negro History,* XII (April, 1927), 345–46.

FICTION

JOHNSON, JAMES WELDON. *The Autobiography of an Ex-colored Man.* New York: A. A. Knopf, Inc., 1927.

APPENDIX

NOTES FOR CHAPTER I

1. Mrs. Varina Davis, *Memoirs of Jefferson Davis* (New York, 1890), II, 934.

2. "Marster" with the broad *a* has been said to be the form of address generally used by slaves to masters. "Massa" seems to be a corruption brought in by writers who attempted to reproduce the word for publication. "Mars" was apparently the elided form of "marster."

3. Whitelaw Reid, *After the War: A Southern Tour from May, 1865, to May, 1866* (London, 1866), pp. 568–69.

4. G. W. Featherstonehaugh, *Excursion through the Slave States from Washington on the Potomac to the Frontier to Mexico with Sketches of Popular Manners and Geological Notes* (New York, 1844), p. 29.

5. John Spencer Bassett (*The Southern Plantation Overseer: As Revealed in His Letters* [Northampton, Mass., 1925], p. 8) mentions that " 'buckra' is a word expressing scorn for a man of no standing." F. C. Adams (*Manuel Pereira: Or the Sovereign State of South Carolina* [Washington, 1853], pp. 50, 184, 223, 269, 277) implies that the Sea Island slaves used the term to refer to nonslaveholding white men and that "poor buckra" was a degree lower in the scale. Victoria V. Clayton (*White and Black under the Old Regime* [Milwaukee, 1899], p. 172) believed that the term carried with it a bit of contempt. But Elizabeth Ware Pearson (ed.) (*Letters from Port Royal; Written at the Time of the Civil War* [Boston, 1906], p. 141) and Frances Anne Kemble (*A Journal of Residence on a Georgia Plantation in 1838–1839* [New York, 1863], pp. 65–66) seem to consider the word in general use, as a term of reference only.

6. J. S. Buckingham, *The Slave States of America* (London, 1842), I, 480.

7. Harriet Martineau, *Society in America* (New York, 1837), I, 222.

8. "Le nouveau savoir-vivre," quoted in *American Weekly*, May 31, 1931, pp. 1–2.

9. "Usages are folkways which contain no principle of welfare, but serve convenience, so long as all know what is expected to be done. . . . . It is an advantage that there should be a usage and that all should know and observe it" (W. G. Sumner, *Folkways* [New York, 1910], p. 57). Sir Henry Maine, describing the written Roman code of law, and mentioning that it belongs to a class of codes, says: "Their value does not consist in any approach to symmetrical classification, or to terseness and clearness of expression, but in their publicity, and in the knowledge which they furnish to everybody as to what he was to do and what not to do" (*Ancient Law* [3d Amer. ed., from the 5th London ed.; New York, 1888], p. 25).

10. *Principles of Sociology* (London, 1882), II, 3.

11. *My Bondage and Freedom* (New York, 1855), p. 138.

12. Sumner, *op. cit.*, p. iii.

13. Clayton, *op. cit.*, p. 68.

14. *Op. cit.*, p. 77.

15. Douglass, *Narrative of the Life of Frederick Douglass* (Boston, 1849), p. 79.

16. *Following the Color Line: An Account of Negro Citizenship in the American Democracy* (New York, 1908), p. 63. The statement is not wholly accurate. Slaves addressed strange white men, supposedly of the upper class, as "Boss" and "Cap'n."

The change seems to be that now Negroes address white men in general with those terms, especially if the given name or surname is unknown.

17. Sumner, *op. cit.*, pp. 77–78.

18. Baker, *op. cit.*, p. 64.

19. Robert Russa Moton, *What the Negro Thinks* (Garden City, N.Y., 1929), pp. 29 and 49.

NOTES FOR CHAPTER II

1. See, e.g., Nehemiah Adams, *A South-Side View of Slavery* (Boston, 1854), p. 18.

2. William Ferguson, *American by River and Rail* (London, 1856), p. 128.

3. Robert Russa Moton, *What the Negro Thinks* (Garden City, N.Y.: Doubleday-Doran, 1929), p. 12 (by permission).

4. Joseph Holt Ingraham, *The Sunny South: Or the Southerner at Home* (Philadelphia, 1860), pp. 58 and 86.

5. Elizabeth Ware Pearson, *Letters from Port Royal; Written at the Time of the Civil War* (Boston, 1906), p. 35; William R. Russell, *My Diary, North and South* (Boston, 1863), p. 257; Adams, *op. cit.*, p. 73.

6. Russell, *op. cit.*, p. 262.

7. Edward A. Pollard, *The Southern Spy: Or Curiosities of Negro Slavery in the South* (Washington, 1859), p. 10.

8. Pearson, *op. cit.*, p. 20; Ingraham, *op. cit.*, pp. 218–19.

9. Pearson, *op. cit.*, pp. 121–23; Ingraham, *op. cit.*, p. 234; T. D. Ozanne, *The South as It Is: Or Twenty-one Years' Experience in the Southern States* (London, 1863), pp. 75–76; Kimball Young, *Source Book for Social Psychology* (New York, 1927), p. 498 (quoting from William I. Thomas, "The Psychology of Race Prejudice," *American Journal of Sociology*, XVI, 745–47); Thomas Nelson Page, *The Old South: Essays Social and Political* (New York, 1892), pp. 165–66.

10. Frederick Law Olmsted reports the meeting of a family in Virginia, which had returned from a long journey: "Black and white met with kisses, and the effort of a long-haired sophomore to maintain his supercilious dignity, was quite ineffectual to kill the kindness of a fat mulatto woman, who joyfully and pathetically shouted, as she caught him off the gang-plank, 'O, Massa George, is you come back?'" (*A Journey through the Seaboard Slave States; with Remarks on Their Economy* [New York, 1886], I, 150; *The Cotton Kingdom: A Traveler's Observation on Cotton and Slavery in the American Southern States* [New York, 1861], I, 142). F. D. Srygley reports that he refused to kiss his "mammy" upon an occasion when she met him with a young woman and says, "I have never fully recovered my self-respect" (*Seventy Years in Dixie: Recollections, Sermons and Sayings of T. W. Caskey and Others* [Nashville, 1891], p. 48). An old slave man kissed Henry Laurens with a "full buss" of his lips, according to Ulrich Bonnell Phillips (*American Negro Slavery* [New York, 1918], p. 324); and Frances Anne Kemble reports seeing a slave woman kiss the master (*A Journal of Residence on a Georgia Plantation in 1838–1839* [New York, 1863], p. 59). A stewardess kissed Miss Bremer as she was leaving a steamboat on the Ohio River (Frederika Bremer, *Homes in the New World* [New York, 1853], II, 99. John Dixon Long implied that kissing was tabooed (*Pictures of Slavery in Church and State* [Philadelphia, 1857], p. 229).

11. A Northern Man, *The Planter, or Thirteen Years in the South* (Philadelphia, 1853), pp. 256–57.

12. Srygley, *op. cit.*, p. 42; Bremer, *op. cit.*, I, 275.

13. James Redpath, *The Roving Editor: Or Talks with Slaves in the Southern States* (New York, 1859), p. 29; Ingraham, *op. cit.*, p. 32; Arthur Singleton, *Letters from the South and West* (Boston, 1824), p. 80.

14. Olmsted, *A Journey through the Seaboard Slave States*, I, 74; Adams, *op. cit.*, p. 15.

15. Ferguson, *op. cit.*, p. 134; Solomon Northup, *Twelve Years a Slave* (Auburn, N.Y., 1853), pp. 183 and 261.

16. Pearson, *op. cit.*, 90. The Sea Island slaves had corrupted the "sir" to "sarr."

17. *Ibid.*, p. 25.

18. Herbert Spencer, *Principles of Sociology* (London, 1882), II, 141.

19. Redpath, *op. cit.*, p. 290.

20. W. Alexander MacCorkle, *White Sulphur Springs* (New York, 1916), pp. 210–11.

21. "Missy" was used as early as the beginning of the eighteenth century, as was "massa" (see St. John de Crevecoeur, *Sketches of Eighteenth Century America: More Letters from an American Farmer*, ed. Henri L. Bourdin, Ralph H. Gabriel, and Stanley Williams [New Haven, 1925], pp. 268; Ingraham, *op. cit.*, p. 52; Pearson, *op. cit.*, p. 150.

22. Ingraham, *op. cit.*, p. 454; Pearson, *op. cit.*, p. 34.

23. D. R. Hundley, *Social Relations in Our Southern States* (New York, 1860), p. 88; C. H. J. Taylor, *Whites and Blacks* (Atlanta, 1889), p. 6; Northup, *op. cit.*, p. 261.

24. Booker T. Washington, *Up from Slavery* (New York, 1901), p. 12; Pearson, *op. cit.*, p. 31.

25. *Narrative of the Life of Frederick Douglass, an American Slave; Written by Himself* (Boston, 1849), p. 53. Joseph Redd, of Newsome's Station, Tenn., says that "master" was used toward the overseer. He was a slave, though young, when the war ended.

26. Pearson, *op. cit.*, p. 75.

27. Ingraham (*op. cit.*, p. 68) says that all old slaves were called "Uncle" or "Auntie" as the case may be (cf. Long, *op. cit.*, p. 21).

28. William Reynolds Vance, *Slavery in Kentucky* (Lexington, Va., 1895), p. 62.

29. Moton, *op. cit.*, p. 190 (cf. Long, *op. cit.*, p. 21).

30. Hundley, *op. cit.*, p. 88; A Northern Man, *op. cit.*, p. 219.

31. Hundley, *op. cit.*, pp. 88–89.

32. Pollard, *op. cit.*, p. 58.

33. Olmsted (*op. cit.*, I, 231) reports the use of this title in Virginia.

34. A Northern Man, *op. cit.*, pp. 99–100; Bremer, *op. cit.*, I, 278; II, 503.

35. *My Bondage and Freedom* (New York, 1855), pp. 70 and 115.

36. *Op. cit.*, p. 150; see also Washington, *op. cit.*, p. 23.

37. Washington, *op. cit.*, p. 23; Moton, *op. cit.*, p. 190.

38. *Op. cit.*, p. 52.

39. Douglass, *Narrative of the Life of Frederick Douglass*, p. 18; Lewis and Milton Clarke, *Narratives of the Sufferings of Lewis and Milton Clarke; Sons of a Soldier of the Revolution, during a Captivity of More than Twenty Years among the Slaveholders of Kentucky, One of the So-called Christian States of North America, Dictated by Themselves to M. C. Lovejoy* (Boston, 1846), p. 33.

40. *The Cotton Kingdom* (New York, 1861), I, 318–19.

41. F. C. Adams, *Manuel Pereira: Or the Sovereign State of South Carolina* (Washington, 1853), p. 70; Clarke, *op. cit.*, p. 94; Douglass, *My Bondage etc.*, pp. 309, 312, 314.

42. *Op. cit.*, p. 170. T. W. Higginson remarks that the term was used more often by his Negro soldiers than by "well-bred" slaveholders (*Army Life in a Black Regiment* [Boston, 1870], p. 28).

43. J. S. Buckingham, *The Slave States of America* (London, 1842), II, 293.

44. F. C. Adams, *op. cit.*, pp. 76 and 127; Douglass, *My Bondage and Freedom*, p. 125; *Narrative of the Life of Frederick Douglass*, pp. 24, 33, 95; Pollard, *op. cit.*, p. 8; N. Adams, *op. cit.*, p. 93.

NOTES FOR CHAPTER III

1. According to U. B. Phillips' classification a large plantation was an organization with over fifty slaves, not necessarily all workers; the small plantation counted from ten to fifty active "hands"; while the farm counted fewer than ten slaves in all. Ralph Betts Flanders seeks to describe the plantation organization in Georgia by noting both the size of the farm and the number of workers (*Plantation Slavery in Georgia* [Chapel Hill, N.C., 1933], pp. 94–132).

2. Interesting descriptions of plantation life are given in Austin Steward, *Twenty-two Years a Slave, and Forty Years a Freeman* (Rochester, N.Y., 1857), pp. 20 ff.; Frederick Douglass, *My Bondage and Freedom* (New York, 1855), pp. 64 ff.; Frederick Law Olmsted, *A Journey through the Seaboard Slave States* (New York, 1856), II, 48; Ulrich Bonnell Phillips, *Life and Labor in the Old South* (Boston, 1929), pp. 188–218; *American Negro Slavery* (New York, 1918), chap. xvi, pp. 309–30.

3. *Op. cit.*, p. 26. J. W. Loguen, in his autobiography (*As a Slave and as a Freeman: A Narrative of Real Life* [Syracuse, N.Y., 1859], p. 154), tells of an incident where "Jarm immediately rose to his feet and took off his hat, as is the custom of slaves, in the presence of white persons."

4. Harriet Martineau, *Society in America* (New York, 1837), I, 123.

5. Olmsted, *op. cit.*, I, 49–50; *The Cotton Kingdom: A Traveler's Observation on Cotton and Slavery in the American Southern States* (New York, 1861), p. 54.

6. William Ferguson noted his surprise when a slave corrected a visitor about the time of his breakfast, when the conversation was between master and visitor (*America by River and Rail* [London, 1856], p. 111).

7. *Op. cit.*, I, 123.

8. Joseph Holt Ingraham, *The Sunny South: Or the Southerner at Home* (Philadelphia, 1860), p. 53.

9. Orland Kay Armstrong, *Old Massa's People* (Indianapolis: Bobbs-Merrill, 1931), p. 32 (by permission); Olmsted, *A Journey in the Back Country; in the Winter of 1853–54* (New York, 1860), p. 153. See also Solomon Northup, *Twelve Years a Slave: Narrative of Solomon Northup, a Citizen of New York: Kidnapped in Washington City in 1841 and Rescued from a Cotton Plantation near the Red River in Louisiana, in 1853* (Auburn N.Y., 1853), pp. 93 and 158.

10. Lewis and Milton Clarke, *Narratives of the Sufferings of Lewis and Milton Clarke; Sons of a Soldier of the Revolution, during a Captivity of More than Twenty Years among the Slaveholders of Kentucky, One of the So-called Christian States of North America, Dictated by Themselves to J. C. Lovejoy* (Boston, 1846), p. 14.

11. Elizabeth Ware Pearson (ed.), *Letters from Port Royal; Written at the Time of the Civil War* (Boston, 1906), pp. 121 and 123.

12. Victoria V. Clayton, *White and Black under the Old Regime* (Milwaukee, 1899), p. 23; Pearson, *op. cit.*, p. 45

13. Clayton, *op. cit.*, pp. 22 and 25.

14. Edward A. Pollard (signer of Preface), *The Southern Spy; or Curiosities of Negro Slavery in the South* (Washington, 1859), p. 34.

15. Clayton, *op. cit.*, p. 25; A Northern Man, *The Planter, or Thirteen Years in the South* (Philadelphia, 1853), p. 33; James J. McDonald (ed. J. A. C. Chandler), *Life in Old Virginia* (Norfolk, Va., 1907), p. 150.

16. Herbert Spencer (*Principles of Sociology* [London, 1882], II, 111) says that the visit of ceremony is regarded as due from an inferior to a superior and is generally taken as a condescension when reversed. Presents, too, when given by inferiors, are symbolic of loyalty, reverence, and continued fidelity to the superior and his interests.

17. James Battle Avirett, *The Old Plantation: How We Lived in the Great House and Cabin before the War* (New York, 1901), p. 47.

18. Pearson, *op. cit.*, p. 119.

19. *Op. cit.*, p. 36.

20. Ingraham *op. cit.*, p. 29.

21. D. R. Hundley, *Social Relations in Our Southern States* (New York, 1860), p. 33.

22. *Op. cit.*, p. 37.

23. St. John de Crevecoeur (*Sketches of Eighteenth Century America: More Letters from an American Farmer*, ed. Henri L. Bourdin, Ralph M. Gabriel, and Stanley Williams [New Haven, 1925], p. 148) noted the ceremony as early as the eighteenth century. Northup (*op. cit.*) says that slaves in Louisiana were provided with passes during the Christmas season, permitted to visit, to ride, or to renew old friendships, or to go where they pleased "within a limited distance." If they worked during the period, they were paid for it. For other observations as to the nature of the celebration see Hundley, *op. cit.*, p. 359; Booker T. Washington, *Up from Slavery* (New York, 1901), p. 133; Olmstead, *Seaboard Slave States*, I, 82–83; *The Cotton Kingdom* (New York, 1861), I, 79; Frederika Bremer, *Homes in the New World* (New York, 1853), II, 190; Ulrich B. Phillips and James D. Glunt, *Florida Plantation Records: From the Papers of George Noble Jones* ("Publications of the Missouri Historical Society" [St. Louis, 1927]), p. 31.

24. Hundley, *op. cit.*, p. 361.

25. Avirett, *op. cit.*, pp. 179–80. Shoes were a common gift near Newsome Station, Tenn. Moreover, presents were expected of visitors as well as from the family (see also C. G. Parsons, *An Inside View of Slavery; or a Tour among the Planters* [Boston, 1855], p. 41).

26. Avirett, *op. cit.*, p. 180; Thomas Nelson Page, *The Old South: Essays Social and Political* (New York, 1892), p. 183. The meal might be served at the cabins, or on the veranda, for house servants (Armstrong, *op. cit.*, p. 137). The meal was supper in Louisiana. See Northup (*op. cit.*, pp. 215 and 286) for a description of such an occasion, with the whites standing, while the slaves were separated by sex at the table.

27. Walter L. Fleming, *Home Life in Alabama during the Civil War* ("Publications of the Southern History Association," Vol. VIII [1904]), p. 99; F. D. Srygley, *Seventy Years in Dixie: Recollections, Sermons, and Sayings of T. W. Caskey and Others* (Nashville, 1891), pp. 298–99.

28. *Op. cit.*, p. 142.

29. *Ibid.* It may have been that this was an inspection to discover if slaves from other plantations were present. But it resembles more a procession of ceremony, rendering thanks to the master for his kindness, and was perhaps as formal as a military inspection of today.

30. Booker T. Washington, *Story of the Negro*, I, 160.

31. *Op. cit.*, p. 146.

32. MacCorkle, *op. cit.*, pp. 109 ff.

33. A Northern Man, *op. cit.*, p. 71; Armstrong, *op. cit.*, p. 171.

34. T. D. Ozanne, *The South as It Is: Or Twenty Years' Experience in the Southern States* (London, 1863), p. 76.

35. There has been much discussion concerning the marriage of slaves before the Civil War and of the legal status of such marriages. Some contend that there was no marriage, others say that there was. It does, however, appear that, even though there may have been no legal justification or recognition, the ceremony was nevertheless observed in many instances. The house servants especially were permitted to "go through

the motions" of the marriage ceremony. Though these marriages might later be broken at the discretion of the master, the ceremonial aspects must have operated to make them more binding (Avirett, *op. cit.*, p. 124; N. Davis, *Narrative of a Colored Man* [Baltimore, 1859], p. 26; Olmsted, *A Journey in the Back Country; in the Winter of 1853-1854*, p. 154). Phillips and Glunt (*op. cit.*, pp. 93 and 128) show that slaves on overseer-controlled plantations obtained consent from the master through the overseer. Higginson, who commanded a regiment of black soldiers in the Lower South, remarked that "the men have somehow got the impresssion that it is essential to the validity of a marriage that they come to me for permission, just as they used to go to the master" (*Army Life in a Black Regiment* [Boston, 1870], pp. 42-43).

36. Slaves from different plantations were frequently married. The woman was then called a "broad-wife." Ingraham (*op. cit.*, p. 143) saw such a marriage. Washington (*Up from Slavery*, p. 24) relates that his mother was so married. Nehemiah Adams (*A South-Side View of Slavery* [Boston, 1854], p. 82) thought the custom was at least looked upon sympathetically. Phillips (*op. cit.*) takes the custom for granted. Others who testify that the custom was frowned upon for one or more reasons were John Spencer Bassett, *The Southern Plantation Overseer; as Revealed in His Letters* (Northampton, 1925) p. 17; Edward Dicey, *Six Months in the Federal States, in 1862* (London, 1863), I, 260; and Srygley, *op. cit.*, pp. 254-56. Higginson (*op. cit.*, p. 258) remarks, concerning the derivation of term, "It was not uncommon for men to have two or three wives in different plantations—the second, or remoter, partner being called a 'broad-wife,'—i.e., wife abroad."

37. Page, *op. cit.*, p. 183; McDonald, *op. cit.*, p. 96; Avirett, *op. cit.*, p. 124.

38. McDonald, *op. cit.*; Avirett, *op. cit.*

39. Ingraham, *op. cit.*, p. 144. The incident occurred in Tennessee. Fleming (*op. cit.*, p. 99) recounts a similar instance in Alabama.

40. That the occasions cited were separate instances, though the time and place are not cited, will be shown by references to two or more sources (C. P. Patterson, *The Negro in Tennessee* [Austin, 1922], p. 18; Page, *op. cit.*, p. 183; Avirett, *op. cit.*, pp. 124-25). This was the occasion where the families were "invited into the dining-room."

41. Olmsted, *Journey in the Seaboard Slave States*, II, 70; Patterson, *op. cit.*; Fleming, *op. cit.*, p. 99.

42. Olmsted, *op. cit.*, in *loc. cit.*; Page, *op. cit.*; Avirett, *op. cit.*; Patterson, *op. cit.*

43. Ingraham, *op. cit.*, p. 144; Avirett, *op. cit.*

44. Page, *op. cit.*; Ingraham, *op. cit.*, p. 144.

45. Avirett, *op. cit.*, p. 127.

46. Ingraham, *op. cit.*, p. 144; Avirett, *op. cit.*, p. 127; Armstrong, *op. cit.*, p. 168.

47. Clayton, *op. cit.*, pp. 130-31.

48. Albert Bushnell Hart, *The American Nation: A History*, Vol. XVI: *Slavery and Abolition, 1831-1841* (New York, 1906), p. 103. The instance appears to be fiction, as indicated by the forms used—"pa" and "ma" and "your pa's wife's weddin' gloves." It is, however, true enough to life to be used here. Note "Marster," the whites standing at the tables, and the supper in the kitchen. See also Bremer (*op. cit.*, I, 376), who saw a slave wedding.

49. McDonald, *op. cit.*, p. 96; William Reynolds Vance, *Slavery in Kentucky* (Washington and Lee University dissertation [privately printed], 1895), p. 67.

50. *Op. cit.*, p. 183.

51. Patterson, *op. cit.*, p. 18; Olmsted, *op. cit.*, II, 70; Page, *op. cit.*, p. 183.

52. Armstrong, *Old Massa's People* (Indianapolis: Bobbs-Merrill), p. 164 (by permission). See also H. N. McTyeire, C. P. Sturgis, and A. T. Holmes, *Duties of Master. to Servants* (Charleston, S.C., 1851), p. 30.

53. Armstrong, *op. cit.*, p. 166.

54. W. P. Starke, "Account of John C. Calhoun's Early Life," *Report of the American Historical Association*, II (1899), 75. The name of the planter is not given, but he lived near the Calhoun plantation. See also an instance in J. E. Kirbye (*Puritanism in the South* [Boston, 1908], p. 133), where the slaves of one master were brought to Charleston and from the plantation to bid the master goodbye.

55. Steward, *op. cit.*, p. 86.

56. Clarke, *op. cit.*, p. 113.

57. Mrs. D. Giraud Wright, *A Southern Girl in '61: The War-Time Memories of a Confederate Senator's Daughter* (New York, 1905), p. 79, quoting an undocumented reference to *Blackwood's Magazine;* Charles Ball, *Slavery in the United States: A Narrative of the Life and Adventures of Charles Ball, a Black Man* (Lewiston, Pa., 1836), p. 301; Bremer, *op. cit.*, I, 374.

58. Arthur Singleton, *Letters from the South and West* (Boston, 1824), p. 77.

59. Avirett, *op. cit.*, p. 129.

60. Steward, *op. cit.*, p. 39.

61. A Northern Man, *op. cit.*, p. 256.

62. Olmsted, *A Journey through the Seaboard Slave States*, II, 34. This is a border-line case, i.e., it was accepted but perhaps not expected. It doubtless showed the affection of a mistress for a favorite slave. Another one was found, in the journal of a planter, a form by which the stonecutter was to be guided perhaps:

Sunday
July 10, 1853
Peyton is no more
Aged 42
Though he was a bad man in many respects
Yet he was an excellent field
hand, always at his
post on this place for 21 years
Except the measles and its sequence, the
injury received by a mule last Nov'r and its sequence
he has not lost 15 days work, I verily believe, in
the remaining 19 years. I wish we could hope for his
eternal state

Taken from Phillips, *American Negro Slavery* (New York: D. Appleton, 1918), p. 292 (by permission).

63. *Op. cit.*, p. 119.

64. *Op. cit.*, p. 74.

65. Phillips, *American Negro Slavery*, pp. 84 and 228; Bremer, *op. cit.*, I, 367; John Fiske, *Old Virginia and Her Neighbours* (Boston, 1901), II, 328.

66. Phillips, *American Negro Slavery*, p. 280; Bassett, *op. cit.*, p. 3.

67. Francis Pendleton Gaines, *The Southern Plantation* (New York, 1925), p. 190.

68. John C. Fitzpatric, *The Diaries of George Washington* (Boston, 1925), I, 138.

69. Bassett, *op. cit.*, p. 3.

70. *Op. cit.*, pp. 147 and 189.

71. Srygley, *op. cit.*, pp. 270-71; Phillips, *American Negro Slavery*, p. 282; Gaines, *op. cit.*, p. 189; Avirett, *op. cit.*, pp. 117-18. See Bassett (*op. cit.*, pp. 7 and 92) for a description of the worst type of overseer, like Ephraim Beanland on President James K. Polk's plantation in Tennessee.

72. McTyeire, Sturgis, and Holmes, *op. cit.*, p. 87.

73. Edward Ingle, *Southern Sidelights: A Picture of Social and Economic Life in the South, a Generation before the War* (New York, 1896), p. 270.

74. Bassett, *op. cit.*, pp. 32 and 53 (quoting from J. D. B. DeBow, *Review*, XII, 38–44)..

75. Phillips, *American Negro Slavery*, p. 275; Phillips and Glunt, *op. cit.*, pp. 577–78; Bassett, *op. cit.*, p. 33.

76. Steward, *op. cit.*, p. 23. References to the duties of overseers may be found in Phillips, *op. cit.*, pp. 261-90.

77. Phillips, *American Negro Slavery*, pp. 281–82.

78. *Ibid.*, p. 304; see also Bassett, *op. cit.*, pp. 18 and 263.

79. Phillips and Glunt, *op. cit.*, p. 150.

80. *Florida Plantation Records, etc.* (St. Louis: Mo. Hist. Soc., 1927), p. 130 (by permission).

81. Marshall Hall, *The Two-Fold Slavery of the United States: With a Project of Self-Emancipation* (London, 1884), p. 34.

82. "The Negro in America" (unpublished lectures).

83. The rules laid down in printed contracts of Richard Corbin (of Virginia, in 1759), of C. Weston (South Carolina, 1856), of Charles Manigault (Georgia), of one Fowler (of the Yazoo-Mississippi Delta, 1857), and of Joseph Acklen (Louisiana, 1861) may be found as documents in Phillips, *Plantation and Frontier Document: 1649–1863* (Cleveland, 1902), I, 109–29. Acklen's rules were first submitted to DeBow (*op. cit.*, XXI, 607–20; XXII, 376–81) in 1856 and 1857, respectively.

84. Bassett, *The Southern Plantation Overseer: As Revealed in His Letters* (Northampton, Mass., Smith College), pp. 262–63 (by permission); see also Lady Emmeline Wortley, *Travels in the United States during 1849–1850* (New York, 1851), p. 120; and John Dixon Long, *Pictures of Slavery in Church and State* (Philadelphia, 1857), pp. 15 and 19.

85. Bassett, *op. cit.*, p. 274.

86. Ball, *op. cit.*, p. 107; Olmsted, *A Journey in the Back Country; in the Winter of 1853-1854*, pp. 72–92; Bremer, *op. cit.*, I, 285–86; Wortley, *op. cit.*, p. 119. The duties, prerequisites, and disabilities of overseers have been well treated by Olmsted, *A Journey in the Back Country, etc.*, pp. 52–62.

87. Bassett, *op. cit.*, p. 226.

88. Samuel Walker, a partner of James K. Polk, dismissed an overseer because he had "too much company around him" (Bassett, *op. cit.*, p. 174). Stancil Barwick, overseer on a plantation near Americus, Georgia, wrote his employer: "Ever since I have been on the place I have not been to three neighbors houses since I have been hear I com hear to attend to my Business" (Phillips, *Plantation and Frontier Records*, I, 313).

89. See correspondence of two overseers and George Noble Jones, an employer, where one said, "I would not think of getting a wife without your consent," and the second wrote "I Expect to Mary Say in the course of two or three months. . . . . My Marring will Not interfere with your business. I shall always attend to My duty as I have bin doing and I think a little Better if I get the right kind of wife . . . ." (Phillips and Glunt, *op. cit.*, pp. 100 and 135 [by permission]).

90. John Evans, one of the overseers referrred to above, wrote his employer to re-sign his place, saying: "Now when I am married and might natu[r]ally expect the friends of my wife and self to visit us in a reasonable manner your expression about this matter the other day at your house was enough to let me know that you did not want my friends to come and see me" (*ibid.*, p. 150 [by permission]).

91. *Ibid.*, pp. 154, 158. Mrs. McCall did, in fact, die, as a later letter mentions.

92. Bassett, *op. cit.*, p. 5. Dr. Park remarks that "relations between the overseer

and the slave dealer were rather close, but the net result of them was to create in both of these types a certain amount of cynicism in regard to the black men under their control. This cynicism is itself an interesting social phenomenon. It seems to be a sort of protective device, the function of which is to make men immune to the sentiments which the conditions of persons with whom they are associated would naturally inspire" ("The Negro in America" [unpublished lectures]).

93. *Life and Labor in the Old South* (Boston, 1929), p. 290.

94. Phillips, "The Origin and Growth of the Southern Black Belts," *American Historical Review*, XI (July, 1906), 807 n. Ethelred Brantley was an overseer who became so enthusiastic over Nat Turner's preaching that they went to a mill pond and "baptized each other." Drewry records that "this man was a respectable overseer, but after his intercourse with Nat, no one would have anything to do with him, so, it is said, he left the State." Our judgment is that the ostracism was partly, if not wholly, due to the fact that Turner was an insurrectionist, as well as a Negro (W. S. Drewry *Southampton Insurrection* [Washington, 1900], p. 33 and n. 1).

95. James Redpath, *The Roving Editor: Or Talks with Slaves in the Southern States* (New York, 1859), p. 290. A Texas former slave reported that they used "Boss", but a Tennessee former slave remembered that they used "Marster," in addressing the overseer.

96. Cf. Bassett (*op. cit.*, p. 8), where he says that "buckra" is a word which expresses scorn for a person of no standing.

97. Phillips and Glunt, *op. cit.*, p. 157.

98. John Evans left four children by a slave woman on El Destino plantation in Florida (*ibid.*, p. 25). Frances Anne Kemble (*A Journal of Residence on a Georgia Plantation in 1838–1839* [New York, 1863], pp. 140–41, 209–10, 162) mentions two instances where the overseer took the head-driver's wife, had a child by her, and then returned the woman to her husband. Joseph Acklen, of Louisiana, included in the "constitution" of his plantation provisions to the effect that "any overseer having connection with the female servants" would be dismissed, with "no excuse taken" (Phillips, *American Negro Slavery*, pp. 273–74). A Mississippi planter discovered two women on his plantation pregnant simultaneously to the overseer (Phillips, *Life and Labor in the Old South*, p. 323). James Tait, of Elbert County, Georgia, dismissed an overseer for "making my Negro men run away by interfering with their women, or on account of the women," among other things (*ibid.*, p. 282). See also McTyeire, Sturgis, and Holmes, *op. cit.*, p. 87.

NOTES FOR CHAPTER IV

1. Phillip A. Bruce, *An Economic History of Virginia in the Seventeenth Century: An Inquiry into the Material Condition of the People Based on Original and Contemporary Records* (New York, 1896), II, 64.

2. Bruce, *Institutional History of Virginia in the Seventeenth Century* (New York, 1910), I, 37.

3. Helen T. Catterall, *Judicial Cases concerning American Slavery and the Negro* (Washington, 1926), I, 57.

4. Cf. James Curtis Ballagh, *A History of Slavery in Virginia* (Baltimore, 1902), p. 47; John Henderson Russell, *The Free Negro in Virginia, 1619–1865* (Baltimore, 1913), p. 39; George Washington Williams, *A History of the Negro Race in America* (New York, 1882), I, 123; Catterall, *op. cit.*, I, 60.

5. Bruce (*An Economic History, etc.*, II, 97) states frankly that the law was enacted because so many Negroes had been escaping slavery by being baptized; cf. Russell, *op. cit.*, p. 39.

6. On this point see Catterall, *op. cit.*, I, 57; and Ballagh, *op. cit.*, p. 45.

7. The statement appeared in the correspondence of "a lady of Barbadoes to God-wyn, the author of the 'Negro's and Indian's Advocate' " (Bruce, *An Economic History, etc.*, II, 93–94).

8. John Evjen, *Scandinavian Immigrants in New York, 1630–1674* (Minneapolis, 1916), p. 358.

9. Wesley M. Gewehr, *The Great Awakening in Virginia, 1740–1790* (Durham, N.C., 1930), p. 249. The "evangelical churches" are Methodist, Baptist, and Presbyterian. The latter was well established in the Shenandoah Valley (*ibid.*, pp. 72 and 237).

10. Noah Davis, *Narrative of a Colored Man* (Baltimore, 1859), p. 25.

11. *Ibid.*, p. 33.

12. John S. Bassett, *Slavery in the State of North Carolina* ("Johns Hopkins University Studies in Historical and Political Science," Ser. XVII, Nos. 7–8 [Baltimore, 1899]), p. 52.

13. William R. Vance, *Slavery in Kentucky* (Washington and Lee University dissertation [privately printed], 1895), p. 68.

14. D. Giraud Wright, *A Southern Girl in '61; the War-Time Memories of a Confederate Senator's Daughter* (New York, 1905), pp. 14–15. Negroes were admitted to the Methodist church of Tennessee as early as 1791. There were many members by 1824. See Caleb P. Patterson, *The Negro in Tennessee, 1790–1865* (University of Texas Bull. 2205 [February, 1922]), p. 117.

15. I. T. Tichenor, *Work of Southern Baptists among Negroes*, quoted in Walter L. Fleming, *A Documentary History of the Reconstruction* (Cleveland, 1907), II, 247.

16. J. Edward Kirbye, *Puritanism in the South* (Boston, 1908), pp. 67 and 77.

17. *South-Side View of Slavery* (Boston, 1854), p. 53.

18. A Northern Man, *The Planter: Or Thirteen Years in the South* (Philadelphia, 1853), p. 76.

19. *Ibid.*, p. 139.

20. T. D. Ozanne, *The South as It Is: Or Twenty-one Years' Experience in the Southern States* (London, 1863).

21. Mrs. Sea states that 466,000 slaves were members of white churches by that date, dividing them as follows: Methodists, 200,000; Hardshell Baptists, 170,000; Old and New Presbyterians, 18,000; Cumberland Presbyterians, 20,000; Episcopalians, 7,000; all others, 51,000—a total of 466,000. (Sophie Fox Sea, *Slavery in the United States: A Brief Synoptical Review* [Louisville, n.d.], pp. 16–17).

22. *Slave Life in Georgia: A Narrative of the Life, Sufferings, and Escape of John Brown, a Fugitive Slave* (London, 1855), pp. 139–40.

23. Bassett, *op. cit.*, pp. 57–58.

24. "The idea of equality was especially prominent among the Methodists and even among the Baptists. . . . . An officer (of King William County, Va.) charged that Methodists and Baptists were meeting two or three times every week after dark, and calling in slaves to attend the meetings. . . . . The Methodists not only set out to proselyte among the slaves, but there was a strong tendency to run counter to the Virginia slave code and social conventions" (Luther P. Jackson, "Negro Religious Development in Virginia," *Journal of Negro History*, XVI [April, 1931], 172 [by permission]).

25. D.R. Hundley, *Social Relations in Our Southern States* (New York, 1860), p. 342; Bassett, *op. cit.*, p. 52.

26. Albert Bushnell Hart, *The American Nation: A History*, Vol. XVI: *Slavery and Abolition, 1831–1841* (New York, 1906), pp. 105–6.

27. Bassett, *op. cit.*, pp. 52 and 60.

28. Patterson, *op. cit.*, p. 124.

29. Adams, *op. cit.*, p. 29.

30. Frederick Law Olmsted, *A Journey through the Seaboard Slave States; with Remarks on Their Economy* (New York, 1856), II, 85, 86.

31. J. S. Buckingham, *The Slave States of America* (London, 1842), I, 483.

32. *Ibid.*, II, 481.

33. *Ibid.*, p. 274.

34. John Preston McConnell, *Negroes and Their Treatment in Virginia from 1865 to 1867* (Pulaski, Va., 1910), p. 107. A. A. Taylor (*The Negro in the Reconstruction of Virginia* [Washington, 1926], p. 174) remarks that, about 1860, urban Negroes were permitted to worship in separate churches directed by white ministers, while the rural Negroes worshiped in the master's church but seated in a separate section. The development seems to have been the other way around. City slaves did worship in masters' churches and later in separate churches; but evidence indicates that the plantation slaves might have churches or chapels serving them, in the main.

35. Patterson, *op. cit.*, p. 146.

36. William Ferguson, *America by River and Rail* (London, 1856), p. 115.

37. Olmsted, *op. cit.*, II, 284.

38. McConnell, *op. cit.*, p. 107.

39. Davis, *op. cit.*, p. 18.

40. Tichenor, *op. cit.*, quoted in Fleming, *op. cit.*, II, 247.

41. Bassett, *op. cit.*, p. 71.

42. Patterson, *op. cit.*, p. 146.

43. Ulrich Bonnell Phillips, *American Negro Slavery* (New York, 1918), p. 318.

44. *Ibid.*, p. 321.

45. Harriet Martineau, *Society in America* (New York, 1837), I, 123. Miss Martineau thought that this example was particularly odious.

46. Joseph Holt Ingraham, *The Sunny South: Or the Southerner at Home* (Philadelphia, 1860), p. 205.

47. Anne Royall, *Mrs. Royall's Southern Tour: Or Second Series of the Black Book* (Washington, 1830), I, 134.

48. Bassett, *op. cit.*, p. 52.

49. William Goodell, *Slavery and Anti-slavery: A History of the Great Question in Both Hemispheres, with a View of the Slavery in the United States* (New York, 1855), p. 200.

50. John Dixon Long, *Pictures of Slavery in Church and State* (Philadelphia, 1857), p. 164, and Bassett, *op. cit.*, p. 71.

51. Patterson, *op. cit.*, p. 124.

52. William Sidney Drewry, *Slave Insurrections in Virginia* (Johns Hopkins University dissertation [Washington, 1900]), p. 23.

53. *Op. cit.*, II, 275.

54. A Northern Man, *op. cit.*, p. 61.

55. C. G. Parsons, *An Inside View of Slavery: Or a Tour among the Planters* (Boston, 1855), pp. 273–74.

56. Davis, *op. cit.*, p. 25.

57. Cf. Frances Anne Kemble, *A Journal of Residence on a Georgia Plantation in 1838–1839* (New York, 1863), pp. 85 and 140.

58. Ulrich B. Phillips and James D. Glunt, *Florida Plantation Records: From the Papers of George Noble Jones* ("Publications of the Missouri Historical Society" [St. Louis, 1927]), p. 31.

59. *Ibid.*, p. 31 (by permission). James Page was a Negro minister.

60. Cf. Bruce, *An Economic History, etc.*, II, 86; C. B. Marryat, *A Diary in America; with Remarks on Its Institutions* (Paris, 1839), p. 177; Long, *op. cit.*, p. 15.

61. Phillips, *Life and Labor in the Old South* (Boston, 1929), p. 110.

62. Arthur Singleton, *Letters from the South and West* (Boston, 1824), p. 74.

63. *Op. cit.*, pp. 69–70.

64. A Northern Man, *op. cit.*, p. 98.

65. Ferguson (*op. cit.*, p. 149) observed white teachers in Charleston, and Davis (*op. cit.*, p. 44) saw them in Baltimore—both instances occurring in 1855.

66. *My Bondage and Freedom* (New York, 1855), p. 194.

67. Phillips, *American Negro Slavery*, p. 316; Frederika Bremer, *Homes in the New World* (New York, 1853), I, 307.

68. Douglass, *op. cit.*, p. 194.

69. *Ibid.* See J. W. Loguen, *As a Slave and as a Freeman: A Narrative of Real Life* (Syracuse, N.Y., 1859), p. 139.

70. Orland Kay Armstrong, *Old Massa's People* (Indianapolis: Bobbs-Merrill, 1931), pp. 223 and 224 (by permission).

71. Phillips, *American Negro Slavery*, p. 318.

72. Ozanne, *op. cit.*, p. 135.

73. Olmsted (*op. cit.*, I, 136) inferred that Negroes were expected and encouraged to unite in services in the churches. Phillips (*American Negro Slavery*, pp. 418–19) notes that they did participate in the ritual of the Catholic and Episcopal churches. Long (*op. cit.*, p. 161) mentions that they were given definite parts in Methodist love feasts.

74. Patterson, *op. cit.*, p. 124; Armstrong, *op. cit.*, p. 36; Bassett, *op. cit.*, p. 52; Adams, *op. cit.*, p. 56.

75. Cf. Olmsted, *op. cit.*, I, 126; Taylor, *op. cit.*, p. 174.

76. *Op. cit.*, p. 270.

77. Walter L. Fleming, *Home Life in Alabama during the Civil War* ("Publications of the Southern Historical Association," Vol. VIII [1904]), p. 99.

78. Minutes of the Presbytery (April 3, 1855) quoted in Rev. H. H. Allen, *The General Assembly and Its Accusers* (Louisville, 1867), p. 39.

79. Minutes of the General Assembly (1801) quoted in *ibid.*, p. 31.

80. Minutes of the Presbytery (September 25, 1833) quoted in *ibid.*, p. 39.

81. Davis, *op. cit.*, pp. 27–28.

82. Quoted in Fleming, *A Documentary History of the Reconstruction*, II, 247.

83. James J. McDonald, *Life in Old Virginia*, ed. J. A. C. Chandler (Norfolk, Va., 1907), p. 103.

84. *Negro Year Book* (Tuskegee Institute, 1925), p. 258.

85. McDonald, *op. cit.*, p. 103; Adams, *op. cit.*, p. 188.

86. Patterson, *op. cit.*, pp. 118–19. The latter two preached only to Negroes it seems.

87. Bassett, *op. cit.*, pp. 67 and 73.

88. Taylor, *op. cit.*, p. 189.

89. Cf. on this point Hundley, *op. cit.*, p. 89; Armstrong, *op. cit.*, pp. 36 and 224; and a so-called "slave sermon" in the latter reference, p. 340.

90. Phillips, *American Negro Slavery* (New York: D. Appleton, 1918), p. 269 (by permission).

91. The point is disputed (see Drewry, *op. cit.*, p. 32; and "Nat Turner's Insurrection," *Atlantic Monthly*, VIII [August, 1881], 175). Relations, later unfriendly, had been so harmonious about 1831 that both races in Fredericksburg, Virginia, contributed to the erection of a monument at the grave of a slave preacher, Alexander Daniel (Davis, *op. cit.*, p. 28).

92. *Op. cit.*, p. 147.

93. *Op. cit.*, p. 57.

94. *Op. cit.*, II, 34–35.

95. Phillips, *op. cit.*, p. 318.

96. Cf. Davis, *op. cit.*, p. 28; and Minnie Claire Boyd, *Alabama in the Fifties: A Social Study* ("Columbia University Studies in History, Economics, and Public Law," No. 353 [New York, 1931]), p. 167.

97. Patterson, *op. cit.*, p. 152.

98. Edward Ingle, *Southern Sidelights: A Picture of Social and Economic Life in the South, a Generation before the War* (New York, 1896), p. 273.

99. *Op. cit.*, p. 148. The separation in this church was not complete, for whites sat around the altar at the front.

100. McConnell, *op. cit.*, p. 107.

101. *Op. cit.*, I, 126.

102. Marshall Hall, *The Two-Fold Slavery of the United States; with a Project of Self-Emancipation* (London, 1884), p. 147.

103. *Op. cit.*, p. 203.

104. Bassett, *op. cit.*, p. 60.

105. Ozanne, *op. cit.*, p. 128.

106. Mary Boykin Chestnut, *A Diary from Dixie* (New York, 1905), p. 354.

107. *Op. cit.*, p. 124 (by permission).

108. Cf. H. N. McTyeire, C. F. Sturgis, and A. T. Holmes, *Duties of Masters to Servants: Three Premium Essays* (Charleston, S.C., 1851), pp. 44–45.

109. *Ibid.*, p. 114.

110. Patterson, *op. cit.*, p. 147 (by permission).

111. Parsons, *op. cit.*, p. 271.

112. *Ibid.*, p. 274.

113. Vance, *op. cit.*, p. 68.

114. Edward A. Pollard (signer of Preface), *The Southern Spy: Or Curiosities of Negro Slavery in the South* (Washington, 1859), pp. 23–24.

115. Cf. Beverly B. Mumford (*Virginia's Attitude toward Slavery and Secession* [New York, 1909], p. 71) for an instance where such a master not only emancipated his slaves but also made provisions for their colonization in Liberia.

116. Francis P. Gaines, *The Southern Plantation* (New York, 1925), p. 235 n. Phillips (*American Negro Slavery*, pp. 269 and 278) quotes instructions from a Mr. Fowler to his overseer given in R. Collins (*Essays on the Management of Slaves* [Boston, 1852]), showing the development of this idea among masters.

117. Bassett, *op. cit.*, p. 87; Patterson, *op. cit.*, p. 124.

118. McTyeire, Sturgis, and Holmes, *op. cit.*, pp. 119–20.

119. Victoria V. Clayton, *White and Black under the Old Regime* (Milwaukee, 1899), pp. 58–59.

120. Cf. Patterson, *op. cit.*, p. 124.

121. Cf. Sea, *op. cit.*, p. 17; A Northern Man, *op. cit.*, p. 254; Olmsted, *op.cit.*, II, 80.

122. *Op. cit.*, pp. 131–32.

123. *Op. cit.*, pp. 66–67.

124. F. D. Srygley, *Seventy Years in Dixie: Recollections, Sermons, and Sayings of T. W. Caskey and Others* (Nashville, 1891), p. 297.

125. Phillips, *Life and Labor, etc.*, p. 253, quoting from *Farmers Register*, VII, 698–703, and Collins in ("Southern Historical Association Publications," Vol. VI [1902]), pp. 24–25.

126. Phillips, *Life and Labor, etc.*, p. 201.

127. Ingraham, *op. cit.*, p. 68.

128. William H. Russell, *My Diary, North and South* (Boston, 1863), p.147; Guion Griffis Johnson, *A Social History of the Sea Islands* (Chapel Hill, N.C., 1930), pp. 147–50.

129. Elizabeth Ware Pearson (ed.), *Letters from Port Royal; Written at the Time of the Civil War* (Boston, 1906), p. 20 n.

130. Cf. Adams, *op. cit.*, p. 54.

131. Cf. McTyeire, Sturgis, and Holmes, *op. cit.*, p. 38.

132. Phillips (*American Negro Slavery*, pp. 422–23) says that the church was organized in 1841. *The Negro Year Book, 1925–1926* (p. 256) places the date of organization as 1780.

133. Buckingham, *op. cit.*, II, 454.

134. Phillips, *American Negro Slavery*, pp. 423–24; cf. Hart (*op. cit.*, pp. 105–6), Patterson (*op. cit.*, p. 146), and Vance (*op. cit.*, p. 68) for a statement of the practice in general.

135. *The Cotton Kingdom: A Traveler's Observations on Cotton and Slavery in the American Southern States* (New York, 1861), I, 308–9; Sea, *op. cit.*, p. 17.

136. *Niles Register*, XLIX (1835), 72. Davis (*op. cit.*, p. 35) found thirteen Negro churches in that year, eleven of which were Methodist. Jeffery R. Brackett (*The Negro in Maryland* ["Johns Hopkins University Studies" (Baltimore, 1889)], p. 206), found thirteen Negro churches but says ten were Methodist.

137. Sea, *op. cit.*, p. 17.

138. *Op. cit.*, p. 167.

139. Phillips, *American Negro Slavery* (New York: D. Appleton–Century, 1918), pp. 420–21 (by permission).

140. *Op. cit.*, I, 165. The church was founded in 1773, according to the *Negro Year Book, 1925–1926*, p. 256.

141. *Op. cit.*, I, 121. Cf. *Negro Year Book, 1925–1926*, p. 256.

142. *Seaboard Slave States*, II, 34. Some eleven Negro churches were established before 1800. The lives of many slave preachers are recorded in the *Negro Year Book, 1925–1926*, along with notes of the establishment of churches (pp. 256–61).

143. *Op. cit.*, I, 351 and 354. Perhaps "Abraham Marshall," white founder of the church, whose first pastor was a Negro, Andrew Bryan.

144. Adams, *op. cit.*, p. 53; Hundley, *Social Relations, etc.*, pp. 350–51, quoted in Phillips, *American Negro Slavery*, p. 423.

145. C. H. Phillips, *History of the Colored Methodist Episcopal Church* (Jackson, Tenn.: C.M.E. Publishing House, 1925), pp. 23–26, 247, 376.

146. *Ibid.* (by permission).

147. See also Carter G. Woodson, *The History of the Negro Church* (2d ed.; Washington, 1925), pp. 193–97.

NOTES FOR CHAPTER V

1. W. A. MacCorkle, *White Sulphur Springs* (New York, 1916), p. 212. This was, perhaps, as close as some Negroes could get to the pronunciation of "mistress," hence "mistis" became conventionalized.

2. E. Pearson (ed.), *Letters from Port Royal* (Boston, 1906), p. 192.

3. Francis Pendleton Gaines (*The Southern Plantation* [New York, 1925], p. 46) refers to *Manuel Pereira* as literature. That is, the author wove some scenes into a background which would assist in presenting his point of view. We believe, however, that the instances quoted are accurate enough to be considered genuine.

4. V. V. Clayton, *Black and White under the Old Regime* (Milwaukee, 1899), p. 172.

5. See F. C. Adams, *Manuel Peirera* (Washington, 1853), pp. 50, 184, 223, 269, and 277. The slaves in Georgia also used the term "buckra" (see F. Kemble, *A Journal of Residence on a Georgia Plantation in 1838–1839* [New York, 1863], pp. 65–66).

6. G. W. Dyer, *Democracy in the South* (Nashville, 1905), p. 88.

7. J. G. Palfrey, *Papers on the Slave Power* (Boston, 1846), pp. 52–53.

8. Pearson, *op. cit.*, pp. 43, 45, 61. Cf. T. W. Higginson, *Army Life in a Black Regiment* (Boston, 1870), pp. 35, 39, 91, 93, 151. "Secesh" was a corruption of "secessionist."

9. Ulrich Bonnell Phillips, *Life and Labor in the Old South* (Boston, 1929), p. 166.

10. J. D. Wheeler, *A Practical Treatise on the Laws of Slavery* (New York, 1837), p. 11.

11. C. G. Parsons, *An Inside View of Slavery; or a Tour among the Planters* (Boston, 1855), p. 282.

12. John Spencer Bassett, *The Southern Plantation Overseer; as Revealed in His Letters* (Smith College Fiftieth Anniversary Publication [Northampton, Mass., 1925]), p. 162 (by permission); E. Pollard (signer of Preface), *The Southern Spy* (Washington, 1859), pp. 58–59.

13. U. B. Phillips and J. D. Glunt, *Florida Plantation Records* (St. Louis, 1927), p. 33.

14. Phillips (*American Negro Slavery* [New York, 1918], p. 275) says: "A female negro is called a 'wench' or a 'woman'; and it is this perhaps, which makes the term 'woman' so offensive to American ears, when applied to white females, who must all be called 'ladies.' " See also J. S. Buckingham, *The Slave States of America* (London, 1842), II, 29–30; Adams, *op. cit.*, p. 162.

15. E. Dicey, *Six Months in the Federal States* (London, 1863), II, 83–84.

16. Marshall Hall, *The Two-Fold Slavery of the United States; with a Project of Self-Emancipation* (London, 1854), p. 33.

17. Buckingham, *op. cit.*, pp. 29–30; H. Martineau, *Society in America* (New York, 1837), p. 381.

18. *Dissertation on Slavery* (Philadelphia, 1796; reprint, New York, 1861), *passim*.

19. J. Redpath, *The Roving Editor* (New York, 1859), p. 87; Hall, *op. cit.*, p. 27.

20. Redpath, *op. cit.*, pp. 47–48. Joseph Holt Ingraham (*The Sunny South: Or the Southerner at Home* [Philadelphia, 1860], p. 448) records such an instance in Thibodeaux, Louisiana, about 1858.

21. "C. says he overheard Amaritta say to him, 'You free man? I t'ot so, when I see you walk wid buckra.' " The conversation is reported to have occurred between a slave and a Negro who had come to South Carolina from Boston (Pearson, *op. cit.*, p. 225).

22. Redpath, *op. cit.*, pp. 105–6 (Richmond, Va., 1854).

23. Frederick Law Olmsted, *A Journey through the Seaboard Slave States; with Remarks on their Economy* (New York, 1856), I, 31; also *The Cotton Kingdom; a Traveler's Observations on Cotton and Slavery in the American Southern States* (New York, 1861), I, 47.

24. *Op. cit.*, II, 112.

25. *Op. cit.*, pp. 288–89.

26. S. Northup, *Twelve Years a Slave* (Auburn, N.Y., 1853), p. 269.

27. The statement that families were separated in slavery, except for reasons of dire necessity, is one that has aroused much argument. Slave-breeding was almost universally denied in the South and quite as universally believed in the North, especially by abolitionists. Arguments in denial of the contention may be found in T. D. Ozanne, *The South as It Is* (London, 1863), pp. 15–16, and Nehemiah Adams, *A South-Side View*

of Slavery (Boston, 1854), p. 78. The reverse contention may be found in Hall, *op. cit.*, pp. 26–27; H. Latham, *Black and White* (London, 1867), p. 269, and A. A. Taylor, *The Negro in the Reconstruction of Virginia* (Washington, 1926), p. 203. That the slave population traveled southward—either being sent or growing by natural increase —is indicated by population statistics and changes in the center of the Negro group from 1790 to 1840. E. Ingle (*Southern Sidelights: A Picture of Social and Economic Life in the South, a Generation before the War* [New York, 1896], p. 17) seems to think that the trend was not due to natural increase.

28. Pearson, *op. cit.*, p. 226. Since this section was written the author has seen letters, over one hundred years old, written by slaves, in Arkansas and Mississippi, to one another.

29. J. B. Avirett, *The Old Plantation* (New York, 1901), p. 168; Buckingham, *op. cit.*, I, 124; II, 335–36.

30. White Sulphur Springs, Virginia, 1839: "The orchestra was filled by negro musicians, the bands being almost always formed of negro musicians. Every door and window, at which, if unoccupied, fresh air might have come in, was crowded by negro servants or visitors" (Buckingham, *op. cit.*, II, 335–36). "They stand in the doors and otherwise vacant places of the ballroom, and laugh, and are as much at home as 'massa and missis.' They come and go as they please. A favored aunty will even ask you, 'Please, missis, stand dis way a little bit so I can see!' and her 'missis' complies as rapidly as if a lady had asked her" (Ingraham, *op. cit.*, p. 205 [Tennessee, *ca.* 1853]).

31. Redpath (*op. cit.*, p. 313) quotes a former slave, in Kansas, as saying that "colored people and whites associate more in the South than in the North. They go to parties together, and dance together. Colored people enjoy themselves in the South more than in any part of the world." The first and last statements are doubtless true, but the one concerning the races dancing together must be taken with reservations.

32. *Ibid.*, p. 4.

33. Orland Kay Armstrong, *Old Massa's People* (Indianapolis, 1931), p. 97. Miss Frederika Bremer was an eyewitness and reported that "during the procession a whole crowd of Negroes leaped about the streets, looking quite entertained, as they are by any pomp" (*Homes in the New World*, I, 305).

34. Buckingham (*op. cit.*, II, 61–62) reported the Athens funeral.

35. MacCorkle, *op. cit.*, p. 398.

36. *Ibid.*, pp. 400–401 (by permission).

37. *Op. cit.*, p. 63. A slave did not ride horseback while the master walked. Northup (*op. cit.*, p. 148) records that, having escaped from his plantation and being retaken, he and his master were returning home: "Master Ford urged me to take his place occasionally on the horse to rest me; but I said 'no,' I was not tired, and it was better for me to walk than him."

38. G. W. Featherstonehaugh, *Excursion through the Slave States, etc.* (New York, 1844), p. 43.

39. *Ibid.*, p. 31.

40. *A Journey through the Seaboard Slave States, etc.*, I, 370.

41. *Ibid.*, pp. 19–20.

42. *Ibid.*, p. 19. Parsons (*op. cit.*, p. 298) saw a "middle-aged slaveholder with a black woman and her infant child," seated together while traveling from Georgia to Pennsylvania. They remained thus until they reached Philadelphia.

43. *A Journey through the Seaboard Slave States, etc.*, I, 353.

44. Olmsted, *The Cotton Kingdom*, I, 39.

45. Redpath, *op. cit.*, p. 96 n.

46. *A Journey through the Seaboard Slave States, etc.*, I, 344.

47. *Ibid.*, pp. 59–60.
48. J. Stirling, *Letters from the Slave States* (London, 1857), p. 53.
49. *Op. cit.*, II, 36.
50. *A Journey through the Seaboard Slave States, etc.*, II, 20–21.
51. *Ibid.*, p. 22. There was also small railway mileage in the United States until after 1835. In the southern states, as late as 1860, mileage was distributed as follows:

State	R.R. Mileage	State	R.R. Mileage
Delaware	127	Florida	402
Maryland District of Columbia	386	Alabama	743
		Mississippi	862
Virginia	1,379	Tennessee	1,267
West Virginia	352	Kentucky	534
North Carolina	937	Louisiana	535
South Carolina	973	Arkansas	38
Georgia	1,420	Texas	307

Taken from *Statistical Abstracts, No. 23, 1900* [Washington, 1901], pp. 374–75.
52. Olmsted, *A Journey through the Seaboard Slave States, etc.*, II, 216 (Mobile, Alabama, to New Orleans), *ibid.*, p. 203 (Montgomery to Mobile, Alabama).
53. *Ibid.*, p. 207.
54. *Ibid.*, p. 265; *The Cotton Kingdom*, I, 350.
55. The incident of dining has been related in chap. i. It is found in Buckingham, *op. cit.*, I, 479–80.
56. *Ibid.*
57. *The Cotton Kingdom*, I, 351.
58. *Seaboard Slave States*, I, 417.
59. Herbert Spencer, *Principles of Sociology* (London, 1882), II, 187.
60. Perhaps "cotton osnaburgh" (see M. B. Chestnut, *A Diary from Dixie* [New York, 1905], p. 139; Phillips and Glunt, *op. cit.*, p. 518; Bassett, *op. cit.*, pp. 268–69; Minnie Claire Boyd, *Alabama in the Fifties: A Social Study* [New York, 1931], p. 54; and Olmsted, *The Cotton Kingdom*, I, 46).
61. *The Cotton Kingdom*, I, 105.
62. *Op. cit.*, p. 128.
63. "An' de chillum? When dey big 'nough ter put on anything, it's a shirt. Boys and gals de same. Run 'roun' in dat shirt-tail. Some de gals tie belt 'roun' de middle, and dat's de only diffrunts. . . . . Dis hyar shu't wuh made jest like a sack. Got hole in de top to' de haid, an' holes fo' de arms. Pull it over yoah haid, push yo' arms t'rough de side holes, an' dar yo' is!" (Armstrong, *Old Massa's People* (Indianapolis: Bobbs-Merrill, 1931), pp. 72 and 73 [by permission]; cf. Olmsted, *The Cotton Kingdom*, I, 105).
64. Olmsted, *A Journey through the Seaboard Slave States, etc.*, I, 29; *The Cotton Kingdom*, I, 45.
65. Olmsted, *The Cotton Kingdom*, I, 46.
66. A. Steward, *Twenty-two Years a Slave* (Rochester, 1857), p. 41.
67. W. H. Russell, *My Diary, North and South* (Boston, 1863), p. 157.
68. *Op. cit.*, p. 3; cf. Armstrong, *op. cit.*, pp. 349–50.
69. Olmsted, *Seaboard Slave States*, II, 32; Robert Ferguson, *America during and after the War* (London, 1866), pp. 129–30.
70. Phillip Alexander Bruce, *An Economic History of Virginia in the Seventeenth Century: An Inquiry into the Material Condition of the People Based on Original and Contemporary Records* (New York, 1896), II, 38–39.

71. Buckingham, *op. cit.*, II, 424.

72. Charles Ball (*Slavery in the United States* [Lewiston, Pa., 1836], p. 287) saw many of these hired slaves in Savannah. D. Nason (*Journal of a Tour from Boston to Savannah* [Cambridge, 1849], p. 33) testified that among Savannah slaves carpenters masons, truckmen, and laborers could be found. Some of the women took in washing at "fifty cents a dozen," with which they met the payments. Redpath (*op. cit.*, p. 173) met a slave in Montgomery, Alabama, who paid $300 per year "body-rent," who boarded and clothed himself, who had saved $100 the previous year, and had saved $930 in all. Olmsted (*Seaboard Slave States*, II, 196) met a carpenter in Montgomery who was earning three dollars per day, out of which he paid his master. He was not required even to consult his master about contracts.

73. See Olmsted (*The Cotton Kingdom*, I, 300–301) for an article from the *New Orleans Crescent* showing this hostility; also E. Pollard, *op. cit.*, pp. 40–43.

74. See Parsons, *op. cit.*, p. 221.

75. *Op. cit.*, pp. 150–51.

76. Anne Royall, *The Black Book* (Washington, 1830), I, 110. Mrs. Royall further remarked that the slave, Clayburn Gladman by name, "is a gentleman in his manners, and deserves the patronage of the public."

77. *Ibid.*, II, 132–33.

78. *Ibid.*

79. *Op. cit.*, pp. 150–51.

80. George Washington Williams, *A History of the Negro Race in America* (New York, 1882), I, 121.

81. J. C. Ballagh, *Slavery in Virginia* (Baltimore, 1902), p. 44. Edward B. Reuter (*The Mulatto in the United States* [Boston, 1918], p. 129) says that the laws began as early as 1663. He must, however, refer to Maryland, as Virginia's law was enacted a year earlier. Laws passed referring to cohabitation and marrriage between the races occurred in: Maryland, 1715, 1717, 1728; Virginia, 1662, 1753, 1798; North Carolina, 1715, 1741. Cf. C. G. Woodson, *Free Negro Heads of Families in 1830* (Washington, 1925), pp. vii ff.; "Beginnings of Miscegenation of Whites and Blacks," *Journal of Negro History*, III, No. 4 (1918), 335–53; Caleb Perry Patterson, *The Negro in Tennessee, 1790–1865* (University of Texas Bull. 2205 [February, 1922]), p. 18.

82. *Op. cit.*, II, 37.

83. "It is true that the licentious passions of men overcome the natural repugnance, and find gratification in intercourse with females of the other race. But this is a very different thing from making her the associate of his life. . . . . Him who would contemplate such an alliance, or regard it with patience, when proposed for a son or daughter or sister, we should esteem a degraded wretch . . . . if found among ourselves (*Memoirs on Slavery* [Charleston, 1838], pp. 57–58]).

84. Cf. A. Hart, *Slavery and Abolition* (New York, 1906), pp. 80–81; L. M. Child, *Anti-slavery Catechism* (Newburyport, Mass., 1836), p. 17; Kemble, *op. cit.*, pp. 140, 162, 199, 208–10; Woodson, *Free Negro Heads of Families in 1830*, p. xiv.

85. This was due, said Phillips (*Life and Labor, etc.*, p. 205), to the fact that the regime of slavery not only made black women subject to white men's wills but also to the fact that it promoted intimacy and weakened racial antipathy.

86. *Slavery in the State of North Carolina* (Baltimore, 1899), p. 46.

87. Vance, *op. cit.*, p. 67.

88. He also intimates that decrease of these relationships occurred between poor whites and Negroes, as these developed a mutual contempt; and among house servants, as these were instructed in the white moral code (*American Race Problem* [New York, 1927], pp. 127–31). See G. McD. Stroud (*Sketch of the Laws Relating to Slavery* [Phila-

delphia, 1827], p. 9) and Woodson (*Free Negro Heads of Families*, pp. vi ff.), indicating that all contacts were not of white men with Negro women but also occasionally the reverse.

89. Buckingham (*op. cit.*, II, 245) states that a vice-president of the United States had "colored children by mulatto mothers." And also that he had later married one of these women. Parsons (*op. cit.*, pp. 193–94) relates a similar instance; but the man was a "city surveyor" who had married his "black female cook." It is not certain that either of these authors distinguished between "marriage" and "cohabitation."

90. See Woodson, "An Open Letter to Miss Carrie Gleed," *Journal of Negro History*, XII (1927), p. 346); cf. also Reuter, *American Race Problem*, p. 130, where it is stated that relatively little miscegenation occurred in Alabama, Mississippi, and, outside of New Orleans, in Louisiana. See also Woodson (*The Education of the Negro prior to 1861* [New York, 1915], p. 110) for a statement that the practice was extensive in Richmond, Petersburg, and Norfolk, in Virginia.

91. Reuter, *American Race Problem*, p. 129; Woodson, *The Education of the Negro prior to 1861*, p. 22; *The Free Negro Heads of Families*, p. xiv.

92. Adams (*op. cit.*, p. 27) is replying to an assertion by a certain Mr. Durkee, a member of Congress, that a Negro had been condemned to be hanged in Charleston for resisting the attempt of his master to make a mistress of his wife. On the other hand, Adams' book is not supposed to be an authentic interpretation of the conditions it describes. See Gaines, *op. cit.*, p. 46.

93. Adams, *op. cit.*, p. 30.

94. Grace King (*New Orleans, the Place and the People* [New York, 1895], p. 342) mentions that these quadroons were *gens de couleur libres* predominantly. They had come to New Orleans during the revolution in Haiti and San Domingo, around the 1790's. Miss Kemble (*op. cit.*, p. 14) notes the presence of this class of women, "with whom no gentleman in the city thinks from associating." She had not seen them, perhaps, but was writing from Philadelphia, in 1838. The incident, however, shows that the custom was widely known. On the other hand, Arthur Singleton (*Letters from the South and West* [Boston, 1824], p. 127) denies the practice, saying that, "if it has been rumoured, it is not to be believed, much less repeated, that to be a gentleman here, like foreign princes and lords of nobility, one must patronize a yellow miss." Miss Martineau (*op. cit.*, I, 116–17) wrote: "The Quadroon connexions in New Orleans are almost universal, as I was assured by ladies on the spot, who can not be mistaken. The Quadroon girls are brought up by their mothers to be what they have been; the mistresses of white gentlemen. . . . . The girls are often highly educated, externally, and are probably as beautiful and accomplished a set of women as may be found. Every young man early selects one, and establishes her in one of those pretty and peculiar houses, whole rows of them may be seen in the Remparts. The connexion lasts for life, now and then; usually for several years. In the latter case, when the time comes for the gentleman to take a white wife, the dreadful news reaches his Quadroon partner either by a letter entitling her to call the house and furniture her own, or by a newspaper, which announces his marriage. . . . . Some men, continue the connexion after marriage."

95. Featherstonehaugh, *op. cit.*, pp. 141–42.

96. Featherstonehaugh (*ibid.*, p. 142) relates an incident of a guest who asked a certain French resident of the city the size of his family. The man named three establishments, in which there were nine children. These were in addition to his home with his wife, where there were three children. Moreover, the incident occurred in the presence of the wife. The related conversation was: "Combine d'enfants, monsieur? Ah, voyons un peu, si on pourrait vous dire, cela! Nous avons d'abord, oui, nous avon

quatre, nes a la Rue Royale, puis trois en haut la de la Rue Chartres; il y a encore les deus Montbrillons, mon fils qui est au sucrier, et puis les trois petites que vous voyez." 97. *Op. cit.*, p. 348.

NOTES FOR CHAPTER VI

1. James Redpath, *The Roving Editor, or Talks with Slaves in the Southern States* (New York, 1859), *passim*. His method of investigation deserves notice if not criticism. He says: "Not one man, not even a Northerner in ten, who speaks with the slaves on the subject of their bondage, ascertains their sincere opinions. They will never learn what they are until they address the slaves, not as bondsmen, but as brothers. This is the secret of my universal success with the slaves. I have been their favored confident wherever I have gone, because I have never adopted the shiftless policy of addressing them as if conscious of being a scion of a nobler race" (p. 157).

2. *A South-Side View of Slavery* (Boston, 1854), p. 28.

3. "We must put ourselves in the position of the subject who tries to find his way in the world, and we must remember, first of all, that the environment by which he is influenced, and to which he adapts himself, in *his* world, not the objective world of science,—is nature and society as he sees them, not as the scientist sees them. The individual subject reacts only to his own experience, and his experience is not everything that an absolutely objective observer might find in the portion of the world within the individual's reach, but only what the individual himself finds. And what he finds depends upon his practical attitudes towards his environment, the demands he makes upon it, his control over it, the wishes he seeks to satisfy, and the way in which he tries to satisfy them" (W. I. Thomas and Florian Znaniecki, *The Polish Peasant in Europe and America* [New York: A. A. Knopf, Inc., 1927], II, Part IV, 1847 [by permission]).

4. C. G. Parsons (*An Inside View of Slavery: Or a Tour among the Planters* [Boston, 1855], pp. 29–30 and Frederick Douglass (*My Bondage and Freedom* [New York, 1855], p. 116) say that the slave was taught to say that he was content. James Stirling (*Letters from the Slave States* [London, 1857], p. 47) admits discontent but offers no evidence. Albert Bushnell Hart (*Slavery and Abolition, 1831–1841* [New York, 1906]) and G. W. Cable ("The Freedman's Case in Equity," *Century Magazine*, XXIX, No. 3 [January, 1885], 409–18) mention the slave codes and fugitive slaves in refutation of the notion of contentment among the slaves. Edward Dicey (*Six Months in the Federal States in 1862* [London, 1863], I, 256–57) says that newspapers printed only advertisements of "runaways committed to jail" and thus gave the impression that most slaves would run away if they could. J. S. Buckingham (*The Slave States of America* [London, 1842], I, 377) found the white inhabitants relating with "the utmost coolness" that slaves would not accept freedom if it were offered, and citing instances in which numerous slaves, having been freed, returned to bondage. He mentions that he could "never discover any well-authenticated instance of this." Yet, Rev. T. D. Ozanne (*The South as It Is: Or Twenty-one Years Experience in the Southern States* [London, 1863], pp. 30–33) and U. B. Phillips (*Life and Labor in the Old South* [Boston, 1929], p. 265) mention one instance each. Booker T. Washington (*Up from Slavery* [New York, 1901], p. 15) says that he never saw a slave who did not wish to be free, nor one who would return to slavery. Robert Russa Moton (*What the Negro Thinks* [Garden City, N.Y., 1929], p. 9) states that modern Negroes resent the "assertion that they were contented as slaves." Stirling (*op. cit.*, p. 201), William Ferguson (*America by River and Rail* [London, 1856], p. 146), and Frederick Law Olmsted (*A Journey through the Seaboard Slave States; with Remarks on Their Economy* [New York, 1856], II, 343) did, however, mention instances of slaves in Georgia, South Carolina, and

Louisiana who expressed a desire to be free. The literature of the opposite contention is voluminous and will be quoted as occasion requires.

5. "Accommodation in the area of personal relations tends to take the form of subordination and superordination. Even where accommodation has been imposed by force, the personal relations of master and slave are invariably supported by appropriate attitudes and sentiments. . . . . Attitudes of superordination and subordination may find expression in the sentiments of a conscientious self-complacent paternalism on the part of the master and of an ingratiating and reverential loyalty on the part of the slave. . . . . The sentiments of subordination which have grown up in conformity with an accepted situation eventually become the basis of a life-philosophy of the person" (R. E. Park and E. W. Burgess, *Introduction to the Science of Sociology* [2d ed.; Chicago, 1924], pp. 667–68 [by permission]).

6. John Spencer Bassett, *The Southern Plantation Overseer, Revealed in His Letters* (Smith College Fiftieth Anniversary Publication [Northampton, Mass., 1925]), p. 161 (by permission).

7. "Along with ways of propitiating the victor, the master, the ruler, will naturally come speeches which, beginning with confessions of defeat by verbal assumptions of its attitude, will develop into varied phrases acknowledging servitude" (Herbert Spencer, *Principles of Sociology* [London, 1882], II, 142).

8. Edward A. Pollard (signer of Preface), *The Southern Spy: Or Curiosities of Negro Slavery in the South* (Washington, 1859), pp. 46–47.

9. Frances Anne Kemble, *A Journal of Residence on a Georgia Plantation in 1838–1839* (New York, 1863), p. 255.

10. Elizabeth Ware Pearson (ed.), *Letters from Port Royal; Written at the Time of the Civil War* (Boston, 1906), p. 45. The term was much used in this section (cf. Thomas Wentworth Higginson, *Army Life in a Black Regiment* [Boston, 1870], p. 28).

11. Joseph Holt Ingraham, *The Sunny South: Or the Southerner at Home* (Philadelphia, 1860), p. 86.

12. *Ibid.*, pp. 416–17.

13. *Ibid.*, p. 33.

14. *Op. cit.*, pp. 210–11.

15. Austin Steward, *Twenty-two Years a Slave, and Forty Years a Freeman* (Rochester, N.Y., 1857), p. 101.

16. Douglass, *Narrative of the Life of Frederick Douglass, an African Slave; Written by Himself* (Boston, 1849), p. 20, and *My Bondage and Freedom*, p. 118.

17. F. D. Srygley, *Seventy Years in Dixie: Recollections, Sermons, and Sayings of T. W. Caskey and Others* (Nashville, 1891), p. 260.

18. Douglass, *Narrative of the Life of Frederick Douglass*, p. 20.

19. Srygley, *op. cit.*; Frederika Bremer, *Homes in the New World* (New York, 1853), I, 386.

20. William Reynolds Vance, *Slavery in Kentucky* (Washington and Lee University dissertation [privately printed], 1895), p. 65.

21. *Op. cit.*, p. 101.

22. James Battle Avirett, *The Old Plantation: How We Lived in the Great House and Cabin before the War* (New York, 1901), pp. 111–12.

23. *Op. cit.*, II, 345. The point of view that the Negro "because of his natural attachment to known familiar objects, persons, and places, is pre-adapted to conservatism and to local and personal loyalties," is advanced by Park (*op. cit.*, p. 137).

24. William H. Russell, *My Diary, North and South* (Boston, 1863), p. 91; see also Allan Nevins (ed.), *American History as Recorded by British Travellers* (New York, 1923), p. 383.

25. It would be interesting to discover whether the whites called older slaves "uncle" and "auntie" because they wished to indicate respect for such servants, or whether the practice was established by the slaves, since they were not expected to use "Mr." or "Miss" or "Mrs." to other slaves and wished, nevertheless, to show some respect for these persons. In the latter case, of course, the white persons would take over the conventional practices of the slaves. But they themselves would also wish to express respect for the older slaves; hence the origin of the practice would have a common source. "An absent master wrote: 'I wish to be remembered to all the servants, distinguishing Andrew as the head man, Katy as the mother of the tribe. Not forgetting Charlotte as head of the culinary department, nor Marcus as the Tubal Cain of the community, hoping that they will continue to set a good example and that the younger generation will walk in their footsteps' " (Phillips, *op. cit.*, quoted from J. P. Carson, *Life of James Louis Pettigru*, p. 421).

26. Douglass (*My Bondage and Freedom*, p. 69) and Russell (*op. cit.*, p. 146) attest that such terms were used by children and younger slaves.

27. Ferguson (*op. cit.*, p. 118) relates how a black gardner referred to field hands as "them black fellows." "Aunt Debby," according to Pollard (*op. cit.*, p. 10), "had a habit of designating every one of her own color not admitted to equality as 'de nigger.' " Ingraham (*op. cit.*, pp. 462–63) relates how one Uncle Ned, a helmsman of a boat on Bayou La Fourche, drew himself up in the presence of these "colored Folk" who were field hands.

28. Arthur Singleton, *Letters from the South and West* (Boston, 1824), p. 74.

29. *Op. cit.*, p. 35 (Tennessee, *ca.* 1853).

30. James J. McDonald (ed. by J. A. C. Chandler), *Life in Old Virginia* (Norfolk, Va., 1907), p. 96.

31. *My Bondage and Freedom*, p. 109.

32. Olmsted (*op. cit.*, II, 49) says that "it is a punishment for a field hand to employ him in menial duties at the house, as it is to set a sneaking sailor to do the work of a cabin-servant; and it is equally a punishment to a neglected house servant to banish him to the field-gangs."

33. Steward, *op. cit.*, pp. 31–32.

34. *Op. cit.*, pp. 179–80; and see Thomas J. Wertenbaker, *Planters of Colonial Virginia* (Princeton, N.J., 1922), pp. 156–57.

35. *Op. cit.*, p. 149.

36. James M. Wright, *The Free Negro in Maryland* ("Columbia University Studies in History, Economics, and Public Law," Vol. XCVII, No. 3, Whole No. 222 [New York, 1921]), p. 335 (by permission).

37. Ingraham, *op. cit.*, p. 209 (Beaver Dam Springs, Tennessee, 1853).

38. G. W. Featherstonehaugh, *Excursion through the Slave States; from Washington on the Potomac to the Frontier of Mexico, with Sketches of Popular Manners and Geological Notes* (New York, 1842), p. 22. This author wrote in 1834, while Ingraham wrote about 1853. It is possible that the latter took information from the former.

39. W. Alexander MacCorkle, *White Sulphur Springs* (New York, 1916), pp. 317–18.

40. Ingraham, *op. cit.*, pp. 209–10. This is the only instance discovered where slaves ate in the dining-room. We do not know how accurate the description is, but we should expect that, where so rigid an etiquette was observed among white people, it was doubtless also reflected among their slaves.

41. Adam Hodgson, *Letters from North America*, I, 97, quoted in Phillips, *American Negro Slavery*, p. 416.

42. Olmsted, *op. cit.*, p. 197; Mary Boykin Chestnut, *A Diary from Dixie* (New York,

1905), p. 217. The illustration also implies that slaves occasionally referred to themselves as "ladies" or "gentlemen."

43. Orland Kay Armstrong, *Old Massa's People* (Indianapolis: Bobbs-Merrill, 1931), p. 24 (by permission).

44. Documents of an old slave, collected by Miss Ophelia Settle.

45. Lady Emmeline Wortley, *Travels in the United States, during 1849–1850* (New York, 1851), pp. 118-19.

46. Olmsted, *op. cit.*, I, 377.

47. *Ibid.*, II, 1-2.

48. Olmsted, *A Journey in the Back Country; in the Winter of 1853-54* (New York, 1860), I, 170.

49. Douglass, *My Bondage and Freedom*, pp. 252-53.

50. Bremer, *op. cit.*, I, 393.

NOTES FOR CHAPTER VII

1. For cases in point see John Henderson Russell, *The Free Negro in Virginia, 1619-1865* (Baltimore, 1913), pp. 25 and 33.

2. Free Negroes, as manumitted slaves rather than as released indentured servants, began to increase about 1662 in Virginia; about 1664 in Maryland. See James Curtis Ballagh, *A History of Slavery in Virginia* (Baltimore, 1902), pp. 34-44; Carter G. Woodson, *Free Negro Heads of Families in the United States in 1830* (Washington, 1925), p. xv; George Washington Williams, *A History of the Negro Race in America* (New York, 1882), I, 123; George McDowell Stroud, *A Sketch of the Laws Relating to Slavery in the Several States* (Philadelphia, 1827), p. 9. Helen Tunnicliff Catterall (*Judicial Cases concerning American Slavery and the Negro* [Washington, 1926], I, 58-59, 72) says that the first *will* of emancipation was dated 1645; Russell (*op. cit.*, p. 39) and St. George Tucker (*A Dissertation on Slavery; with a Proposal for the Gradual Abolition of It in the State of Virginia* [2d ed.; New York, 1861], p. 34) show that the first *record* of emancipation in Virginia was in 1668—a law subjecting "Negroe Women set free to a tax on titheables." Ulrich Bonnell Phillips (*Life and Labor in the Old South* [Boston, 1929], p. 170) dates the period as the closing decades of the seventeenth century.

3. John Fiske, *Old Virginia and Her Neighbors* (Boston, 1901), II, 199; Woodson, *op. cit.*, p. xxi.

4. See above, pp. 34-35. The legislature of Virginia, in 1667, enacted the law declaring: "Whereas some doubts have arisen whether children that are slaves by birth . . . . should by vertue of their baptisme be made free; It is enacted . . . . that the conferring of baptisme doth not alter the condition of the person as to his bondage or freedom" (Catterall, *op. cit.*, I, 57 [by permission]).

5. See Bevereley B. Mumford, *Virginia's Attitude toward Slavery and Secession* (New York, 1909), p. 51.

6. Slaves were not recruited at the beginning of the Revolution. However, when instances began to appear that they had deserted to the British, it was suggested that they "be given the sword with which to prove their right to freedom" (Woodson, *The Negro in Our History* [Washington, 1927], pp. 123 ff.).

7. North Carolina, for instance, directly after the Revolution, prohibited manumission "except for meritorious services." Later, however, the legislature removed even these restrictions. See Caleb Perry Patterson, *The Negro in Tennessee* (University of Texas Bull. 2205 [Austin, 1922]), p. 17; George Livermore, *Historical Research Re-Soldiers* (Boston, 1862), pp. 109-10.

8. James M. Wright, *The Free Negro in Maryland* ("Columbia University Studies

in History, Economics, and Public Law," Vol. XCVII, No. 3, Whole No. 222 [New York, 1921]), pp. 47 ff.

9. John Spencer Bassett, *Slavery and Servitude in the State of North Carolina* ("Johns Hopkins University Studies in Historical and Political Science," Ser. XVII, Nos. 7–8 [Baltimore, 1899]), pp. 51–55.

10. Catterall, *op. cit.*, I, 109, quoting from Hening, *Statutes at Large*, chap. xxi, p. 39; and *Charles* v. *Hunnicutt*, 5 Call 311 (October, 1804).

11. *Ibid.*, p. 114 (case of *Whiting* v. *Daniel*, 1 Hening and Marshall 390).

12. *Ibid.*, I, 200 (citing *Newton* v. *Poole*, 12 Leigh 112 [March, 1841]). See also *ibid.*, p. 206 (*Lucy and Others* v. *Cheminant*, 2 Grattat 36 [April, 1845]), where some slaves were set free by will, while others were left enslaved; and see *ibid.*, p. 181 (*Miars* v. *Bedford*, 9 Leigh 361), where a man who had two slaves manumitted one and gave the other to a friend (quoted by permission).

13. Catterall (*ibid.*, p. 72) mentions that a certain Lilly was set free "on account of several very acceptable services done by her." She also (*ibid.*, p. 98) records that Joseph Mayo set free all his slaves "on account of their services," as well as the will of Matthew Maben, who freed a slave "in consideration of faithful services, since a child."

14. *Ibid.*, p. 128 (citing *Lemon* v. *Reynolds*, 5 Mumford 552 [April, 1817] [Washington: Carnegie Inst., 1926] [quoted by permission]).

15. *Ibid.*, p. 74.

16. *Ibid.*, p. 318 (citing *Patton* v. *Patton*, J. J. Marshall 389 [April, 1831] [quoted by permission]).

17. *Ibid.*, p. 119 (citing *Bates* v. *Holman*, 3 Hening and Marshall 502 [quoted by permission]).

18. Booker T. Washington, *The Story of the Negro* (New York, 1909), I, 195–96. The essential difference between manumission on principle and manumission because of claims seems to lie in the relation between master and slave. In the former case the slave was conceived as a member of a group, hence the act of manumission was a benevolent act, redounding to the benefit of the master. In the latter case manumission was an act dictated by sentiment or emotion—each case was separate action, the slave was thereby individualized—and both the master and the slave were believed to benefit by the act. This latter procedure was, most likely, the outcome of long association and common experiences on the small farm or small plantation.

19. *Op. cit.*, pp. 70–71. He noted that "upwards of ten thousand had been manumitted since the Revolution." See also Mumford (*op. cit.*, p. 42), who places the number at 13,000 in Virginia, by 1810. A detailed discussion of the point is found in Livermore, *op. cit.*, pp. 113–200. Data on free Negroes before 1790 are very scattered.

20. Census Bureau, *A Century of Population Growth* (Washington, 1909), p. 80, gives the following data:

Year	Number of Slaves	Number of Free Negroes
1790	697,897	59,557
1860	3,953,760	488,070

The statistics for slaves in 1790 show a slight discrepancy (Census Bureau, *Negro Population in the United States, 1790–1915*, p. 55). Otherwise the figures check. A table of growth by census years is found in the latter citation.

21. Woodson, *Free Negro Heads, etc.*, pp. xxiii and xviii.

22. See Tables A and B in Appendix. Interesting notes on conditions in North Caro-

lina and Georgia are found in O. W. Blacknall (David Dodge, pseudonym), "Free Negroes in North Carolina, "*Atlantic Monthly*, LVIII (January, 1886), 23; and Ralph Betts Flanders, "The Free Negro in Ante-bellum Georgia," *North Carolina Historical Review*, IX, No. 3 (July, 1932), 250–59. See also Washington, *op. cit.*, p. 195.

23. Census Bureau, *Negro Population in the United States, 1790–1915*, p. 55, gives the following data:

PERCENTAGE OF TOTAL FREE NEGRO POPULATION BY AREAS

Year	S. Atlantic	E. South Central	North	W. South Central
1790	53.8	.8	45.4	....
1810	51.9	1.8	42.3	4.1
1830	47.9	3.6	43.2	5.3
1860	44.6	4.4	46.2	3.9

Woodson (*The Negro in Our History*, p. 244) mentions that the increase after 1830 was due largely to natural causes since only a few free Negroes had immigrated, or were added by acquisition of new territory, while manumissions had greatly decreased. Patterson (*op. cit.*, p. 179) believes that the influence of North Carolina had extended into Tennessee.

24. *Op. cit.* (New York: Author's copyright, 1921) pp. 346–47 (by permission).

25. Catterall, *op. cit.*, I, 72.

26. Tucker, *op. cit.*, p. 19.

27. Mumford, *op. cit.*, p. 60.

28. *Ibid.*, pp. 92–93.

29. This was in the form of a resolution requesting the governor to communicate with the president of the United States, concerning the problem. Similar resolutions were passed in 1805 and 1816 (see Mumford, *op. cit.*, p. 60).

30. The Society was frequently aided, "on principle," by the more humane churches —notably the Presbyterians of Kentucky. See, on this point, Rev. Heman B. Allen, *The General Assembly and Its Accusers; Being a Compilation from Official Records of the Deliverances of the Church (Presbyterian) on Civil Affairs and Slavery* (Louisville, 1867), pp. 38–40, for minutes and records to this effect.

31. For cases in point see Catterall, *op. cit.*, I, 73–74; *ibid.*, p. 193, *Maund v. McPhail*, 10 Leigh 199 (April, 1839); *ibid.*, p. 206, *Binford v. Robin*, 1 Grattan 327 (January, 1845); *ibid.*, p. 233, *Young v. Vass*, 1 Patton and Heath 167 (January, 1855), where a master provided that two manumitted slaves should be sent to North Carolina; and (*ibid.*, p. 204) the case of John Randolph of Roanoke, who provided in his will that all his slaves—near four hundred in number—be manumitted and "sent to some other State or territory of the United States" and suggested that the executor of the will would be "too wise, just, and humane, to send them to Africa or the West Indies." He likewise provided for the support of the slaves, wherever they were sent. Wm. Fitzhugh left his slaves "unconditionally free, with the privilege of having their expense paid to whatever place of residence they may select" (see Theodore M. Whitfield, *Slavery Agitation in Virginia, 1829–1932* [Baltimore, 1930], p. 10).

32. Washington, *op. cit.*, I, 193. See Tucker, *op. cit.*, p. 88; Blacknall, *op. cit.*, p. 20.

33. George Fitzhugh, *Sociology for the South; or the Failure of Free Society* (Richmond, Va., 1854), p. 271.

34. See Distinguished Southern Writers, *The Pro-slavery Argument* (Charleston, 1852), p. 435.

35. Patterson (*op. cit.*, p. 156) quotes Judge Catron. Edward Ingle (*Southern Side Lights: A Picture of Social and Economic Life in the South, a Generation before the War* [New York, 1896], pp. 279–80) summarizes the laws enacted to prevent free Negroes from "becoming an element of disturbance among the slaves." Travelers, such as Arthur Singleton (*Letters from the South and West* [Boston, 1824], pp. 80–81) and J. C. Buckingham (*The Slaves States of America* [London, 1842], I, 242), also note the situation, the latter saying: "In Charleston, the number of free blacks was very considerable; and as many of them had leisure and means, and communicated freely with slaves, a union and concentration—of their sympathies, made them much more dangerous. . . . ."

36. It is not to be understood that all masters freed their natural children, for, by 1850, 60 per cent of the mulatto population was still enslaved. E.g., C. B. Marryat (*A Diary in America; with Remarks on Its Institutions* [Paris, 1839], p. 252) notes that a member of Congress for Georgia "brought up a fine family of children, his own issue by a female slave; permitted them to call him by the endearing title of 'papa,' but lived to see them sold at a public auction." On the other hand, not all mulattoes were children of masters. Some were offspring of mulatto parents, of masters' sons, and, in certain cases, of overseers. In general, however, none of these latter had power to manumit. Yet, it is significant that 8 per cent of the slave population was mulatto, while 37 per cent of the free Negroes was of this type. The percentage of mulattoes was also considerably "higher in the slave than in the free states" (see, on this point, Edward Byron Reuter, *The Mulatto in the United States; Including a Study of the Role of Mixed-Blood Races throughout the World* [Boston, 1918], pp. 113 and 116).

37. Reuter, *The American Race Problem* (New York, 1927), 131; *The Mulatto, etc.* p. 114.

38. This was especially true in New Orleans, Mobile, Charleston, and Richmond. In Charleston the class was known as "bright fellows" or "white niggers" (F. C. Adams, *Manuel Pereira*, pp. 160, 162, 163 n.).

39. Woodson, *Education of the Negro, etc.*, p. 110. There was "an almost universal feeling that the privilege of this class should differ from that of the whites. . . . . But, the best people early learned to show much interest in a considerable number of thrifty free persons of color" in Richmond, Petersburg, and Norfolk, in Virginia, "where there had been an extensive miscegenation of the races" (by permission).

40. Some persons thought that mulattoes should not be slaves. Others felt that they should be granted privileges not given to blacks. Some of the mulatto slaves had imbibed this idea, one mulatto boy asking Mrs. Kemble for permission to carry a gun, "on account of his color," while a mulatto woman slave asked to be excused from field labor for the same reason (Frances Anne Kemble, *A Journal of Residence on a Georgia Plantation in 1838–1839* [New York, 1863], pp. 131, 193–94). But, again, the notion that mulattoes were inferior to, and worse than, blacks existed even among certain Africans, where, it is said, "they bore the worst of characters" (Nicholas Owen [Eveline Martin, ed.], *Journal of a Slave-Dealer—a View of Some Remarkable Incidents in the Life of Nics. Owen on the Coast of Africa and America from the Year 1746 to the Year 1757* [London, 1930]). See Catterall (*op. cit.*, I, 201–2) for a criminal case where a white man murdered another, after heaping vituperation on him, rising crescendo to a "damned, free Negro, mulatto looking, S—— of a B——." All persons evidently did not believe in mulatto superiority and privileges.

41. Woodson, *Free Negro Heads, etc.*, p. xxi.

42. Washington, *op. cit.*, pp. 198–99. Previous exclusion, as we have noted, tended be on the basis of Christianity.

24. *Ibid.*, p. 9.

25. Quoted as a document in Wright, *op. cit.*, p. 168. See also, on the point, Washington, *Story of the Negro*, II, 5.

26. For example, in Helena, Arkansas, where there were, in fact, few slaves, and where relations between master and slave had been less intimate than in the older regions, deserting blacks congregated three thousand or more strong (T. S. Staples, *Reconstruction in Arkansas* [New York, 1923], p. 53).

27. William H. Russell, *My Diary, North and South* (Boston, 1863), pp. 78–79 (dated April 16, 1861).

28. *Op. cit.*, pp. 15, 52, 181. The instances appeared between March and June of 1861. Was this suspicion?

29. Washington, *The Story of the Negro*, II, 9.

30. This point of view is expressed by William T. Alexander, *History of the Colored Race in America* (Kansas City, Mo., 1887), p. 148; T. D. Ozanne, *The South as It Is: Or Twenty-one Years' Experience in the Southern States* (London, 1863), pp. 72–73; M. Evans, *Black and White in the Southern States* (London, 1915), p. 87; and Robert Park and Ernest W. Burgess, *Introduction to the Science of Sociology* (Chicago, 1921), p. 137. Ulrich Bonnell Phillips (*Life and Labor in the Old South* [Boston, 1929] pp., 234–35, 258, 259) shows, however, that many did desert and concluded that the trait was not instinctive.

31. William Reynolds Vance, *Slavery in Kentucky* (Washington and Lee University dissertation [privately printed], 1895), p. 55; John Spencer Bassett, *Slavery in the State of North Carolina* ("Johns Hopkins University Studies in Historical and Political Science," Ser. XVII, Nos. 7–8 [Baltimore, 1899]), p. 108.

32. Henry Latham, *Black and White: A Journal of a Three Months' Tour in the United States* (London, 1867), pp. 264 and 275.

33. Chestnut, *op. cit.*, pp. 93 and 224.

34. Edward Ruffin, "Extracts from the Diary of Edward Ruffin, on the Conduct of Negroes during the War, 1861–1865," *William and Mary Quarterly*, XXIII (1913), 258–63.

NOTES FOR CHAPTER IX

1. "When the habits are running smoothly the attention is relaxed; it is not at work. But when something happens to disturb the run of habit the attention is called into play and devises a new mode of behavior which will meet the crisis. That is, the attention establishes new habits, or it is its function to do so. . . . . But crisis is not to be habitually regarded as violent. It is simply a disturbance of habit, and it may be no more than an incident, a stimulation, a suggestion . . . . such conditions as the exhaustion of game, the intrusion of outsiders, defeat in battle, floods, drought, pestilence, and famine illustrate one class of crisis" (W. I. Thomas, *Source Book for Social Origins* [Boston, 1909], pp. 16–18).

2. Robert E. Park, "Negro Race Consciousness as Reflected in Race Literature," *American Review*, I, No. 5 (1923), 510.

3. C. H. J. Taylor, *Whites and Blacks* (Atlanta, 1899), p. 7; F. D. Srygley, *Seventy Years in Dixie* (Nashville, 1891), p. 50; Whitelaw Reid, *After the War: A Southern Tour* (London, 1865), p. 273; V. V. Clayton, *Black and White under the Old Regime* (Milwaukee, 1899), p. 172; Booker T. Washington, *Up from Slavery* (New York, 1901), p. 22.

4. For cases in point see Washington, *op. cit.*, pp. 13–14; G. Campbell, *White and Black—Outcome of a Trip to the United States* (London, 1879), p. 341; and David Macrae, *Americans at Home* (Edinburgh, 1870), I, 171.

5. E. King, *The Great South* (Hartford, 1875), p. 553; James J. McDonald, *Life in Old Virginia* (Norfolk, Va., 1907), p. 173.

6. McDonald, *op. cit.*, p. 173.

7. Reid, *op. cit.*, pp. 100 and 112; see also King, *op. cit.*, p. 299.

8. Campbell, *op. cit.*, p. 349; King, *op. cit.*, p. 430.

9. Reid, *op. cit.*, pp. 93, 111, 120.

10. Robert Somers, *The Southern States since the War* (New York, 1871), p. 130.

11. King, *op. cit.*, p. 303.

12. *Ibid.*, p. 788.

13. Reid, *op. cit.*, p. 502.

14. J. T. Trowbridge (*The Desolated States, and the Work of Restoration, 1865-1868* [Hartford, 1868], pp. 162–63) recorded an instance of this kind in Virginia.

15. Alrutheus A. Taylor, *The Negro in the Reconstruction of Virginia* (Washington 1926), p. 54. Gilbert T. Stephenson (*Racial Distinctions in American Law* [New York, 1910], p. 117) shows that Tennessee did, in fact, pass just such a law. Only one group of Negroes—a delegation attending the constitutional convention of 1867-68—had sought to sit in the dress circle of any theater of Richmond. When these were directed to the gallery and refused to go, they had their admissions returned.

16. A. A. Taylor, *op. cit.*, p. 53.

17. Stephenson (*op. cit.*, p. 137) advances this idea, with much evidence to support it.

18. Reid, *op. cit.*, pp. 299 and 507; King, *op. cit.*, p. 436.

19. Reid, *op. cit.*, p. 509.

20. Especially in South Carolina were these relations cordial, according to Reid (*op. cit.*, p. 130); Mary Boykin Chestnut, *Diary from Dixie* (New York, 1905), pp. 381, 385, 387, 395; McDonald, *op. cit.*, p. 172; Francis Butler Simpkins and Robert Hilliard Woody, *South Carolina in Reconstruction* (Chapel Hill, N.C., 1932), pp. 338–72. Cf. Robert E. Park, "Racial Assimilation in Secondary Groups," *American Journal of Sociology*, XIX (1913–14), 606–23.

21. Srygley, *op. cit.*, pp. 302–3; King, *op. cit.*, pp. 567 and 789; Reid, *op. cit.*, p. 143.

22. King, *op. cit.*, p. 789. Another example in point is that of the bartender at White Sulphur Springs, Virginia. "With a venerable head of gray wool, the bartender mixes his juleps with a flourish, as if keeping time to the music. 'Haven't I waited on you befo', sah? At Capon Springs? Sorry, sah, thought I knowed you. Sorry, but glad to know you now, sah. If that julep don't suit you, sah, th'ow it in my face'" (W. Alexander MacCorkle, *White Sulphur Springs* [New York, 1916], p. 300).

23. Clayton, *op. cit.*, pp. 180–83.

24. *Ibid.*, pp. 170–72.

25. Even in the halls of legislature, after Negroes began to attend, the practice of separation, and the rule that Negroes must not sit while white people sat, was observed (Campbell, *op. cit.*, pp. 309 and 374).

26. Somers, *op. cit.*, p. 51; Reid, *op. cit.*, p. 34.

27. "The new situation has the nature of a crisis, and in a crisis the individual tends either to reorganize his life positively, adopt new habits and standards to meet the new situation, or to repudiate his old habits and their restraints without reorganizing his life—which is demoralization" (Robert E. Park and Herber A. Miller, *Old World Traits Transplanted* [Chicago, 1925], p. 61 [by permission]).

28. King, *op. cit.*, p. 304.

29. See, on this point, statements in A. A. Taylor, *The Negro in South Carolina during Reconstruction*, p. 21; G. W. Cable, "The Freedman's Case in Equity," *Century Magazine*, XXIX, No. 3 (January, 1885), 412; and C. H. J. Taylor, *op. cit.*, pp. 8 and 10.

30. Cf. C. Johnson, *Highways and Byways of the South* (New York, 1895), p. 278; John Preston McConnell, *Negroes and Their Treatment in Virginia* (Pulaski, Va., 1910),

p. 79; Henry Latham, *Black and White: A Journal of a Three Months' Tour in the United States* (London, 1867), p. 144; King, *op. cit.*, pp. 38 and 617.

31. Kelley Miller, e.g., offers the explanation that the field hand displayed more belligerence and independence in freedom (see *Baltimore Afro-American*, October 23, 1923, p. 16).

32. A. A. Taylor, *op. cit.*, p. 9; C. H. J. Taylor, *op. cit.*, pp. 10–11.

33. See two cases given in Reid, *op. cit.*, pp. 417 and 419.

34. Washington, *op. cit.*, pp. 23–24; Robert Russa Moton, *What the Negro Thinks* (Garden City, N.Y., 1929), p. 190; Orland Kay Armstrong, *Old Massa's People* (Indianapolis, 1931), p. 60.

35. Robert Ferguson, *America, during and after the War* (London, 1866), p. 216.

36. Chestnut, *op. cit.*, p. 389; see also Johnson, *op. cit.*, p. 332. Both instances were, of course, resented by white people.

37. E. Franklin Lee (*Social Solidarity and Race Inequalities in the South* [Columbia University dissertation (privately printed), 1911], p. 16) testifies that the usage became quite general.

38. See Reid, *op. cit.*, pp. 84–85; Trowbridge, *op. cit.*, p. 206.

39. See, on the point, Charles William Ramsdell, *Reconstruction in Texas* ("Columbia University Studies in History, Economics and Public Law," Vol. XXXVI, No. 1 [New York, 1910]), p. 71; Ferguson, *op. cit.*, p. 229.

40. The testimony on this point is overwhelming. See Trowbridge, *op. cit.*, pp. 205–6; Campbell, *op. cit.*, p. 150; McConnell, *op. cit.*, pp. 19–20, 22, 29; King, *op. cit.*, *passim.* "There was one difference between slavery and freedom which was very real to the freedman. And this was the liberty to move. To move from one plantation to another in case he was discontented was one of the ways in which a freedman was able to realize his freedom and make sure that he possessed it" (Robert E. Park and Ernest W. Burgess, *Introduction to the Science of Sociology* [2d ed.; Chicago, 1926], p. 623 [by permission]).

41. A. A. Taylor, *The Negro in the Reconstruction of Virginia*, p. 68; King, *op. cit.*, p. 32; Booker T. Washington and W. E. B. Dubois, *The Negro in the South* (Philadelphia, 1907), p. 45.

42. A. A. Taylor, *op. cit.*, p. 16.

43. Ferguson, *op. cit.*, p. 230; C. H. J. Taylor, *op. cit.*, p. 7. Yet, in some cases of agreement, the wages were not paid (see Campbell, *op. cit.*, p. 316; Trowbridge, *op. cit.*, pp. 155–56).

44. McDonald, *op. cit.*, pp. 176–77; see also Somers, *op. cit.*, p. 280.

45. Somers, *op. cit.*, p. 130.

46. Elizabeth Ware Pearson (ed.), *Letters from Port Royal; Written at the Time of the Civil War* (Boston, 1906), pp. 102 and 181.

47. Campbell, *op. cit.*, pp. 144 and 308.

48. A. A. Taylor, *op. cit.*, p. 16.

49. The actual vagrancy may have been less than it was pictured. Before the war Negroes had not moved about so much but had been kept at work and did not excite alarm because of idleness. See, this on point, McConnell, *op. cit.*, p. 49.

50. *Ibid.*, pp. 40–42; Reid, *op. cit.*, pp. 343, 344, 373.

51. Reid, *op. cit.*, p. 373; Latham, *op. cit.*, pp. 271–72. When the Freedman's Aid Bureau interfered with these practices, the cry went up that legislation should be invoked to make Negroes work.

52. Reid, *op. cit.*, p. 151; cf. Trowbridge, *op. cit.*, p. 393.

53. P. Clayton, *Aftermath of the Civil War in Arkansas* (New York, 1915), p. 208; Reid, *op. cit.*, pp. 416–17.

54. See, e.g., Trowbridge, *op. cit.*, pp. 367–68.

55. See cases in Reid, *op. cit.*, p. 325; McConnell, *op. cit.*, p. 36; A. A. Taylor, *op. cit.*, p. 82.

56. If this plan served to bring adjustment, it is not clear how it was done. Negroes seemed unwilling to work under overseers of their own racial group (see Reid, *op. cit.*, p. 462; Trowbridge, *op. cit.*, p. 483).

57. See George K. Holmes, "Peons of the South," *Annals of the American Academy of Political and Social Science*, IV (September, 1893), 265–74.

58. See Walter L. Fleming (*Laws Relating to Freedmen* [Morgantown, W.Va., 1904], *passim*), where all the laws of this period are given; A. A. Taylor, *op. cit.*, pp. 16 and 18; McConnell, *op. cit.*, pp. 49–52, 54–55, 101; and Carter G. Woodson, *The Rural Negro* (Washington, 1930), p. 67.

59. For parades see Ferguson, *op. cit.*, p. 218; Somers, *op. cit.*, p. 55; A. A. Taylor, *op. cit.*, p. 64.

60. A. A. Taylor, *op. cit.*, pp. 62–66; King, *op. cit.*, p. 580.

61. Fleming, *A Documentary History of the Reconstruction* (Cleveland, 1907), II, 270; Reid, *op. cit.*, pp. 298 and 386; King, *op. cit.*, p. 778; McConnell, *op. cit.*, p. 106.

62. Details of this riot may be found in A. A. Taylor, *op. cit.*, p. 23; and McConnell, *op. cit.*, p. 74.

63. Chestnut, *op. cit.*, p. 347.

64. See Fleming, *The Sequel to Appomattox: A Chronicle of the Re-union of the States* ("Chronicles of America" series, Vol. XXXII [New Haven, 1921]), p. 42.

65. Unpublished lectures on "The Negro in America."

66. Mississippi and South Carolina in 1865; Alabama in 1866; Georgia in 1868. Fleming, *Laws Relating to Freedmen*, pp. 14, 17, 32; *Documentary History of the Reconstruction*, II, 266; A. A. Taylor, *op. cit.*, pp. 56–62. Ferguson (*op. cit.*, p. 236) was present at the actual passage of the Alabama bill. See Stephenson (*op. cit.*, p. 81) for a summary of the laws—constitutional and statutory.

67. Trowbridge (*op.cit.*, p. 111) and Fleming (*Documentary History of the Reconstruction*, II, 292) give cases where Negro men married white women; Somers (*op. cit.*, p. 226) and King (*op. cit.*, p. 320) cite instances where Negro women were married to white men.

68. Latham, *op. cit.*, p. 276.

69. David Quinn, *Petition and Memorial Addressed to the United States Congress Asking for a Re-establishment of Slavery in the United States* (Chicago, 1866), p. 11.

70. Julian Ralph, *Dixie: Or Other Southern Scenes and Sketches* (New York, 1895), p. 374.

71. See U.S. Congress, *Report of the Joint Committee on Reconstruction* (39th Cong., 1st sess. [Washington, 1866]), Part II, p. 5; Johnson, *op. cit.*, p. 333; Pearson, *op. cit.*, p. 210.

72. An editorial in the *Richmond* (Va.) *Enquirer*, of September 6, 1866, suggested that white girls should no longer be accompanied by a Negro while riding horseback, even though the Negro was a servant (A. A. Taylor, *op. cit.*, p. 53).

73. See Chestnut, *op. cit.*, p. 345; C. H. J. Taylor, *op. cit.*, p. 10.

74. Reid, *op. cit.*, pp. 84–85.

75. Trowbridge, *op. cit.*, p. 291.

76. McConnell, *op. cit.*, pp. 63–65; Pearson, *op. cit.*, p. 108.

77. Buckner H. Payne ("Ariel," pesudonym), *The Negro: What is His Ethnological Status?* (Cincinnati, 1867), p. 48.

78. See Quinn, *op. cit.*, p. 23.

79. See A. A. Taylor, *op. cit.*, pp. 46–47, 58.

80. Editorial in the *Daily South* (New Orleans), November 19, 1865, quoted in Reid, *op. cit.*, p. 411.

81. Editorial in the *Richmond Dispatch*, January 11, 1871, quoted in A. A. Taylor, *op. cit.*, p. 54.

82. Reid, *op. cit.*, p. 218.

83. Somers, *op. cit.*, p. 58.

84. See instances in Reid, *op. cit.*, pp. 211, 297, 331, 409, 418–420; and Trowbridge, *op. cit.*, pp. 138, 228, 295, 576.

85. A widely known case was the "Dr. Watson case" from Virginia (see A. A. Taylor, *op. cit.*, p. 106; McConnell, *op. cit.*, pp. 66–67).

86. "G—— D—— the infamous, dirty liver-hearted scoundrel. . . . . The dirty Yankee says a nigger is as good as a white man. The old abolition sneak" (Reid, *op. cit.*, p. 342).

87. Charles Nordhoff, *The Cotton States in the Spring and Summer of 1875* (New York, 1876), p. 106.

88. Reid, *op. cit.*, pp. 240 and 256.

89. Campbell, *op. cit.*, p. 299. The first bill was passed in 1866.

90. John Wallace, *Carpet-Bag Rule in Florida* (Jacksonville, Fla., 1888), p. 63; Fleming, *Documentary History of the Reconstruction*, II, 282; Reid, *op. cit.*, p. 259.

91. Reid, *After the War*, pp. 243–44 (Chief Justice Salmon P. Chase).

92. *Report of Freedman's Aid Society* (1874), quoted in Fleming, *Documentary History of the Reconstruction*, II, 256.

93. P. Clayton, *Aftermath of the Civil War in Arkansas* (New York: Neale Publishing Co., 1915), p. 117.

94. Fleming, *Laws Relating to Freedmen*, p. 12.

95. This point of view is expressed by J. K. Commons, *Races and Immigrants in America* (New York, 1924), p. 113; D. A. Mayo, "The Third Estate of the South," *New England Magazine* (November, 1890), p. 308; King, *op. cit.*, pp. 372 and 730; McConnell, *op. cit.*, p. 92; Trowbridge, *op. cit.*, p. 584; and C. H. J. Taylor, *op. cit.*, p. 10.

96. King, *op. cit.*, p. 291.

97. *Op. cit.*, p. 349.

98. King, *op. cit.*, p. 789 (called "niggerisms" by the author).

99. *Ibid.*, pp. 297.

100. *Senate Report on Capital and Labor*, IV (1884), 159; quoted in Fleming, *Documentary History of the Reconstruction*, II, 446.

101. *Op. cit.*, p. 61.

102. See *Pastoral Letter of the Bishops* (M.E. church, South [1865]) and *Resolutions of the Methodist Protestant Church of Alabama; Minutes of the Alabama Baptist State Convention* (1865), as quoted in Fleming, *Documentary History of the Reconstruction*, II, 245, 246, 250.

103. As in South Carolina by Reid (*op. cit.*, pp. 35 and 101) and as in Virginia by Trowbridge (*op. cit.*, pp. 182–83).

104. The whites sat in the front, or occasionally, in the rear (see Reid, [*op. cit.*, p. 79] for South Carolina and King [*op. cit.*, p. 630] for Virginia).

105. Nordhoff, *Communistic Societies in the United States* (New York, 1875), p. 207.

106. Washington, *op. cit.*, p. 157.

107. Cable, *op. cit.*, p. 418.

108. Henry W. Grady, "In Plain Black and White," *Century*, XXIX, No. 6 (April, 1885), 911; Nordhoff, *The Cotton States in the Spring and Summer of 1875*, p. 111; Fleming, *Documentary History of the Reconstruction*, II, 275.

109. *American Annual Encyclopedia* (1866), p. 461; Fleming, *Documentary History of the Reconstruction*, II, 251; McConnell, *op. cit.*, p. 108.

110. See, on the point, McConnell, *op. cit.*, pp. 28–29.

111. See Fleming, *Documentary History of the Reconstruction*, II, 218; A. A. Taylor, *op. cit.*, p. 178.

112. See two illustrations in C. H. J. Taylor, *op. cit.*, p. 45—one recording that a carriage was sent to escort a Negro bishop to a church where he was engaged to preach to white people; and another stating that a southern town was thrown open to a Negro conference.

113. E.g., the Methodist Episcopal church, South, provided a separate organization of its Negro members at Jackson, Tennessee, in 1870, ordained its bishops, and gave it the name of the "Colored Methodist Episcopal church" (William A. Bell, "Missions and Co-operation of the M.E. Church, South, with the C.M.E. Church" [mimeographed; Nashville, 1933], pp. 42 and 46).

114. McConnell, *op. cit.*, p. 109; McDonald, *op. cit.*, p. 276; King, *op. cit.*, p. 608; and Campbell, *op. cit.*, p. 52.

115. Ulrich B. Phillips, *History of the Transportation in the Eastern Cotton Belt to 1860* (New York, 1908), p. 396.

116. The practice was noted by travelers in Virginia (1867), in Georgia (1870), and in Mississippi (1874). See Latham, *op. cit.*, p. 97; Somers, *op. cit.*, p. 82; King, *op. cit.*, pp. 554 and 782.

117. See cases in Reid, *op. cit.*, p. 421; A. A. Taylor, *op. cit.*, p. 52; and Cable, *op. cit.*, p. 415. Latham (*op. cit.*, p. 97) remarked that it was "not the right thing to do" for white men to sit in the smoker with Negroes. Florida law prohibited Negroes from entering any public assembly of whites, as early as 1866 (Fleming, *Laws for Freedmen*, p. 30).

118. *Op. cit.*, p. 783. He also noted separate waiting-rooms in the depots but remarked that the practice had died out, save in some sections of Georgia, by 1874 (p. 782). He also found a Negro who remarked that he "was damned if he appreciated" the separation (*ibid.*).

119. Latham, *op. cit.*, p. 143; Somers, *op. cit.*, p. 216; Trowbridge, *op. cit.*, p. 393.

120. Trowbridge (*op. cit.*, p. 352) records the first instance; King (*op. cit.*, p. 72) mentions the latter.

121. A. A. Taylor, *op. cit.*, p. 52.

122. Nordhoff, *The Cotton States in the Spring and Summer of 1875*, p. 106.

123. See Woodson, *The Education of the Negro prior to 1861* (New York, 1915), *passim*.

124. Washington, *The Story of the Negro* (New York, 1909), II, 116–17; C. W. Birnie, "The Education of the Negro in Charleston, South Carolina, before the Civil War," *Journal of Negro History*, XII (January, 1927), 20–21.

125. *Story of the Negro*, II, 115–16, 133.

126. Washington, *Up from Slavery*, p. 80.

127. *American Annual Encyclopedia* (1866), pp. 376–77. The quotation from this source may also be found in A. A. Taylor, *op. cit.*; McConnell, *op. cit.*, p. 93; and Trowbridge, *op. cit.*, p. 228.

128. Separate schools were established by statute or constitutional provision in the following order: Louisiana, 1852; Tennessee, 1866; Arkansas, 1867; Kentucky, Maryland, and Virginia, 1870; Georgia, 1872; Alabama and North Carolina, 1875; Texas, 1876; Mississippi, 1878; Florida, 1887. The laws of Arkansas, South Carolina, Mississippi, and Louisiana were subject to repeal or revision by legislatures of which Negroes were members. Yet, they later reverted to the original separation scheme. See, on the point, *Negro Year Book* (1926), pp. 285–87; Stephenson, *op. cit.*, pp. 170–86; Somers, *op. cit.*, pp. 19–20, 228; A. A. Taylor, *op. cit.*, pp. 146–54; King, *op. cit.*, pp. 97–98, 135,

267, 294, 463, 470, 712; Fleming, *Documentary History of the Reconstruction*, II, 189, 203–5.

129. Hampton Institute, at Hampton, Virginia, did at first, however, accept Indians as students.

130. On the point see King, *op. cit.*, p. 601.

131. See Trowbridge, *op. cit.*, p. 392; King, *op. cit.*, p. 370.

132. Fleming, *Documentary History of the Reconstruction*, II, 165–66.

133. See Campbell, *op. cit.*, p. 356; McConnell, *op. cit.*, p. 24. "The Southern whites .... complained that the teachers were political emissaries and taught doctrines of social equality, that they made the blacks dislike the whites, that the teachers were fanatical or of bad character, that the schools were centers of trouble, and that in the white schools, textbooks hostile to the South were used and the pupils forced to sing Northern songs of the war" (Fleming, *Documentary History of the Reconstruction*, II, 157, 183–84; cf. Nordhoff, *The Cotton States in the Spring and Summer of 1875*, p. 106; Macrae, *op. cit.*, I, 238).

134. See Reid, *op. cit.*, 46; Ferguson, *op. cit.*, p. 199; Trowbridge, *op. cit.*, p. 188; King, *op. cit.*, p. 599.

135. Ferguson, *op. cit.*, p. 200.

136. Woodson, *The Negro in Our History*, pp. 103–4; Somers, *op. cit.*, p. 155.

137. Ferguson, *op. cit.*, p. 204; Reid, *op. cit.*, p. 248.

138. See Fleming (*Documentary History of the Reconstruction*, II, 177–80, 196) for cases in point.

139. See Campbell, *op. cit.*, p. 313.

140. Fleming, *Documentary History of the Reconstruction*, II, 181. Washington (*Story of the Negro*, II, 139) thought that white southerners who did teach Negroes directly after the war did so as a means to "eke out a livelihood." Yet the practice may have been governed largely by local traditions, as in Georgia. Cf. the statement of the superintendent of education (1867) in *Negro Year Book* (1926), p. 286, where "lawyers, ministers, physicians, editors, and all classes of white people" applied for positions to teach freedmen. Occasionally a Confederate soldier, or his daughter, might be discovered teaching freedmen (King, *op. cit.*, p. 782; A. A. Taylor, *op. cit.*, pp. 150–52). Or, as in Virginia, southern white people might, in the cities, instruct the freedmen, while freedmen, in the rural districts, might be found instructing one another (A. A. Taylor, *op. cit.*, p. 153; Reid, *op. cit.*, p. 511).

141. See cases in Fleming, *Documentary History of the Reconstruction*, II, 176; Reid, *op. cit.*, p. 511.

142. U.S. Congress, *op. cit.*, Part II, pp. 195, 249–50; Pearson, *Letters from Port Royal*, p. 65; Washington, *Story of the Negro*, II, 139.

143. Pearson, *op. cit.*, pp. 208–9.

144. Washington, *Story of the Negro*, II, 28 ff.; A. P. Stokes, *Tuskegee Institute, the First Fifty Years* (Tuskegee, Ala., 1931), pp. 7–8.

145. Ramsdell, *op. cit.*, pp. 45 and 47.

146. V. V. Clayton, *op. cit.*, p. 162.

147. Ramsdell, *op. cit.*, p. 45.

148. See Fleming, *Laws Relating to Freedmen*, *passim*; Trowbridge, *op. cit.*, pp. 369 ff.; McConnell, *op. cit.*, pp. 61 and 104; Nordhoff, *The Cotton States. etc.*, p. 92.

149. See "The City Ordinances of Opelousas, Louisiana," in Fleming, *Laws Relating to Freedmen*, pp. 30–32; Thomas S. Staples, *Reconstruction in Arkansas* ("Columbia University Studies in History, Economics and Public Law," Vol. CIX, Whole No. 254 [New York, 1923]), pp. 83, 213–14.

150. Washington, *Story of the Negro*, II, 8–9, 10.

151. The history and dates of the several enactments may be found in Stephenson, *op. cit.*, pp. 35 ff.; and Fleming, *Documentary History of the Reconstruction*, II, 102 ff.; also see A. A. Taylor, *op. cit.*, pp. 22–23.

152. Proposed in 1869; proclaimed in force in 1870.

153. *Story of Negro*, II, 28.

154. See, on the point, *ibid.*, pp. 13–16; and Staples *op. cit.*, 219. The first move to obtain some part in the government, says Washington, was made by the free Negroes of New Orleans. They asked to be permitted to take part in the establishment of the new government under the convention plan. Some meetings were held in South Carolina to which all people, without distinction of color, were invited. In 1865 the Negroes called a state convention to confer and deliberate so that the black codes might be removed. They addressed a communication to the whites bringing out these facts. Colored Conservatives met at Nashville, Tennessee, April 5, 1867, saying that they took their stand with the Union Conservatives of Tennessee and invited their race to do the same.

155. Nordhoff (*The Cotton States, etc.*, p. 12) gives a brief, but excellent, description of this situation.

156. Washington, *The Story of the Negro*, II, 10 ff.

157. *Ibid.*, p. 22.

158. Campbell, *op. cit.*, p. 181.

159. C. H. J. Taylor, *op. cit.*, p. 19.

160. Washington, *Up from Slavery*, p. 111. A comment to the same effect is found in Thomas Nelson Page, *The Old South* (New York, 1892), pp. 311–12.

161. See Wallace, *op. cit.*, p. 42; Fleming, *Documentary History of the Reconstruction*, II, 4–5, 27, 88–89; McConnell, *op. cit.*, p. 27.

162. C. H. J. Taylor, *op. cit.*, p. 19; Fleming, *Documentary History of the Reconstruction*, II, 283.

163. Nordhoff, *The Cotton States, etc.*, pp. 34, 36, 39, 74; Campbell, *op. cit.*, p. 309; King, *op. cit.*, pp. 113, 426, 427.

164. The point has been touched upon by historians, but we refer to testimony of eyewitnesses, such as Somers, *op. cit.*, pp. 17, 41; King, *op. cit.*, pp. 129, 333, 461; Nordhoff, *The Cotton States, etc.*, p. 49; Washington, *Story of the Negro*, II, 22.

165. See James S. Pike (*The Prostrate State: South Carolina under Negro Government* [New York, 1874], pp. 15, 42, 63, 110) and Somers (*op. cit.*, pp. 226–27) on the point.

166. King, *op. cit.*, pp. 281–82, 315, 420.

167. See Stephenson, *op. cit.*, p. 79; McConnell, *op. cit.*, pp. 118–19; Nordhoff, *The Cotton States, etc.*, p. 35; Wallace, *op. cit.*, p. 86; Fleming, *Documentary History of the Reconstruction*, II, 285–88.

168. King, *op. cit.*, p. 461; Latham, *op. cit.*, p. 218; William A. Dunning, *The American Nation: A History*, Vol. XXII: *Reconstruction: Political and Economic* (New York, 1907), p. 114.

169. Armstrong, *Old Massa's People* (Indianapolis: Bobbs-Merrill, 1931), p. 328 (by permission).

170. See, on the point, Washington, *Up from Slavery*, p. 84; A. A. Taylor, *op. cit.*, p. iii; Nordhoff, *The Cotton States, etc.*, p. 17.

171. The condition was true as late as 1910, says McConnell (*op. cit.*, p. 14).

172. Maurice S. Evans, *Black and White in the Southern States* (London, 1915), p. 53. Perhaps on hearsay alone.

173. Pike, *op. cit.*, p. 21.
174. Staples, *op. cit.*, p. 218 (by permission).
175. Macrae, *op. cit.*, I, 248.
176. *Ibid.*, p. 161.
177. Cf. King, *op. cit.*, pp. 89, 298; Staples, *op. cit.*, p. 129.
178. Cable, *op. cit.*, p. 412; Page, *op. cit.*, pp. 342–43; Somers, *op. cit.*, pp. 89 and 298.
179. Joseph Alexander Tillinghast, *The Negro in Africa and America* (New York, 1902), p. 194; Fleming, *Documentary History of the Reconstruction*, II, 226, 265–66.
180. P. Clayton, *op. cit.*, p. 307; Nordhoff, *The Cotton States, etc.*, p. 77; King, *op. cit.*, p. 96.
181. See comments offered by Somers, *op. cit.*, p. 153; and King, *op. cit.*, p. 715.
182. *Op. cit.*, p. 583.
183. *Op. cit.*, pp. 784–85.
184. Fleming, *Documentary History of the Reconstruction*, II, 34–35.
185. Cf. *Negro Year Book* (1925–26), pp. 232–33; and *Atlantic Monthly*, XXIX, 909.
186. The thought, while agreed with here, is from Washington, *Story of the Negro*, II, 13, 31.
187. A classic statement of this position is found in Grady, *op. cit.*, pp. 909–17. Similar positions are taken by Tillinghast (*op. cit.*, p. 194), Latham (*op. cit.*, p. 277), and Page (*op. cit.*, pp. 305–6).
188. See Washington, *Story of the Negro*, II, 54.
189. The evidence on this point is overwhelming (see Washington, *op. cit.*, II, 29; Reid, *op. cit.*, p. 244; Pearson, *op. cit.*, p. 124; U.S. Congress, *op. cit.*, Part II, p. 259; A. A. Taylor, *op. cit.*, p. 12; Pike, *op. cit.*, pp. 276–77; Staples, *op. cit.*, pp. 204–5; Chestnut, *op. cit.*, p. 397).
190. O. W. Blacknall (David Dodge, pseudonym), "Free Negroes of North Carolina," *Atlantic Monthly*, LVII (January, 1886), 29; King, *op. cit.*, p. 453; Fleming, *Documentary History of the Reconstruction*, II, 279.
191. Ferguson (*op. cit.*, p. 262) says that the movement started in 1865 in Nashville, Tennessee.
192. See A. A. Taylor, *op. cit.*, p. 160; Grady, *op. cit.*, p. 912; Campbell, *op. cit.*, p. 384.
193. *Senate Report on Capital and Labor*, IV, 454—quoted in Fleming, *Documentary History of the Reconstruction*, II, 446.
194. McConnell, *op. cit.*, pp. 40–41.
195. Trowbridge, *op. cit.*, p. 287; A. A. Taylor, *op. cit.*, p. 131.
196. *Op. cit.*, p. 258.
197. *Ibid.*, p. 194.

NOTES FOR CHAPTER X

1. William Archibald Dunning (*Studies in Southern History and Politics* [New York, 1914], p. 241) dates the beginning of the modern period in politics, in 1890, from the adoption of the Mississippi constitution providing that election or registration officers could exclude Negroes from voting by certain tests. Booker T. Washington (*Story of the Negro* [New York, 1909], II, 28) uses the date of the last speech of a Negro in Congress, before De Priest, as the beginning of a new era. The speech was in 1899.

2. Cf. John Dewey (*Human Nature and Conduct* [New York, 1922], p. 108), where, among other things, he says, "Political and legal institutions may be altered, even abolished; but the bulk of popular thought which has been shaped to their patterns persists."

3. Robert Russa Moton (*What the Negro Thinks* [Garden City, N.Y., Doubleday-Doran, 1929], pp. 52–53) remarked that this legislation "looked to a re-establishment of disabilities such as the federal law would allow, and that would effectively remove the Negro from contact with the white man's world except where he could be used to personal or general advantage." Cf. also G. W. Cable, "The Freedman's Case in Equity," *Century*, XXIX (1885), 409–18.

4. Clarence E. Cason, "Middle Class and Bourbon," in W. T. Couch (ed.), *Culture in the South* (Chapel Hill, N.C.: University of North Carolina Press, 1934), pp. 497–98 (by permission).

5. William Graham Sumner, *Folkways* (New York, 1910), p. 78; see also Joseph Alexander Tillinghast, *The Negro in Africa and America* (New York, 1902), p. 194.

6. Ray Stannard Baker, *Following the Color Line: An Account of Negro Citizenship in the American Democracy* (New York, 1908), p. 55.

7. The *Oklahoma City Black Dispatch*, October 20, 1929. Maurice S. Evans (*Black and White in the Southern States* [London, 1915], p. 183) relates that a white man, accused not only of associating with Negroes but of actually being one, had to procure documentary evidence to the contrary. T. Bailey (*Racial Orthodoxy in the South* [New York, 1914], p. 292) tells of a white man who took two witnesses with him against his attendance at a Negro meeting, and who "thought it best to tell no one."

8. Julian Ralph, *Dixie: Or Other Southern Scenes and Sketches* (New York, 1895), p. 382.

9. *The Crisis*, January, 1912, p. 99.

10. See J. L. Gillin, *Criminology and Penology* (New York, 1926), p. 74.

11. Gilbert T. Stephenson (*Racial Distinctions in American Law* [New York, 1910]) has given a résumé of all such laws prior to 1910. See especially his distinction drawn between law and custom (*ibid.*, p. 5).

12. Cf. J. W. Johnson and H. Seligmann, "Legal Aspects of the Negro Problem," *Annals of the American Academy of Political and Social Science*, CXXXX (1928), 91–92; Bailey, *op. cit.*, pp. 30–38; Dunning, *op. cit.*, p. 310.

13. Alabama and Texas in 1922 and 1923, respectively, sought to exclude Negroes from the Democratic primary (Johnson and Seligmann, *op. cit.*, pp. 91–92); while Republicans of Florida and Virginia, in 1929, sought also to exclude Negroes (*Jacksonville* [Fla.] *Sentinel*, October 18, 1929). Tennessee, in 1932, witnessed a gubernatorial campaign in which one candidate sought to pledge all candidates to the policy of exclusion of Negroes from the Democratic primary (*Nashville* [Tenn.] *Independent*, June 11, 1932; see also *ibid.*, July 16, 1932).

14. Sam Small, "A Statement to the Forum Magazine concerning Southern Race Prejudice," *Atlanta* (Ga.) *Constitution* (1927), Vol. LX, No. 75.

15. Charles Horton Cooley, *Social Organization* (New York, 1914), p. 219.

16. Senator W. F. George in *Liberty*, April 21, 1928, quoted by Johnson and Seligmann, *op. cit.*, p. 90.

17. Social equality, says Alfred H. Stone, "may be said to carry with it a conception of any form, or even appearance of equality between the two races, or between individual members of the two races" ("Recent Race Problem Literature" [review], *Southern History Association Publication*, VIII [1904], 453; see also Cooley, *op. cit.*, pp. 218–19). It, however, usually refers to intermarriage and sex contacts, the former of which laws of fifteen southern states forbid, and the latter of which taboos and custom regulate. This would make the Negro a caste, if, with Sighele, we agree that "the prohibition of intermarriage, observed in its most rigid form is the fundamental distinction of caste" (quoted in R. E. Park and E. W. Burgess, *Introduction to the Science of Sociology* [Chicago, 1921], p. 722). See also Carl Kelsey, *The Physical Basis of Society* (New

York, 1928), pp. 400 and 428. A summary and digest of these laws may be found in the *Negro Year Book* (1926), pp. 241–43; and in Stephenson, *op. cit.*, pp. 82 ff.

18. *Op. cit.*, pp. 92–93. It is not clear from the context whether Mr. Bailey is presenting his own views or merely summarizing the views of others.

19. Stone, "Is Race Friction between Blacks and Whites in the United States Growing and Inevitable?" *American Journal of Sociology*, XIII (1907), 677–96, quoted in Park and Burgess, *op. cit.*, pp. 635–36.

20. *Op. cit.*, pp. 310–11.

21. Robert E. Park, Racial Assimilation in Secondary Groups," *American Journal of Sociology*, XIX (1913), 616.

22. Herbert Spencer, *Principles of Sociology* (London, 1882), II, 3.

23. H. M. Bond, "A Negro Looks at His South," *Harpers*, CLXIII (1931), 103 (by permission).

24. Clifton Johnson, *Highways and Byways of the South* (New York, 1895), pp. 37–38.

25. The *Chicago Defender* (November 14, 1931) reports that a Negro at Smartt's Station, Tennessee, was killed for violating the rule.

26. Baker, *op. cit.*, p. 72.

27. Moton, *op. cit.*, p. 194.

28. *Ibid.*, p. 252; cf. Johnson (*op. cit.*, p. 331) for cases in refutation.

29. Moton, *op. cit.*, pp. 185 and 186. Negroes use the term "nigger" themselves (*ibid.*, pp. 187–88, and Edward King, *The Great South* [Hartford, Conn., 1875], p. 786).

30. At the Democratic national convention in Chicago in 1932 Senator Huey Long, of Louisiana, refused to shake hands with a Negro delegate (*Nashville Independent*, July 9, 1932). Bailey (*op. cit.*, p. 86) tells of an incident where, while taking a walk, a toddling Negro child touched his coat. He ends, however, by saying that "pretty soon he will know better."

31. The practice is so universal that it, perhaps, needs no documentary evidence. A Negro teacher in a southern city told the author that it was the practice of the white superintendent of schools not to remove his hat, nor the cigarette which he invariably was smoking, when he visited Negro schools. This was done even on occasions where he addressed the children.

32. Moton, *op. cit.*, pp. 191–92. Mr. J. S. Bassett consistently referred to "Mr. John Chavis," when writing *Slavery in the State of North Carolina* (Baltimore, 1899). This probably was not a "slip," for it is said that white persons generally used the title in speaking of, or to, Mr. Chavis.

33. *Nashville* (Tenn.) *Banner*, April 21, 1932, p. 17 (A.P. item).

34. Moton, *op. cit.*, pp. 188–89. See also a discussion of changing trends with reference to the use of the lower-case and capital letter in spelling "Negro" in the *Negro Year Book* (1931–32), pp. 21–26.

35. Cf. his statement in *op. cit.*, p. 252.

36. Negroes use the term "nigger" freely among themselves as a term of reference (see Washington, *Up from Slavery*, p. 141).

37. *Op. cit.*, p. 189.

38. Johnson, *op. cit.*, pp. 331–32; Bailey, *op. cit.*, p. 86.

39. As a matter of fact, Negroes, in general, do not have the word "woman" in their vocabulary. Every woman, white or black, is a lady. On the other hand, pressure is generally felt to call every white woman a "lady" (see Bailey, *op. cit.*, p. 368).

40. See Moton, *op. cit.*, p. 164. Eddie Tolan and Ralph Metcalfe, two Negro entrants and successful competitors in the Olympic games of 1932, were referred to, in every dispatch that we saw, as "Negroes." Other contestants were "Germans,"

"French," or what-not; but these boys were never "Americans." The practice was not modified in 1936.

41. See above, chap. i.

42. See amusing incidents related by Washington in *Up from Slavery*, pp. 226 ff. and 289.

43. *Ibid.*, p. 247. A cartoon in the *New Orleans Daily States*, in 1924, was titled "Mr. Colored Man, Read, Ponder This." The cartoon was issued in an attempt to stop migration of Negroes (*Negro Year Book* [1925–26], p. 7).

44. Moton, *op. cit.*, p. 191. E. Franklin Frazier ("Pathology of Race Prejudice," *Forum*, LXXVII [June, 1927], 857) remarks that "a White woman who addresses a Negro as 'mister' is immediately asked whether she would want a Negro to marry her sister. . . . ." Edmund DeS. Brunner (*Immigrant Farmers and Their Children* [Garden City, N.Y., 1929]), pp. 209–10), referring to the Czechoslovakians of Petersburg, Virginia, noted a *past* tendency for that group to eat and to shake hands with Negroes— "even to have called them 'Mister.' That is not so true now, if it ever was," he adds.

45. Private document.

46. The *Augusta* (Ga.) *Chronicle* is the newspaper in point. A resident of the city tells me that the custom recently has been dropped by that journal, which now uses the conventional "Mr.," "Mrs.," and "Miss." The *Augusta Herald*, however, retains it, it is alleged.

47. Moton, *What the Negro Thinks* (Garden City, N.Y.: Doubleday-Doran, 1929), pp. 187–88 (by permission); see also King, *op. cit.*, p. 786.

48. See a summary of such laws in Stephenson, *op. cit.*, pp. 88 ff., 146–49, 190 ff.

49. See George S. Schuyler, "Keeping the Negro in His Place," *American Mercury*, XVII, No. 68 (August, 1929), 469; Baker, *op. cit.*, p. 46; and *The Crisis*, March, 1912, p. 8. The latter reference is to the case of a Negro in Spartanburg, S.C., who was fined $100 because he admitted having dined with white people. Documents collected in connection with this study seem also to support the generalization that this function is tabooed.

50. *Op. cit.*, p. 352; see also Ralph, *op. cit.*, p. 374; and *The Crisis*, July, 1913, p. 120.

51. Documents from Selma (Ala.), Chattanooga (Tenn.), and Georgetown (Ky.) mention Negroes entering from the front. A document from Birmingham (Ala.) mentions that white people boycotted a theater where this form was practiced; one from Owensboro (Ky.) states that the form, once practiced, was later dropped; and while still another from Huntsville (Ala.) relates that white men assaulted Negroes who had entered a theater there by the front door to go to the balcony.

52. As in Nashville (Tenn.).

53. As in Memphis (Tenn.), and Dallas and Fort Worth (Tex.).

54. Document from Eufaula (Ala.).

55. *Op. cit.*, p. 469. Questionnaires 3, 34, 51; Documents II–10 and 12; *The Crisis*, February, 1911, p. 6.

56. See Evans, *Black and White in the Southern States*, p. 140. Birmingham (Ala.) and Muskogee (Okla.) have in 1923 and 1912, respectively, sought to require entirely separate vehicles for the races (see *Negro Year Book* [1925–26], p. 89; *The Crisis*, March, 1912, p. 8; and Quincy Ewing, "Heart of the Race Problem," *Atlantic Monthly*, CIII [1909], 394).

57. Generally in the rear, but in the front in Birmingham, Ala.

58. Document from Nashville, Tenn. Moton summarizes the complexity of these relations in his book (*op. cit.*, pp. 79–80).

59. A Negro man was shot for violating the rule, in Columbia, S.C. (*The Crisis*, June, 1920, p. 101). Two Negro women, in Texarkana, Tex., were fined ten dollars

each for boarding a car ahead of white women, according to a document from that city (No. VI).

60. *Op. cit.*, pp. 91–92.

61. The notices distinguishing between "people" and members of a "race" are found in Nashville and in other Tennessee towns. The italics are ours.

62. Baker (*op. cit.*, p. 31) is referring to signs in Atlanta cars which read: "White people seat from the front of the car toward the back, and colored people from rear toward front."

63. See an instance reported in *The Crisis*, November, 1918, p. 27.

64. Two documents in our possession report this situation in Nashville, Tenn. The incident was not reported as general but as occurring to individuals.

65. With the possible exception of Missouri. For the laws see Stephenson, *op. cit.*, pp. 190 ff.; Evans, *op. cit.*, pp. 75 and 140. General descriptions of the entire situation are given by Moton, *op. cit.*, p. 69.

66. See Baker, *op. cit.*, p. 34. The author has seen a station in a small Georgia town where a fence to separate the races extended from the station almost to the tracks.

67. The practice is so general as to be a subject of discussion; however, one person thought to mention it in a document (No. 38).

68. Johnson, *op. cit.*, pp. 330–31.

69. Personal observation, August 31, 1930.

70. Park, "Bases of Race Prejudice," *Annals*, CXXXX, 19.

71. Moton, *op. cit.*, p. 75; *The Crisis*, July, 1913, p. 120.

72. Park, "Bases of Race Prejudice," *Annals*, CXXXX, 19. A Judge in Shreveport, La., however, decided that a colored woman could not occupy a berth in a Pullman car, even as a servant (*The Crisis*, December, 1911, p. 56).

73. See *Negro Year Book* (1925–26), p. 3; and Baker, *op. cit.*, p. 52.

74. Moton, *op. cit.*, p. 76; Questionnaire No. 2 (Fort Smith, Ark.).

75. The Republican postmistress in a Mississippi village made the statement to Ralph (*op. cit.*, pp. 374–75).

76. See Baker, *op. cit.*, pp. 54 and 55. Principals and school nurses in the Richmond (Va.) Negro schools were white as late as 1929, but colored principals were elected in 1932 (*Kansas City Call*, August 8, 1933; and Josephus Simpson, "The Best Negroes in the World," *Opportunity*, IX [September, 1931], 283). Charleston (S.C.). Negro schools had white teachers as late as 1922 (*The Crisis*, April, 1927, p. 270). See also Negro Welfare Survey Committee, *The Negro in Richmond*, p. 90.

77. T. J. Woofter, *Negro Problems in Cities* (Garden City, N.Y., 1928), pp. 205–6.

78. The latter practice is customary in Charleston, S.C., according to a document (Questionnaire No. 34).

79. *The Crisis*, September, 1925, p. 230. On the entire point, showing provisions for hospitalization of Negroes in southern states, see Esther Balderston Jones, "Where Should a Negro Get Hurt?" *Christian Index*, LXI (August 25, 1932), 9–10. The article concludes: "So it is really best for a Negro not to get hurt at all anywhere."

80. As in a prominent university hospital (Document XVIII).

81. Stephenson, *op. cit.*, p. 137; Johnson, *op. cit.*, p. 90.

82. *The Crisis*, January, 1920, p. 147.

83. Documents (II and VII) from Savannah (Ga.) and Georgetown (Ky.).

84. Baker, *op. cit.*, p. 36. This practice is also occasional.

85. See Stephenson (*op. cit.*, pp. 146–48) for a summary of the laws.

86. *The Crisis*, April, 1911, p. 6; *Negro Year Book* (1925–26), p. 91.

87. Cf. n. 17, this chap., and Kelly Miller, "Government and the Negro," *Annals*, CXL (1928), 102.

88. It seems to be generally conceded that, in the states where intermarriages are not prohibited by law, they are nevertheless not general.

89. This is said in the face of attempts to repeal intermarriage laws, as occasionally occurs in cases of Negro organizations. The rationalization is that these organizations seek to improve the bastardy laws, which is impossible in face of prohibitory inter-marriage laws.

90. *Negro Year Book* (1925–26), p. 75; quoting from an editorial in the *Christian Index*.

91. See *Race Adjustment: Essays on the Negro in America* (Washington, 1908) p. 47; cf. also Moton (*op. cit.*, p. 183), who adopts a more restrained view.

92. Baker, *op. cit.*, p. 40.

93. The *Chicago Defender*, March 21, 1931.

94. Dunning (*op. cit.*, p. 308) implies that the rule works only in those cases where Negro men would work side by side with white women. Cases are, of course, reported where white and Negro men work together (see Ralph, *op. cit.*, p. 245), but either their tasks are separate or somewhere there is, in general, some subtle distinction not visible to the naked eye. A Negro painter, employed by the C.W.A. in 1934, related that, while he received the union rate for painting, the white men insisted that he confine his activities to mixing the paints.

95. Ralph, *op. cit.*, pp. 3, 22–23.

96. Moton, *op. cit.*, p. 165; Edward Byron Reuter, *The American Race Problem* (New York, 1927), p. 242; Evans, *op. cit.*, p. 165; *Negro Year Book* (1925–26), p. 85.

97. W. E. Burghardt DuBois, *The Philadelphia Negro: A Social Study* (Philadelphia 1899); quoted also in Kimball Young, *Source Book for Social Psychology* (New York, 1927), p. 499.

98. Moton, *op. cit.*, p. 199.

99. *Op. cit.*, p. 216.

100. A recent check on the situation shows that previously the postmen were white and the street cleaners colored. The situation is now reversed (Document II, 6); see *The Crisis*, January, 1912, p. 145; January, 1913, p. 118; January, 1920, p. 147.

101. See citations in preceding note.

102. Document from Birmingham, Ala.

103. Document from Fort Worth, Tex.

104. See some interesting cases in *Opportunity*, October, 1929, p. 34; Baker, *op. cit.*, p. 83; *The Crisis*, January, 1913, p. 169; July, 1917, p. 114; and Evans, *op. cit.*, p. 163.

105. Document II, 15 (Miss.).

106. *The Crisis*, June, 1919, p. 97. Other interesting cases are given in the same reference.

107. *Ibid.*, March, 1912, p. 8.

108. Document II, 10 (Tenn.).

109. Even the inclusion of such items in the daily press about Negroes is uncommon. Moton (*op. cit.*, p. 55), referring to the conditions under consideration, says: "In all public matters, it is accepted that the Negro is concerned and included only incidentally; the law is so construed, and the government so administered; and public sentiment so cultivated" (by permission).

110. *Ibid.*, p. 82 (by permission); see also Baker, *op. cit.*, p. 64; Bailey, *op. cit.*, p. 109; Ralph, *op. cit.*, pp. 386–87.

111. The point is discussed at great length in Bertram W. Doyle, "Racial Traits of Negroes as They Assign Traits to Themselves (University of Chicago thesis [unpublished], 1924), pp. 109–22.

112. Eugene Gordon, "The Negro's Inhibitions," *American Mercury*, XIII, No. 50 (February, 1928), 159 to 165; see also Schuyler, "A Negro Looks Ahead," *American Mercury*, XIX, No. 74 (February, 1930), 212-20.

113. Moton, *What the Negro Thinks* (Garden City, N.Y.: Doubleday-Doran, 1929), p. 3; see also *Negro Year Book* (1925-26), pp. 21-26.

114. Bond (*op. cit.*), apparently unconsciously, infers that Negroes would find it easier to look up to white people if the latter were generally of a class to whom Negroes could look up.

115. "Our White Folks," *American Mercury*, XII (December, 1927), 386.

NOTES FOR CHAPTER XI

1. Thomas Flanagan, "From My Window," *Nashville* (Tenn.) *World*, September 16, 1932, p. 6.

2. Robert Russa Moton, *What the Negro Thinks* (Garden City, N.Y.: Doubleday-Doran, 1929), p. 225.

3. Negroes of Shreveport, La., invited Oscar De Priest, the Negro congressman, to address them. Before the date set, however, they sent a delegation to the mayor, sheriff, and other public officials to discover "what they thought." These latter "thought the idea ill-advised," and the engagement was canceled.

4. A Negro who lived in Atlanta, where Negroes board streetcars at the rear, went to Birmingham, where Negroes board streetcars at the front. Hence, on one occasion, when he stopped a streetcar, he got on at the wrong end. He said, however, that he apologized to the conductor by saying that he thought the car was going the other way. As obviously untrue as such a statement was, it served the purpose of relieving an embarrassing moment.

5. The thought is advanced by Dr. R. E. Park in his unpublished lectures on "The Negro in America."

6. See, on the point, E. Franklin Lee, *Social Solidarity and Race Inequalities in the South* (Columbia University dissertation [privately printed], 1911), pp. 107-8; Edgar Gardner Murphy, *Problems of the Present South* (New York, 1905), p. 185; Moton, *op. cit.*, pp. 39 and 203; Thomas P. Bailey, *Racial Orthodoxy in the South* (New York, 1914), p. 108; Maurice S. Evans, *Black and White in the Southern States* (London, 1915), pp. 161-62.

7. Murphy, *op. cit.*, p. 185.

8. Moton, *op. cit.*, p. 178; see also Ray Stannard Baker, *Following the Color Line* (New York, 1908), p. 35.

9. Evans (*op. cit.*, p. 118), quoting the Rev. Snyder in the *Forum*.

10. R. E. Park, "Negro Home Life and Standards of Living," *Annals of the American Academy of Political and Social Science*, XLIX (September, 1913), 155.

11. Ira DeA. Reid (*Negro Membership in American Labor Unions* [New York, 1930], p. 165) says that "on the one hand is the half-hearted interest, and sometimes the total lack of interest of labor leaders who either organize Negroes into separate locals that have little or no bargaining power, or do not organize Negroes at all." See also Edward B. Reuter, *The American Race Problem* (New York, 1927), p. 243; Baker, *op. cit.*, p. 160; Julian Ralph, *Dixie: Or Other Southern Scenes and Sketches* (New York, 1895), p. 368; *Negro Year Book* (1925-26), pp. 11-13; William A. Dunning, *Studies in Southern History and Politics* (New York, 1914), p. 308.

12. See an amusing incident concerning the appointment of a Negro librarian in Jesse O. Thomas, "Social Work among Negroes in the South," *Opportunity*, I (January, 1923), 14.

13. Park, "Racial Assimilation in Secondary Groups with Especial Reference to the Negro," *American Journal of Sociology*, XIX (1913–14), 617.

14. Ernest Watson Burgess, "Residential Segregation in American Cities," *Annals*, CXL (November, 1928), 105.

15. T. J. Woofter, *Negro Problems in Cities* (Garden City, N.Y., 1928), p. 37.

16. Legal aspects of "segregation ordinances" occasionally passed by southern cities, and the extent of such enactments, are given in J. W. Johnson and H. Seligmann, "Legal Aspects of the Negro Problem," *Annals*, CXXXX (1928), 92–93, and Woofter, *op. cit.*, Part II. References to local situations are found in the *Philadelphia Tribune* and the *Atlanta Independent*—both of October 24, 1929—and the *Baltimore Afro-American* of November 24, 1928.

17. *The Negro Yearbook* (1925–26), pp. 385–87, lists seventy-one towns and twenty-three settlements of Negroes; of which fifty-seven towns and nine settlements are in the South. Wybark, Tex.—where it was said to be a breach of etiquette for a white man to remain overnight (*The Crisis*, March, 1912, p. 8)—was not mentioned in the list. Towns in which Negroes are not allowed are more frequent. Bailey (*op. cit.*, p. 79) speaks of one in Mississippi; Evans (*op. cit.*, p. 163) of one in Oklahoma; and Dunning (*op. cit.*, p. 311) states that there is a county in North Carolina where neither a Negro nor a Democrat is permitted to live. The mountaineers of the same state told Johnson that they "busted mighty nigh every nigger" who came through their section (*Highways and Byways of the South* [New York, 1895], p. 334). The *Houston* (Tex.) *Defender* refers to an "old custom in Polk County, Arkansas, which says that 'no Negro can stay over-night' " (II [May 15, 1932], 32).

18. "Racial Assimilation, etc.," *loc. cit.*, p. 618.

19. *Op. cit.*, p. 248.

20. "Bases of Race Prejudice," *loc. cit.*, p. 19.

21. *Op. cit.*, pp. 365–67.

22. *Nashville Evening Tennesseean*, June 9, 1932, p. 9.

23. William I. Thomas, "The Psychology of Race Prejudice," *American Journal of Sociology*, IX (1903-4), 593–611.

24. The practice was reported by Dr. Herbert Blumer.

25. Moton, *op. cit.*, pp. 194–95.

26. *Ibid.*, p. 252.

27. George S. Schuyler, "A Negro Looks Ahead," *American Mercury*, XIX, No. 74 (February, 1930), 219. This is an overstatement to say that "in no case" is segregation observed. Similar cases have come to the attention of the writer, but they are by no means universal, as is implied here.

28. See Paul K. Edwards, *The Southern Urban Negro as Consumer* (New York, 1932).

29. Park, "Bases of Race Prejudice," *loc. cit.*, p. 19.

30. "As far as the South is concerned it is where racial prejudices, and the social order which they perpetuated, are breaking down that racial animosities are most intense. It is when the Negro invades a new region that race riots occur; it is when he seeks a place in a new occupation or a new profession that he meets the most vigorous opposition; it is when he seeks to assume a new dignity that he ceases to be quaint and becomes ridiculous" (*ibid.*, p. 15.)

31. Moton, *op. cit.*, p. 32.

32. See, on the point, Baker, *op. cit.*, p. 241; Johnson, *op. cit.*, p. 331.

33. Agreement on the point expressed by representatives of such different traditions. as Baker (*op. cit.*, p. 248), Evans (*op. cit.*, p. 32), and Bailey (*op. cit.*, p. 30).

34. The point has been advanced by Frank Tannenbaum, *Darker Phases of the South* (New York, 1924), pp. 157–67, but esp. p. 162.

35. See Bailey, *op. cit.*, p. 368; Baker, *op. cit.*, p. 44; Lee, *op. cit.*, p. 88; and Moton, *op. cit.*, p. 212.

36. *Op. cit.*, p. 212; Cable, *op. cit.*, p. 415; Taylor, *op. cit.*, p. 47.

37. Johnson, *op. cit.*, pp. 346–47.

38. Park ("Bases of Race Prejudice," *loc. cit.*, p. 18) says that "it seems as if there are no racial antipathies that cannot be overcome by a scrupulous adherence to etiquette."

39. See, for example, Schuyler, "Our White Folks," *American Mercury*, XII (December, 1927), 385–92, and his "Keeping the Negro in His Place," *ibid.*, XVII, No. 68 (August, 1929), 469–76.

40. Park, "Bases of Race Prejudice," *loc. cit.*, pp. 18–19.

TABLE A*

FREE COLORED POPULATION OF SOUTHERN AND BORDER STATES, 1790–1850

States and Territories	1790	1800	1810	1820	1830	1840	1850
Alabama				571	1,572	2,039	2,265
Arkansas				59	141	465	608
District of Columbia		783	2,549	4,048	6,052	8,361	10,059
Delaware	3,899	8,268	13,136	12,958	15,855	16,919	18,073
Florida					844	817	932
Georgia	398	1,019	1,801	1,763	2,486	2,753	2,931
Kentucky	114	741	1,713	2,759	4,917	7,317	10,011
Louisiana			7,585	10,476	16,710	25,502	17,462
Maryland	8,043	19,587	33,927	39,730	52,938	62,078	74,723
Mississippi		182	240	458	519	1,366	930
Missouri			607	347	569	1,574	2,618
North Carolina	4,975	7,043	10,266	14,612	19,543	22,732	27,463
South Carolina	1,801	3,185	4,554	6,826	7,921	8,276	8,960
Tennessee	361	309	1,317	2,727	4,555	5,524	6,433
Texas							397
Virginia	12,766	20,124	30,570	36,889	47,348	49,852	54,333
Total	32,361	61,241	108,365	134,213	182,070	215,575	265,650

TABLE B*

INCREASE AND DECREASE PERCENTAGE OF FREE COLORED POPULATION IN SOUTHERN AND BORDER STATES, 1790–1850

States and Territories	1800	1810	1820	1830	1840	1850
Alabama				175.30	29.70	11.08
Arkansas				138.98	229.78	30.75
District of Columbia		225.54	58.80	51.97	35.90	20.30
Delaware	112.05	58.87	−1.34	22.35	6.71	6.82
Florida					− 3.19	14.07
Georgia	156.03	76.74	−2.10	41.00	10.74	6.46
Kentucky	550.00	131.17	61.06	87.21	48.81	36.81
Louisiana			38.11	59.50	52.61	−31.52
Maryland	143.52	73.21	17.10	33.24	17.26	20.36
Mississippi		31.86	90.83	13.31	163.19	−31.91
Missouri			−42.83	63.97	176.62	66.32
North Carolina	41.56	45.76	42.33	33.74	16.31	20.81
South Carolina	76.84	42.98	49.89	16.04	4.48	8.26
Tennessee	−14.40	326.21	107.06	67.03	21.27	16.25
Texas						
Virginia	57.63	59.90	20.67	28.35	5.28	8.98

* Data taken from J. D. B. Debow, *Statistical View of the United States: A Compendium of the 7th Census*, pp. 63 and 64.

INDEXES

INDEX OF SUBJECTS

INDEX OF NAMES

43. Gilbert T. Stephenson (*Racial Distinctions in American Law* [New York, 1910], p. 39) has discussed this situation at length. Virginia was one example of a state with both laws. See, on this point, John Preston McConnell, *Negroes and Their Treatment in Virginia, from 1865 to 1867* (Pulaski, Va., 1910), p. 8. On February 2, 1839, Alabama enacted legislation to the effect that:

"1. The master of any vessel bringing in any free Negro must pay $2000 as a guarantee that he will be removed.

"2. Free persons of color may be imprisoned on arrival in the State.

"3. A free Negro returning, after being sent out of the State, shall receive thirty-nine lashes, and sold as a slave if not out of the State in twenty days" (*New Orleans Louisianian*, March 13, 1839). See also Catterall, *op. cit.*, I, 353.

44. Albert Bushnell Hart (*The American Nation: A History*, Vol. XVI: *Slavery and Abolition, 1831–1841* [New York, 1905], p. 90) remarks that "upon no point in history is there less evidence than that of a desire by the free Negro for the comforts of a slave home. The whole system of slave codes was based upon the belief that every slave desired to be free, and every free Negro to remain free." However, Flanders (*op. cit.*, pp. 264–65) gives three cases from Georgia and (p. 263) also shows that free Negroes were frequently enslaved in the same state. See Whitelaw Reid (*After the War: A Southern Tour from May, 1865, to May, 1866* [London, 1866], pp. 189–93) for the story of "Sandy," who, having lost his "free papers" and being on the verge of being returned to slavery, mutilated himself—cutting off his right hand—in order to be less valuable to the slaveholder.

45. North Carolina was known as such a state, which accounts, perhaps, for the relatively large proportion of free Negroes in the state (Blacknall, *op. cit.*, p. 20).

46. Buckingham, *op. cit.*, I, 168.

47. Russell, *op. cit.*, pp. 64–65.

48. This was the resolution already referred to in this chapter (note 29) and was the starting-point of the colonization movement in Virginia, if not in the United States, according to Russell (*op. cit.*, p. 66).

49. *Ibid.*, pp. 66, 140–41.

50. *Ibid.*, p. 144.

51. Flanders, *op. cit.*, p. 263.

52. Bassett, *op. cit.*, p. 34; see also Adams (*op. cit.*, p. 163 n.), for a statement to the effect that the "bright fellows" of Charleston, S.C., also suffered under these new disabilities; "that rights inherited by birth and blood were taken from them; that being subjected to the same law which governed the most abject slave, every construction of it went to degrade them. . . . ."

53. Flanders, *op. cit.*, pp. 268–69, quoting from *Bryan v. Walton*, 14 Georgia 185.

54. Ingle, *op. cit.*, p. 285. See a general comment on the situation in Phillips, *American Negro Slavery* (New York, 1918), p. 453, and a case—recorded in Catterall (*op. cit.*, I, 130–31), *Selden v. Coalter*, 2 Va. CA 553 (November, 1818)—where a man wished to purchase a plot of land in order to prevent the family of a free Negro from being "so near his son Joseph."

55. James Stirling, *Letters from the Slave States* (London, 1857), pp. 243–44.

56. "I wouldn't like to live where niggers was free," said a Tennessean to Olmsted; while a North Carolinian later advanced the same opinion (Frederick Law Olmsted, *A Journey in the Back Country; in the Winter of 1853–1854* [New York, 1860], p. 237).

57. Olmsted, *A Journey through the Seaboard Slave States; with Remarks on Their Economy* (New York, 1856), II, 218–19. See also his *Back Country* (p. 203) for a statement to the same effect from the same state. On the other hand, mountaineers of Tennessee, Alabama, and North Carolina were not generally believed to be friendly to

Negroes, slave or free. The note serves mainly to show the spread of opinion concerning colonization at this time. See William Archibald Dunning (*Studies in Southern History and Politics* [New York, 1914], pp. 3–30) for a summary of the situation.

58. Joseph Holt Ingraham, *The Sunny South, or the Southerner at Home* (Philadelphia, 1860), p. 473.

59. Olmsted, *Seaboard Slave States*, I, 48, 110.

60. A Northern Man, *The Planter, or Thirteen Years in the South*, p. 67.

61. John Dixon Long, *Pictures of Slavery in Church and State* (Philadelphia, 1857), p. 25.

62. "Competition, unqualified and uncontrolled, as with plants, and in the great impersonal life-struggle of man with his kind and with all animate nature, is unconscious. Conflict is always conscious, indeed, it evokes the deepest emotions and strongest passions and enlists the greatest concentration of attention and effort. Both are forms of struggle. Competition, however, is continuous and impersonal; conflict is intermittent and personal" (Robert Park and Ernest W. Burgess, *Introduction to the Science of Sociology* [2d ed.; Chicago, 1926], p. 574 [by permission]).

63. Woodson, *Free Negro Heads, etc.*, p. xxxvi; Phillips, *American Negro Slavery*, p. 403.

64. C. W. Birnie, "The Education of the Negro in Charleston, South Carolina, before the Civil War," *Journal of Negro History*, XII, 17; Woodson, *Negro in Our History*, pp. 246–48.

65. Flanders, *op. cit.*, p. 266.

66. Figures compiled from Census Bureau, *Negro Population, 1790–1915*, p. 511, and J. D. B. DeBow, *Statistical Review of the United States; Being a Compendium of the Seventh Census* (Washington, 1854), p. 51.

67. Bassett, *op. cit.*, p. 45.

68. Patterson, *op. cit.*, p. 11.

69. Buckingham, *op. cit.*, I, 211–12; Flanders, *op. cit.*, p. 271.

70. Woodson, *Free Negro Heads, etc.*, p. xxxvi.

71. Flanders, *op. cit.*, pp. 269–70.

72. Phillips, *American Negro Slavery*, p. 430; quoted also in Flanders, *op. cit.*, p. 270.

73. Woodson, *Education of the Negro, etc.*, pp. 26–27, 33.

74. "Among his pupils were Willie P. Mangum, afterwards United States Senator; and Priestley P. Mangum, his brother; Archibald and John Henderson, sons of Chief Justice Henderson, Charles Manly, afterward Governor of the State . . . . and many more excellent men who did not become so distinguished in their communities" (Bassett, *op. cit.*, pp. 74–75).

75. Of the 184 free Negroes in Chatham County, in 1826, 25 owned from one to twenty-five slaves and real estate holdings ranging from one city lot to two hundred acres. In 1830 free Negroes held small parcels of slaves in thirteen counties of Georgia, the largest being twenty-five (Flanders, *op. cit.*, p. 267). These small parcels could scarcely be called large enough for planters' operations. Olmsted (*Seaboard Slave States*, II, 286–87) mentions the Cane River farmers; Bassett (*op. cit.*, p. 43) and Washington (*op. cit.*, II, 201) refer to the North Carolina farmers. Frederika Bremer (*Homes in the New World* [New York, 1853], II, 527) mentions the situation in Virginia, and the Census Bureau (*Negro Population, 1790–1915*, p. 511) records 158 farmers and 244 planters among the 2,809 free Negroes of Louisiana.

76. One hundred and thirty free Negroes, from 390 taxpayers of that class, in Charleston in 1860 held 390 slaves. There was an "abundance" of such holdings at New Orleans, also. Phillips (*American Negro Slavery*, p. 434) says: "Cyprian Ricard bought at a sheriff's sale in 1851, an estate in Iberville Parish [La.] along with its 91

slaves for a quarter of a million dollars; Marie Metoyer, of Nachitoches Parish, had 58 slaves and more than 200 acres of land. . . . . Charles Roques of the same parish died in 1854, leaving 47 slaves and 100 acres; and Martin Donato, of St. Landry Parish bequeathed liberty to his slave wife and seven children, and left them 89 slaves and 45,000 arpents of land, as well as notes and mortgages to a value of $46,000" (by permission). See also Robert E. Park, "Negro Home Life and Standards of Living." *Annals of the American Academy of Political and Social Science*, XLIX (September, 1913), p. 157; Woodson, *Free Negro Heads, etc.*, pp. xv and xxv, *Negro in Our History*, p. 246, and "An Open Letter to G. D. Eaton," *Journal of Negro History*, XII (April, 1927), 332; Blacknall, *op. cit.*, p. 24; Hart, *op. cit.*, p. 77; Long, *op. cit.*, p. 235; Bremer, *op. cit.*, I, 363.

77. C. G. Parsons, *An Inside View of Slavery; or a Tour among the Planters* (Boston, 1855), p. 297.

78. Olmsted, *Seaboard Slave States*, II, 286–87.

79. *Ibid.*, and *A Journey through Texas; or a Saddle-Trip on the Southwestern Frontier* [New York, 1857], p. 386) recorded the locations of these settlements. Washington (*op. cit.*, II, 207) also notes this but takes the reference from Olmsted.

80. A glance at the census of 1850 shows clearly marked tendencies to settle in colonies in a given county, or in towns. For example: In Alabama the concentration was in Mobile County; in Florida, Escambia County—almost adjacent to Mobile County; in Arkansas, Marion County—near the Missouri line; in Georgia, Chatham (Savannah), Richmond (Augusta), and Warren counties; in Kentucky, Jefferson (Louisville) and Fayette counties; in Louisiana, Orleans (New Orleans), St. Landry, and Nachitoches parishes; in Maryland, Baltimore (Baltimore) County; in Mississippi, Adams (Natchez) County; in Missouri, St. Louis (St. Louis) County; in North Carolina, Craven, Granville, Halifax, Pasquotank, Robeson, and Wake counties—all with more than one thousand free Negroes. In South Carolina the concentration was, of course, in Charleston County; in Tennessee, Davidson County; in Texas, Jefferson; while Virginia had ten counties with one thousand or more, led by Henrico, Accomac and Dinwiddie counties (DeBow, *op. cit.*, pp. 194–320).

81. Phillips, *Life and Labor in the Old South*, p. 172.

82. See G. W. Cable, "The Freedman's Case in Equity," *Century Magazine*, XXIX, No. 3 (January, 1885), 409–18; Stroud, *op. cit.*, p. 68. The original enactment is found also in *Martin's Digest*, I, 640–42.

83. Bassett, *op. cit.*, p. 45.

84. *Ibid.*, p. 44.

85. *Ibid.*, p. 57.

86. *Ibid.*, p. 58.

87. *Op. cit.*, I, 212 (see also Arfwedson, "The United States and Canada in 1833 and 1834," I, 425, quoted as a document in *Journal of Negro History*, III [1918], 196).

88. Bassett, *op. cit.*, p. 75.

89. *Ibid.*

90. Patterson, *op. cit.*, p. 11, quoting from Hale and Merritt, *History of Tennessee* (Chicago, 1913), II, 293.

91. *Seaboard Slave States*, II, 15.

92. See Blacknall (*op. cit.*, p. 29) for a case in point.

93. "The free Negroes were either required not to associate with slaves or they were made to feel that being better than the slaves they should not associate with them. The one was taught to hate the other. The slaves referred to the freedmen as 'the old issue free' and the free Negroes applied to the slaves such epithets as might best express

their haughtiness and superciliousness in dealing with bondsmen occupying a lower status" (Woodson, *Free Negro Heads, etc,.* p. lvii [by permission]).

94. Compare the view given here with that advanced by Phillips, when he says: "Since the whites everywhere held the whip hand and nowhere greatly refrained from the use of their power, the lot of a colored freeman was one hardly to be borne without the aid of habit or philosophy. They submitted to the regime because it was taken mostly as a matter of course, because resistance would surely bring harsher repression, and because there were solaces to be found. . . . . The possession of sincere friends among the whites here and there also helped them to feel that their lives lay in fairly pleasant places; and in their lodges they had a refuge peculiarly their own . . . ." (*American Negro Slavery*, p. 450 [by permission]).

NOTES TO CHAPTER VIII

1. Mary Boykin Chestnut, wife of James Chestnut, Jr., U.S. senator from South Carolina, 1859–61, and afterward aide to Jefferson Davis, and a brigadier-general in the Confederate Army, *A Diary from Dixie* (New York, 1905).

2. *Ibid.*, pp. 112 and 153.

3. *Ibid.*, pp. 84–85.

4. *Ibid.*, pp. 100–101.

5. *Ibid.*, p. 284 (February 5, 1863, Richmond, Va.).

6. *Ibid.*, p. 92 (July, 1861).

7. Mrs. D. Giraud Wright, *A Southern Girl in '61; the War-Time Memories of a Confederate Senator's Daughter* (New York, 1905), pp. 16–17.

8. *Op. cit.*, p. 365 (Lincolnton, N.C., March, 1865).

9. *Ibid.*, p. 28.

10. *Ibid.*, p. 227. The incident was perhaps propaganda directed against the "Yankees." Few, if any, Union officers were likely in Montgomery at the time. The instance, however, is a good one in which to exhibit attitudes of Negro slaves.

11. *Ibid.*, p. 255.

12. *Ibid.*, pp. 394, 402–3.

13. *Ibid.*, p. 38.

14. Elizabeth Ware Pearson (ed.), *Letters from Port Royal; Written at the Time of the Civil War* (Boston, 1906), p. 63 (letter dated July, 1863).

15. *Op. cit.*, pp. 93 and 225.

16. Pearson (*op. cit.*, p. 50) records that a minister, ostensibly Northern, had preached a sermon to Negroes at Hilton Head, South Carolina, and compared them to Israelites. Booker T. Washington says, "They learned early to apply this story to their own case" (*Story of the Negro* [New York, 1909], II, 3).

17. *Op. cit.*, II, 4–5.

18. *Ibid.* He also records (*Up from Slavery* [New York, 1901], p. 7) that the slaves had kept in touch with the abolition movement "from the time that Garrison, Lovejoy, and others began to agitate for freedom."

19. *U.S. Congress, Report of the Joint Committee on Reconstruction* (39th Cong., 1st sess. [Washington, 1866]), Part III, p. 108.

20. Washington, *Up from Slavery*, pp. 7, 19–20. "Grapevine telegraph" was underground information, rumor, gossip (see, on this point, W. E. Burghardt DuBois, *Souls of Black Folk; Essays and Sketches* [Chicago, 1903], pp. 5–6).

21. See Robert Russa Moton, *What the Negro Thinks* (Garden City, N.Y., 1929), p. 10.

22. Chestnut, *op. cit.*, p. 199.

23. Washington, *The Story of the Negro*, II, 8.